1983

Keats: *The Religious Sense*

KEATS

The Religious Sense

by Robert M. Ryan

PRINCETON UNIVERSITY PRESS

PRINCETON, NEW JERSEY

Publication of this book has been aided by a grant
from the Andrew W. Mellon Foundation.

Library of Congress Cataloging in Publication Data will
be found on the last printed page of this book
This book has been composed in Janson type
and designed by Bruce D. Campbell
Printed in the United States of America
by Princeton University Press, Princeton, New Jersey

For My Parents

Contents

Keats: *The Religious Sense*

Foreword

IN the large and still rapidly expanding catalogue of published commentary on the life and poetry of John Keats one finds relatively little attention given to the question of his religious faith. There has been no book-length study dealing specifically and exclusively with the topic (Keats is unique among the major Romantic poets in this regard), and in more general works of biography and criticism the subject has usually been treated perfunctorily, as a matter of no great consequence, or tentatively, as a matter on which no conclusive evidence is available. Only a few authors have considered the question of Keats's religion an important area of investigation, and their treatment of the problem has generally been unconvincing or incomplete.

If called upon to name the standard work on the subject, one would have to cite Hoxie Neale Fairchild's chapter on Keats in *Religious Trends in English Poetry*.[1] Fairchild did take the trouble to marshal most of the relevant texts, using them as the basis for what, at first glance, appears to be an inductive analysis. Unfortunately, he used his own concept of Anglican orthodoxy as the standard by which to judge the soundness of Keats's religious views, and this rendered him incapable of taking the poet's ideas seriously. Dismissing with impatience all evidence to the contrary, he concluded that Keats was little more than a pagan and that "devotion to genius" was "the nearest thing to a religion which can be ascribed to him."[2]

The inadequacy of Fairchild's study results from the author's inability or unwillingness to admit that Keats might have found a legitimate religious alternative to orthodox Christianity. Walter Evert, in his *Aesthetic and Myth in the*

---

[1] Volume III: *1780-1830, Romantic Faith* (New York: Columbia University Press, 1949).
[2] *Ibid.*, p. 460.

Poetry of Keats, criticized Fairchild for his narrowness, for his "blurring of the distinction between general religiosity of outlook and specific sectarian commitment," but in attempting to define the form that Keats's "religiosity" took he came to a conclusion rather like Fairchild's. He too suggested that, having rejected Christianity, Keats had nowhere to turn for religious satisfaction but to a form of paganism: "Here then was Keats's dilemma: Inclined toward speculative activity and a basically religious view of life, yet out of sympathy with the dominant metaphysical mode of organizing experience in that culture to which he must address his poetry, how was he to proceed? . . . Keats met [the problem] by turning to a cultural taproot which had been largely neglected in the poetry of the Neoclassic age, the mythology of classical antiquity."[3] Evert seems to have forgotten that the "dominant metaphysical mode of organizing experience" in Keats's time had been under attack for more than a century and that Keats, like many of his contemporaries, believed that it was fast losing its hold on the minds and hearts of men—"dying like an outburnt lamp," to use the poet's own phrase. In its place, he believed, was arising a more humane and reasonable faith, a revival of the original "natural religion" ordained by God at the beginning of time, and more pleasing in His sight than any more recently organized system of belief. Indeed, it can be argued that in the particular society of artists and intellectuals in which Keats moved, this faith had already become "the dominant metaphysical mode." Benjamin Robert Haydon, a member of that circle, believed that as a Christian he represented an embattled minority besieged on all sides by "the deists," among whom, on occasion, he numbered Keats.

Insufficient attention to Keats's place in the tradition of natural religion has led several other scholars into difficulty when they attempted to deal with the poet's religious

---

[3] *Aesthetic and Myth in the Poetry of Keats* (Princeton: Princeton Univ. Press, 1965), pp. 9, 13f.

FOREWORD

thought. Apparently unaware of the historical roots of
Keats's theological ideas, John Middleton Murry regarded
him as an original religious thinker, almost as a prophet
bringing a special revelation from God.[4] Clarence Thorpe
likewise believed that Keats devised a special religion for
himself, involving a kind of Platonic quest for and worship
of absolute Beauty.[5] An opposite tendency in criticism has
disregarded the evidence of Keats's serious involvement
with religious concerns, speaking of him as though he were
an early exponent of modern secular humanism. This approach often necessitates interpreting Keats's religious language in non-religious terms, as is done in a recent study
when an obvious reference to the Deity ("the great Power") is understood as signifying "an endless potential for
creation, an ideal of beauty latent amid the elements of human perception."[6] The fact is that Keats was neither an
evangelist nor an agnostic. He was an earnest seeker after
truth who believed in the existence of a Supreme Being and
who felt a need to investigate the consequences and ramifications of that belief. He was not an especially original or
creative thinker in theology; most of his ideas were borrowed from friends or from books. But he was determined
to find his own way in religion, and the system of faith he
constructed for himself clearly reflects his own personality.

It will be noticed that in my investigation into the nature
of Keats's religious beliefs I have avoided using the major
poems as primary sources of evidence. With one or two ex-
ceptions, the poetry on which Keats's reputation is based
does not concern itself in any obvious or direct way with
modern religious themes—unless "religious" is defined in
such a way as to make it synonymous with words like
"idealistic" or "poetic." When Earl Wasserman wrote, "The

[4] *Keats and Shakespeare* (1925; rpr. London: Oxford Univ. Press,
1949), pp. 141-48.
[5] *The Mind of John Keats* (1926; rpr. New York: Russell & Russell, 1964), pp. 154-58.
[6] Stuart M. Sperry, *Keats the Poet* (Princeton: Princeton Univ.
Press, 1973), p. 135.

odes on the urn and the nightingale, 'La Belle Dame Sans Merci,' and 'The Eve of St. Agnes' were religious experiences almost terrifying to their maker,"[7] he was using "religious" in an eccentric manner—in a sense that would not be generally understood outside the carefully controlled atmosphere of *The Finer Tone*. In this study, for the sake of clarity and precision, I intend to speak of religion in a rather strict traditional sense, using a definition similar to this one taken from *Webster's Third New International Dictionary*: "A personal awareness or conviction of the existence of a supreme being or of supernatural powers or influences controlling one's own, humanity's or all nature's destiny . . . accompanied by or arousing reverence, gratitude, humility, the will to obey and serve." For a study of Keats's religion in that sense of the term, the relevance of the major poems is questionable. If we come to them knowing nothing of Keats's basic theology, they do not do much to enlighten us. I am not suggesting that the poems cannot enrich our understanding of Keats's religious consciousness; what they tell us about the man's mind is as valuable in this area as in others. But I believe that before one attempts to interpret the religious significance of the poetry, it is useful to have a fairly clear conception of the poet's personal creed. I offer this study, then, as a sort of prolegomenon or preface to any further examination of the religious aspects of Keats's verse. There is another sense, too, in which an understanding of Keats as a religious thinker can contribute to a better understanding of him as a poet. Some of his most important pronouncements on poetry—for instance, his remarks on Negative Capability and on "the truth of Imagination"—were made in the context of religious discussion and cannot be fully or properly understood without reference to that context.

One factor that has encouraged some scholars to use the poems as evidence of Keats's religious ideas is an apparent

[7] *The Finer Tone: Keats's Major Poems* (Baltimore: Johns Hopkins Univ. Press, 1953), p. 56.

paucity of information from other sources. I realize that by excluding the major poetry from consideration I appear to have confined myself to a rather narrow field of investigation. Some passages in the letters and a few short occasional poems dealing explicitly with modern religious concerns—these make up the primary data on which my conclusions will be based. If these items are studied in isolation, within the limited context of Keats's own writings, they do not reveal very much. But I have found that when Keats's remarks are examined in a somewhat larger context they begin to suggest larger meanings. When, for instance, his comments on religion are compared with those of his friends—the men who were his constant companions and in dialogue with whom he formulated his ideas—they take on considerable new significance. And when the context is broadened further to include the general theological concerns of the age in which he lived, his statements become still more suggestive. I will point out, for example, that certain words that have no particular religious significance for us today—words like "identity" and "affection"—had strong theological connotations for Keats and his contemporaries. This book is in many respects a study in contexts: it is an attempt to reconstruct the historical, social, and intellectual environment that influenced and, in a sense, generated Keats's religious ideas.

My examination of the development of his thought will generally follow a chronological pattern. Ideas are the products of moods, and this is particularly true of religious ideas. The intensity of a man's interest in the existence and nature of a transcendent order is often determined by his level of satisfaction with his earthly circumstances. Thus the religious views expressed by Keats during the carefree winter of 1817–1818 are different from those developed in the troubled spring of 1819. While there are some consistent elements in his theology throughout his adult life, an attempt to systematize his religious ideas would distort rather than clarify them. Moreover, the gradual process by which he arrived at certain conclusions is often as interesting as the conclusions themselves. One can learn much about the quality of his mind by following him step by step as he struggles toward the resolution of an intellectual difficulty.

Keats's religious thought developed in observable stages, and I have made those stages the basis of my chapter divisions. My analysis of this development begins with an attempt to reconstruct as far as possible the process by which he abandoned the Christian faith in which he had been brought up. The succeeding chapters examine the important contributions of Leigh Hunt, Benjamin Bailey, and some other friends as he began to formulate his mature views on religion. Chapter Four approaches Keats as an independent thinker coming to grips with the problem of evil, which emerged as the central theological dilemma of his life. Finally, in Chapter Five, we see Keats constructing for himself a system of faith that would serve as an alternative to Christianity and provide an explanation for the mystery of earthly suffering. I have placed the unhappy story of his death in an epilogue because, while it is certainly relevant to this study, it tells us more about the bewilderment and despair of a dying man than about the religious thought of a working poet.

Since this process of development did not take place in a vacuum, I offer an introductory description of the general religious milieu in which Keats lived. I have not attempted anything like a full-scale analysis of the state of religion in England in the early nineteenth century: I wish only to point out a few important facts about the period in order to provide the reader of this study with some added perspective, so that the nature of the poet's personal religious difficulties and his manner of meeting them may be more completely understood.

My understanding of Keats as a religious thinker is founded, inevitably, on my sense of him as man and poet.

For this general understanding I am indebted to a rich tradition of Keats scholarship. I have specified some of this debt in the text and notes, but I feel obliged to mention three writers in particular who have helped me to form the impression of Keats's character and genius that inspired and underlies this book. They are John Middleton Murry, Aileen Ward (whose biography provided my first introduction to the poet), and Walter Jackson Bate. I owe another kind of debt, an immeasurable one, to Carl Woodring, who has been teaching me for ten years what it means to be a scholar (if I have learned the lesson imperfectly, the fault is entirely mine). While this study was taking its original form at Columbia University, I was fortunate also to have the advice and encouragement of Karl Kroeber and Leonard M. Trawick.

Like the man who is the subject of this study, I have been most fortunate in my friends. To them, and especially to my wife, Brighid Blake, I will only say, as Keats said to a friend, "I wish, at one view, you could see my heart towards you."

Part of Chapter Three was originally published as "Keats and the Truth of Imagination," *The Wordsworth Circle*, 4 (1973), 259-66. I am grateful to the Houghton Library at Harvard for permission to print excerpts from the Bailey Scrapbook.

INTRODUCTION

The Religious Milieu

IT should be recalled at the outset that John Keats lived during a very important and unusually lively period of English religious history. There had been for centuries a special relationship between religion and politics in Britain, and when the political atmosphere heated up during the age of revolution, the effects were felt immediately in the religious sphere. Indeed, from the time Edmund Burke, in his *Reflections on the Revolution in France*, linked the welfare of the English State with that of the English Church, and Tom Paine in answer advocated the overthrow of both, it became increasingly difficult to separate political debate from religious apologetics. The rhetoric of both the liberal reform movement and the conservative reaction to it became saturated with religious feeling and vocabulary. Within the ecclesiastical communities themselves, debate and dialectic rose in volume as the Methodist and Evangelical movements went about the work of transforming the complacent worldliness of eighteenth-century religious life into the earnest pietism of the Victorian era.

In our time, when religious convictions generally are politely underplayed, it may be difficult to imagine the fervor and fury with which such debates were carried on in the time of Keats. A sense of the era's enthusiasm for religious argument may be derived from statistics on the number of theological and moral tracts published in the period. Beginning with Hannah More's *Cheap Repository*, which began to appear in 1795 as an attempt to counteract the anticipated ill effects of *The Age of Reason*, England was flooded with countless millions of "penny readings" purveying various aspects of Christian teaching on faith, morality, and politics. They were sold in bookshops and by itinerant peddlers, and the number disposed of was enormous. In its first year of publication alone, two million copies of the *Cheap Repository* were sold.[1] In 1799, the Religious Tract Society—another counterrevolutionary organization—was founded, and by the 1820's was publishing and distributing over ten million tracts a year. The Society for Promoting Christian Knowledge was a much smaller operation, but still managed to produce a million tracts in 1817 alone, as well as 84,000 inexpensive Bibles and New Testaments. These are but a few of the many organizations, within and without the Established Church, that took to the presses in these years in an attempt to sway the minds and souls of the British people.

They found a ready market for their publications. The tracts were read by rich and poor alike. The cataclysm of the French Revolution and the long war that followed frightened the English people into a new interest in religion and morality.

> We have offended, Oh! my countrymen!
> We have offended very grievously,

wrote Coleridge in 1798,[2] and many in England were inclined to agree with him that the unsettling events of the time were a judgment from an "all-avenging Providence." People on every level of society began attending church more regularly, so many that in 1818 Parliament was prevailed upon to allot one million pounds for construction of new churches in the more crowded parishes. Prophets and visionaries arose, like Richard Brothers and Joanna Southcott, attracting thousands of disciples all over the country. While many questioned both the desirability of this rebirth of spiritual ardor and the motivation of some of its instigators, the fact remains that Britain in this period experienced

---

[1] This and the following statistics are taken from Maurice Quinlan's *Victorian Prelude: A History of English Manners, 1700–1830* (1941; rpr. Hamden, Conn.: Archon Books, 1965), pp. 83, 124, 133.

[2] "Fears in Solitude," *The Poems of Samuel Taylor Coleridge*, ed. E. H. Coleridge (London: Oxford Univ. Press, 1961), p. 258.

a religious revival remarkable in its extent and fervor. In 1819 Thomas Moore wrote to Leigh Hunt, cautioning him to keep his theories of religion and morality more to himself, "the mania on these subjects being so universal & *congenital*, that he who thinks of curing it, is as mad as his patients."[3]

Subsisting at the heart of all this agitation was the official religious establishment of the country, the Church of England. This was the community of believers in which Keats was born and brought up, by whose ministers he was baptized and confirmed, and in whose doctrines he was instructed. The Church represented orthodoxy to Keats, the Christian faith in its most traditional and "respectable" form. In attempting to understand his almost total rejection of that faith, we will find it helpful to have some notion of what Christianity meant to him, of the contemporary reality that clothed the ancient ideal. There were, of course, other communities of Christians present and active in Keats's England, and I shall have occasion to refer to some of them from time to time. For now, a sufficient foundation will be provided for this study by focusing attention on that Church of which King George III was sole earthly head.

Historians do not give a flattering account of the condition of England's Church in the period from 1795 to 1821.[4]

[3] *The Letters of Thomas Moore*, ed. Wilfred S. Dowden (Oxford: Clarendon Press, 1964), II, 471.
[4] Among the historians to whom I am indebted for the material that follows are: S. C. Carpenter, *Church and People, 1789-1889* (London: S.P.C.K., 1933); Gerald R. Cragg, *The Church and the Age of Reason, 1648-1789* (Baltimore: Penguin Books, 1966); L. E. Elliott-Binns, *The Evangelical Movement in the English Church* (London: Methuen, 1928) and *Religion in the Victorian Era* (London: Lutterworth Press, 1936); Elie Halévy, *A History of the English People in 1815*, 2nd rev. ed. (New York: Smith, 1949); J. Wickham Legg, *English Church Life from the Restoration to the Tractarian Movement* (London: Longmans, 1914); William Law Mathieson, *England in Transition, 1789-1832* (London: Longmans, 1920) and *English Church Reform* (London: Longmans, 1923); John Henry Overton, *The English Church in the Nineteenth Century* (London:

Although recent scholars have tended to look more kindly upon the Hanoverian Church as a whole than did their nineteenth-century predecessors (many of whom regarded the period before the Oxford illumination as a time of total darkness), the modern rehabilitation of the Church of the Georges has usually focused on the period *up to* the outbreak of the French Revolution. Even the most sympathetic commentators find little to praise in the years that followed. Norman Sykes, who perhaps did more than any other historian to rescue the eighteenth-century Church, said of this period: "The unhappy generation from 1793 to 1826 contributed more than any of its predecessors to the ill-repute of the eighteenth century by its policy of repression and reaction, which, though resolute in opposing all who laid even the mildest hands upon the established order in church and state, allowed the accumulation of anomalies and abuses in such magnitude as to provoke the radical reform epoch which succeeded."[5]

This consideration should be kept constantly in mind during any discussion of Keats's attitude toward Christianity: if the historians of the Church of England were asked to name the period in modern times when that Church was spiritually, intellectually, and structurally in its worst condition, farthest from the ideals of its founders and reformers, and least deserving of the respect of an intelligent and sensitive man, they would be virtually unanimous in choosing a period that coincides almost exactly with the lifetime of John Keats. It should be noted too that the years of his maturity were years when the people of England were becoming progressively more aware of the stains on the Church's garment, and progressively more critical of the

Longmans, 1894); Norman Sykes, *Church and State in England in the XVIIIth Century* (Cambridge: Cambridge Univ. Press, 1934); J. Edward Vaux, *Church Folklore* (London: Griffith, 1894); Alec R. Vidler, *The Church in an Age of Revolution* (Baltimore: Penguin Books, 1962); and R. J. White, *Waterloo to Peterloo* (London: Heinemann, 1957).

[5] *Church and State*, p. 407.

conduct and character of her ministers. It is not my intention to try to prove that Keats would have been a loyal Churchman if the Church had been more deserving of his loyalty. I would suggest, however, that if a time ever came in his adult life when Keats was willing to consider seriously the merits of the Christian faith and to look with renewed interest at the personality and teaching of Jesus, the difficulty of reconciling the Christ of the gospels with the Christianity of his own time could easily have discouraged him from pursuing his investigation.

This is not the place for an exhaustive inventory of the ills that afflicted the Church of England at the turn of the nineteenth century. Many of the most serious abuses (from the historian's point of view) did not become matters of widespread public concern until the very end of the period in question, and many would not have presented themselves directly to Keats's observation. Pluralism, for example—the holding of multiple benefices by a single clergyman—was only beginning to be seen as an evil and was usually excused as a necessary one. The concomitant abuse of nonresidence in cures was not a serious problem in the London area. Beilby Porteus, Bishop of London from 1787 to 1809, had dedicated himself to eradicating the evil and succeeded so well that in 1808 the Archdeacon of Middlesex (where Keats lived most of his life) could report that "on almost every living, the income of which is sufficient to supply the means of maintaining a decent residence for the incumbent, this important object is already attained."[6] It certainly may be questioned whether Keats ever cared enough about the institutional Church to be disturbed or disedified by purely canonical improprieties. But there were other aspects of the Church's life and conduct that must have intruded upon his observation, even as a youth, and made a disagreeable impression.

[6] Quoted by Robert Hodgson, *The Life of Bishop Porteus* (London: Cadell, 1823), p. 107.

One such stumbling block was the role of the Church in contemporary politics. Because episcopal appointments were controlled by the Prime Minister and because the Tories had held power in England nearly uninterruptedly since 1783, the bench of bishops in Keats's time was made up almost entirely of men expected to follow the conservative line. They surpassed expectations. Frightened by the revolution in France and by radical agitation in England, which they saw, not without reason, as a threat to the ecclesiastical Establishment, the hierarchy set itself almost to a man in opposition to the democratic spirit wherever it reared its atheistical head. In times of great economic distress, amid bread riots and hunger marches, most bishops voted consistently against the people's welfare, appealing to the inscrutable designs of a Providence that had sunk the poor in their poverty and obviously intended them to remain in that condition. As for the government, it was only too happy to accept the services of the Church as a retaining wall against the Jacobin tide. Many an embarrassing political question was answered with the cry, "The Church is in danger!"

The ecclesiastical record is a sorry one. Whether one thinks of the persecution of Thomas Williams by Bishop Porteus and the Proclamation Society for selling *The Age of Reason*, or the complicity of the local clergy in the Peterloo Massacre,[7] whether one recalls the comforting counsel of Bishop Paley that "poverty within certain bounds is more enjoyable than wealth,"[8] or the remark of Bishop Howley of London at the time of George IV's divorce that "the King could do no wrong either morally or physically,"[9] the leaders of the Church in this period seem to have placed themselves squarely on the side of legitimacy and repression, in

[7] Mathieson, *English Church Reform*, pp. 27f.
[8] Quoted by Mathieson, *England in Transition*, p. 77.
[9] Quoted by C. K. Francis Brown, *A History of the English Clergy, 1800-1900* (London: Faith Press, 1953), p. 87.

opposition to the forces of liberalism and reform. Words-worth was not overstating the case when he said, in his letter to the Bishop of Llandaff: "With a servility which has prejudiced many people against religion itself, the ministers of the Church of England have appeared as writers upon public measures only to be the advocates of slavery civil and religious."[10] In such a situation, a man growing up with liberal views might well feel that he was confronted with a choice between Christianity and humanitarianism. Many of Keats's contemporaries saw the choice in precisely those terms. To them, and perhaps to Keats himself, one might apply the words of Church historian S. C. Carpenter: "When the great majority of Christians seem with one voice to repudiate the demand for freedom and to applaud coercion, daring and eager spirits with the passion for liberty will assume that Christianity is dead, and will pass by on the other side."[11]

The unloveliness of the Church's external complexion was only a symptom of a serious inanition afflicting its interior life. The second half of the eighteenth century had brought a steady decline in faith and piety among members of the Church, a decline that reached its lowest point at around the time of Keats's birth. The age of reason had not provided a hospitable milieu for religious faith, and, although English theologians led by Bishop Butler (*The Analogy of Religion*, 1736) effectively rebutted the attacks of the Deists from without, the critical spirit had made damaging incursions within the Church itself. Weary of the kind of doctrinal warfare that had torn the seventeenth century, and eager to adapt and simplify Christianity to suit the taste of an enlightened age, liberal ecclesiastics were disposed to gloss over difficult or controversial articles of faith and to

[10] *The Prose Works of William Wordsworth*, ed. W. J. B. Owen and Jane Worthington Smyser (Oxford: Clarendon Press, 1974), I, 31.
[11] *Church and People*, p. 12.

emphasize instead those religious notions, such as the Fatherhood of God and the brotherhood of man, which all believers held in common. This approach to religion stressed the reasonable, common-sense aspects of Christianity over the supernatural and mysterious, making "natural religion" rather than revelation the basis of their faith. The end product was a religion eminently reasonable by contemporary standards, but rather cold and colorless, offering little nourishment to the emotions or to the imagination. The spiritual hunger left by a religion that often seemed little more than a system of polite ethics was satisfied for many by Methodism or Evangelicalism.[12] Others sought their food beyond the pale of Christianity. Meanwhile, among the leaders of the Establishment, theology stagnated, as the frightened conservatism of the clergy made them suspicious of doctrinal speculation, which they saw as a characteristic preoccupation of "infidels and sectaries." Churchmen were content to rest upon the traditional formulations and to enjoin on the faithful, in the words of a London bishop, "that humble docility, that prostration of the understanding and will, which is indispensable to proficiency in Christian instruction."[13]

The clergy, in fact, were hardly qualified to do more than repeat a few, simple religious formulae, most of them having received little or no training in theology. England was probably the only country in Europe where a man might present himself for ordination without having gone through a formal course of instruction in Christian doctrine.[14] It was

[12] The preaching and organizational activities of John Wesley and others had started a widespread revival of religious fervor in eighteenth-century England. The Methodist movement grew up within the Church, though without recognition or support from the hierarchy. After the death of Wesley, most of his followers formed a separate organization, but a good number refused to break formally with the Church. These zealous Churchmen formed a distinct party within the Establishment and eventually came to be called Evangelicals.

[13] *Edinburgh Review*, 37 (1822), 458.

[14] Halévy, p. 391.

left to individual bishops to examine the qualifications of their candidates, and many made this a very perfunctory procedure. The shallowness of the average clergyman's grounding in divinity was reflected in his preaching, and the quality of Sunday sermons was a subject of frequent complaint in this period. "The great object of modern sermons," said a commentator in 1803, "is to hazard nothing: Their characteristic is decent debility."[15] Earlier, the pious Samuel Johnson had made a similar comment on the quality of the preaching in London churches (whose pulpits, one should note, generally attracted the more learned and talented clergy): "I am convinced I ought to be present at divine service more frequently than I am; but the provocations given by ignorant and affected preachers too often disturb the mental calm which otherwise would succeed to prayer. I am apt to whisper to myself on such occasions— How can this illiterate fellow dream of fixing attention, after we have been listening to the sublimest truths, conveyed in the most chaste and exalted language, through a Liturgy which must be regarded as the genuine offspring of piety impregnated by wisdom."[16] Many preachers read the same sermons year after year from crumbling manuscripts or bought new ones ready-made from publishers— sometimes prepared, as one advertisement boasted, "in the form of manuscripts, so as not only to save clergymen the trouble of composing their discourses, but even of transcribing them."[17]

The clergy's lack of training in theology, combined with the Church's general lack of interest in doctrine per se, produced a type of preaching that offered little in the way of solid instruction to listeners. Since the weekly sermon was

[15] *Edinburgh Review*, 1 (1803), 83.
[16] *Johnsonian Miscellanies*, ed. G. Birkbeck Hill (Oxford: Clarendon Press, 1897), II, 319.
[17] Brown, pp. 32f. This particular abuse caught the attention of Keats's friend, John Reynolds, who called it "a gross infringement of the candour and decency of the church." *London Magazine*, 4 (November 1821), p. 516.

usually the sole source of religious education for the laity, it is not surprising that they, too, were largely ignorant of Christian doctrine. In 1812, Leigh Hunt wrote in the *Examiner*: "Of all the respectable people who go to church on Sundays, and who have been in the habit from their infancy of taking their religion for granted, there are probably not a sufficient number out of ten parishes to fill a single pew, who are acquainted with the thirty-nine articles of their faith."[18] From Hunt's point of view such ignorance was salutary. In another context he wrote: "Why should the most obscure mysteries be made the perpetual subject of the pulpit, why should theory and not practice be so everlastingly preached to those who know as much of the theory as they ever will? . . . Mankind will believe a hundred good things, before they do one."[19] This emphasis on doing rather than believing, on practice as opposed to theory, was one that Hunt shared with many more orthodox than he. The most characteristic quality of contemporary religion, at least within the Church, was a kind of pious utilitarianism, concerned much more with morals than with dogma, with the "whole duty of man" rather than with articles of faith. Looking back on this period, James Anthony Froude wrote: "Religion, as taught in the Church of England, meant moral obedience to the will of God. The speculative part of it was accepted because it was assumed to be true. The creeds were reverentially repeated; but the essential thing was practice. People went to church on Sunday to learn to be good, to hear the commandments repeated to them for the thousandth time, and to see them written in gilt letters over the communion table."[20]

If the Church's intellectual life was in a depressed state, its sacramental life was in no better condition, and the communion table of which Froude spoke served most often a

[18] *Examiner*, May 3, 1812, p. 274.
[19] *Ibid.*, May 15, 1808, p. 317.
[20] "The Oxford Counter-Reformation," *Short Studies on Great Subjects*, Fourth Series (New York: Scribner, 1883), p. 156.

purely ornamental function. In the majority of churches the Lord's Supper was celebrated only four times a year (at Easter, Whitsunday, Michaelmas, and Christmas) and even those limited opportunities were not taken by most of the people. It is recorded that in St. Paul's Cathedral on Easter Sunday, 1800, only six persons communicated.[21] The necessary rites of baptism, marriage, and burial, on the other hand, were performed with such frequency that they often could not be celebrated with dignity or even decency in the limited facilities available. The older churches and cathedrals were poorly maintained, and the new buildings erected in an emergency program after 1815 were characterized by "unmitigated ugliness and hopeless inconvenience."[22] Austerity rather than beauty was the guiding principle in church adornment, whitewash being the most usual means of decoration. While artwork like mural paintings was frowned upon as smacking of "popery" (William Blake and Benjamin Robert Haydon were among those who worked to remove this prejudice), the walls and aisles of churches were cluttered with memorial plaques and monuments. As for music, psalmody was in a generally unsatisfactory state, the most commonly used translation of the Psalms being the pedestrian metrical versions in the Prayer Book. Hymns were still considered "methodistical"; only in the 1820's were they adopted on a large scale. All in all, it was as though the external forms and appurtenances of religion had been blighted by the same disease that was afflicting its internal spirit. In a short time, the Tractarian movement would restore to the Church a consciousness of her old identity as mother of the arts and a new realization of the importance of the aesthetic factor in the ritual and environment of worship. In Keats's lifetime, however, the element of beauty was still being conspicuously neglected.

A religious organization intellectually becalmed, spiritually desiccated, and aesthetically impoverished, whose

[21] Vaux, p. 56.   [22] Overton, p. 155.

official spokesmen were worldly, self-serving chaplains to the status quo in a repressive society—this was the Church of England as Keats knew it. Yet, at the very time when the Church's fortunes were at their lowest, the movement that would effect a new reformation was already under way, sending its roots deep into the foundations of the Establishment. And this description of the Anglican Church in Keats's time would not be complete or honest without some allusion to the remarkable company of men and women who worked to accomplish this reformation—the Evangelicals. Remaining loyal members of the Church, these "enthusiasts" witnessed by word and deed against the worldliness and complacency of their coreligionists and unceasingly attacked ecclesiastical corruption. Inspired by an intense personal faith in God and a strong commitment to Jesus Christ as Savior and Master, they succeeded in reviving religious fervor within the Church and in changing radically the moral climate of England. The range of their activities extended to the social and political spheres as well, and, although they subscribed to the view of religion as a specific against revolution, the record shows that their accomplishments in the area of social amelioration far outweigh those of the disciples of Paine and Godwin.

However, recognizing their contributions to Church and State and their genuine virtues, the Evangelicals had certain traits that must certainly have repelled a man like Keats. Their theology had a Calvinist base, with the characteristic belief in natural depravity. This emphasis led them to equate humanism with secularism, and to look upon philosophy, science, and the arts as, at best, unnecessary distractions from "the one thing needful" and, at worst, devices of Satan to lead astray the elect. With a sense of the "high seriousness" of life on earth, they condemned as dangerous dissipations card playing, dancing, and particularly attendance at theaters. Perhaps because he was the chief English dramatist, they reserved some of their choicest damnations for William Shakespeare, singling him out as a great enemy of religion.[23] Even the intelligent, cultivated Hannah More had grave reservations about him: "Who will deny that all the excellences we have ascribed to him are debased by passages of offensive grossness? are tarnished with indelicacy, false taste, and vulgarity?"[24] It was to accommodate such scrupulous readers that Thomas Bowdler produced *The Family Shakespeare* in 1818.

Knowing Keats's almost worshipful attitude toward Shakespeare, we find it easy to imagine his reaction to all of this. In fact, like most liberal intellectuals of the time, he despised the "Methodists."[25] This is a significant point. The one large segment of the Church of England that possessed a vital, living faith in Keats's day, and that was not afflicted with apathy or tainted with corruption, also emerged as an implacable enemy of things as dear to him as life itself. The Evangelicals could have little to say to a man for whom poetry was the one thing needful.

Sometime between his fifteenth and twentieth year, Keats stopped thinking of himself as a member of the Church of England; by the end of 1816 he had come to look upon the religion practiced in the churches as no better than superstition. This repudiation of the faith in which he had been brought up was apparently not a sudden dramatic act of apostasy, but a gradual process of abandoning doctrines and practices that, as he grew older, he found intellectually indefensible or emotionally unappealing. At the end of this winnowing process he had discarded the most distinctive doctrines of Christianity and explicitly disassociated himself from that faith. During the remainder of his life he de-

[23] Quinlan, p. 242.

[24] *The Works of Hannah More* (London: Fisher, 1834-1835), v, xxix.

[25] In the early years of the nineteenth century, the term "Methodist" was often used to describe the new religious enthusiasts within the Church as well as those who had separated from it. The distinction between Methodist and Evangelical was ignored for some time, especially by critics of the movement.

voted much thought to formulating an alternative system of religion, one that would not, as he put it, "affront our reason and humanity." The form of faith he devised for himself was quite personal, but it was not especially original. Many of his specific ideas were borrowed from his friends, Christian and non-Christian. The general nature of his belief belonged to a fairly old tradition in English religious thought: the tradition of natural religion.

Natural religion is based on the proposition that the Supreme Being has endowed man with sufficient reasoning power to enable him, if he will but examine the physical universe around him and study carefully his own interior dispositions, to arrive at certain basic conclusions about his Creator's existence and nature, and about his own duties and destiny as a creature. Natural theology has always been a part of the orthodox Christian tradition, but in the latter half of the seventeenth century it began to receive increased attention. The new science, which proclaimed the perfect order and harmony of the physical universe and thus provided what seemed irrefutable proof of the existence of a beneficent Creator; the new philosophy of Locke, which made "reasonableness" the standard by which all things, including religion, were to be judged; the desire of men weary of doctrinal strife to find a common religious ground on which all parties could meet and agree—these and other factors combined to place natural theology at the center of English religious consciousness at the turn of the eighteenth century.

As long as natural theology was understood to embody only the first premises of religion, premises that needed to be clarified and supplemented by the fuller revelation embodied in Scripture, there was no quarrel between natural religion and Christian orthodoxy. But there suddenly appeared on the scene a group of scholars who proposed natural religion as an *alternative* to Christianity, as a purer, more reasonable, and more authentic form of faith. The Deists, as they came to be called, regarded the Christian system as at best a superfluous complication of the simple natural religion ordained by God from the beginning, and at worst a superstitious perversion of it. Their belief that a true religion ought to be universal and unchanging led them to repudiate the concept of continuing divine intervention in human affairs and a gradually unfolding revelation—a concept that is the foundation of the Judaeo-Christian religious tradition. Beginning as a constructive attempt to make religion more palatable to an enlightened age, Deism soon became essentially negative and critical in character. The Deists seemed more interested in elaborating a radical critique of Christianity than in developing a positive alternative. Their positive creed was rather brief: it included belief in a personal if somewhat aloof Deity who created the universe and continues to sustain it in existence, a recognition of man's obligation to worship the Supreme Being and to live ethically here on earth, and a sometimes unsteady confidence in the existence of an afterlife, in which rewards and punishments will be meted out according to deserts.

Most historians treat Deism as a short-lived phenomenon, a kind of nine decades' wonder. In this view, Deism collapsed about 1750 under a two-pronged assault by orthodox apologetics on one side and the radical skepticism of David Hume on the other. And yet, as late as 1819 one finds Leigh Hunt speaking of Deism as a living, thriving faith and prophesying a bright future for it. "It has been making multitudes of converts for many years past; and who can tell when the *now* of Deism is not to arrive? whether it has not even arrived already, though not as an established or legalized dogma?"[26] In defense of the traditional opinion,

[26] *Examiner*, October 24, 1819, p. 675. Hunt was not alone in his belief that Deism was in a flourishing state. In the same year, a tract was published called *Deism Refuted, or Plain Reasons for Being a Christian* (London, 1819; rpr. Philadelphia: Littell & Henry, 1820). Its author, Thomas Horne, explained his reason for writing the pamphlet thus: "At a time, when the Press teems with invectives against the fundamental doctrines of the Christian Religion, and old

it should be noted that what Hunt and his contemporaries called Deism was rather different in character from the movement that flourished in the early eighteenth century. The positive tenets were the same and the critical attitude toward Christianity had not changed; but the cool rationalism of the Augustan scholars had given way to a much more emotional kind of faith. Deism, as it survived into the nineteenth century, was a "religion of the heart" (in Hunt's phrase) rather than of the head. Men looked into their hearts to find the truths of natural religion inscribed there by God, a God who seemed closer and more accessible than the Great Artificer discovered by reason in the previous century.

It should be pointed out that in Keats's time adherence to natural religion did not automatically necessitate a formal break with the Church of England. There were many who called themselves Churchmen who did not believe in the divinity of Christ and who rejected other important doctrines of the faith. Because of its loose structure the Church had little opportunity, even if it had the will, to discipline its members in orthodoxy. Even the clergy simply ignored dogmas they found intellectually embarrassing; the non-theological character of the age made it relatively easy to get by, as layman or priest, with the barest minimum of doctrine. A man could believe privately what he liked, without ever having his credentials as a Churchman questioned by the authorities.

Indeed, in that sense it might be said that John Keats never "left the Church" at all. Notwithstanding his disdain for the Establishment's doctrine and politics and his general

---

objections against the authenticity and inspiration of the Holy Scriptures are circulated in the shape of compendiums of infidelity, and in the cheapest possible forms, silence on the part of those who believe the Bible to be the Word of God, becomes criminal." Five years earlier, Percy Bysshe Shelley had also published *A Refutation of Deism*, though from rather different motives.

(25)

contempt for its clergy, he was given ecclesiastical burial when he died. At his death, as at his birth, the Church of England claimed him as one of its own. But in those few years when he was able to think and speak for himself, Keats stood stubbornly apart from the Church, striving to find his own way in religion, to define in his own terms the nature of the relationship that existed between himself and the Being whom he called his Creator.

CHAPTER ONE

The Early Years

O N December 18, 1795, in the dark and gloomy church
of St. Botolph, Bishopsgate, the first-born son of the
Keats family was brought to be baptized. Standing at the
marble font, the officiating cleric spoke these words: "We
receive this child into the Congregation of Christ's flock,
and do sign him with the sign of the Cross, in token that
hereafter he shall not be ashamed to confess the faith of
Christ crucified, and manfully to fight under his banner,
against sin, the world, and the devil. . . . Seeing now that
this Child is regenerate, and grafted into the body of
Christ's Church, let us give thanks unto Almighty God for
these benefits; and with one accord make our prayers unto
him, that this child may lead the rest of his life according
to this beginning."[1] But the optimistic hopes of the Church
for this particular child were not to come true: the grafting
was unsuccessful. How Keats's religious views developed,
and how he wandered away from the flock into which he
had been received as an infant, will be the concern of the
following pages.

It will, of course, be impossible to present a completely
documented account of the progress of Keats's disaffection
from the Christian faith. He left us no history of the
"growth of a poet's mind," and the evidence from other
sources concerning his early intellectual development is
rather scanty. But by assembling what biographical data is
available and then filling in some of the gaps with educated
guesses based on knowledge of the social and cultural

[1] *The Book of Common Prayer and Administration of the Sacraments and other Rites and Ceremonies of the Church* . . . (Oxford:
Clarendon Press, 1803). All further citations of the Prayer Book
will be from this edition.

---

milieu in which he lived, it is possible, I think, to construct a relatively coherent and satisfying explanation of the growth of Keats's critical attitude toward Christianity. Many of my conclusions will necessarily be tentative and conjectural, but I feel that the investigation is worthwhile: in a study such as this, one simply cannot pass over in silence a period that comprises four-fifths of the subject's lifetime.

Many years after Keats's death, Benjamin Bailey expressed the opinion that his friend's early religious education had been "greatly or wholly neglected."[2] Before taking exception to this statement, one must concede that of all Keats's acquaintances Bailey was perhaps in the best position to make such a judgment. He was a clergyman, and thus qualified by training to make an evaluation of this kind. Moreover, Keats seems to have discussed religion at greater length with him than with any other of his circle of friends.[3] Yet Bailey's opinion can be challenged on the basis of considerable evidence which suggests that Keats possessed a competent grasp of the essentials of Christian doctrine, and that as a child he had at least the opportunity to receive a fairly thorough grounding in religious knowledge, according to the standards of his time and social class. The discrepancy can, I think, be resolved somewhat by placing Bailey's remark in context. It was part of an attempt to explain Keats's religious skepticism, and to clear his friend's memory as best he could from what he considered a stain upon it. Moreover, Bailey was writing as an archdeacon of the Church in a period much more scrupulous about what constituted a proper religious upbringing. Standards had changed considerably in fifty years as a result of the Evangelical and Tractarian reform movements.

[2] *The Keats Circle*, ed. H. E. Rollins (Cambridge, Mass.: Harvard Univ. Press, 1965), II, 292. Hereafter this collection will be referred to as *KC*.
[3] *KC*, II, 252, 264.

Indeed, by later standards, religious education at the turn of the nineteenth century might be said to have been "greatly or wholly neglected" as a general rule. At Eton, for instance, there was no official program of religious instruction, and a similar gap existed at a number of the other public schools.[4] Even in formally ecclesiastical environments, religious education reflected the utilitarian, anti-doctrinal bias of the age. James Anthony Froude, son of the Archdeacon of Totnes, describes his own experience thus:

My brothers and I were excellently educated, and were sent to school and college. Our spiritual lessons did not go beyond the Catechism. We were told that our business in life was to work and to make an honorable position for ourselves. About doctrine, Evangelical or Catholic, I do not think that in my early boyhood I ever heard a single word, in church or out of it. The institution had drifted into the condition of what I should call moral health. It did not instruct us in mysteries, it did not teach us to make religion a special object of our thoughts; it taught us to use religion as a light by which to see our way along the road of duty.[5]

Given the cultural milieu, and the case of a clergyman's son who never heard "a single word" about doctrine in his boyhood, one might reasonably expect that the religious education of the son of a London hostler would have been minimal—at most. Yet the evidence shows that Keats's upbringing may have been somewhat atypical in this regard and that he had certain opportunities not shared by many children in his class.

To begin with, the family into which he was born had

[4] John Henry Overton, *The English Church in the Nineteenth Century* (London: Longmans, 1894), p. 227.

[5] "The Oxford Counter-Reformation," *Short Studies on Great Subjects*, Fourth Series (New York: Scribner, 1883), p. 158. Froude is speaking here of the 1820's, when the ecclesiastical revival was already under way—though obviously it had not yet penetrated into his father's archdeaconry.

been quite active in ecclesiastical affairs. His maternal
grandfather, John Jennings, held several positions of trust
at the church of St. Stephen, Coleman Street, most notably
that of senior churchwarden, to which office he was elected
in 1789.[6] The position of churchwarden was one of considerable dignity and importance, the occupant bearing responsibility not only for the physical upkeep of the church
building and its written records but also in certain ways for
the moral welfare of the parishioners. The canon law of the
Church lists among the duties of churchwardens "the sup-
pressing of sin and wickedness in their several parishes, as
much as in them lieth, by admonition, reprehension, and
denunciation to their Ordinary."[7] Among the evils they
were responsible for repressing were adultery, prostitution,
incest, drunkenness, swearing, ribaldry, and usury. The
churchwarden's duty of moral surveillance was still being
taken seriously at the beginning of the nineteenth century.[8]
We do not know how much attention John Jennings paid to
his responsibilities, but the very fact that he was chosen for
such a position testifies to his reputation as a worthy
Churchman. It may be of some significance that another of
his grandsons, Midgely John Jennings, was ordained to the
ministry, and that a granddaughter, Midgely's sister, mar-
ried a Canon of St. Paul's Cathedral.[9]

As for Keats's parents, we know little of their religious
habits and attitudes except for an indication by Richard
Abbey (another churchwarden, and one who seems to have
taken seriously his duty as moral overseer) that Mrs.
Keats's behavior was not always that of a respectable
Churchwoman. He described her (to John Taylor) crossing

---

[6] Jean Haynes, "John Jennings: Keats's Grandfather," *Keats-
Shelley Memorial Bulletin*, 13 (1962), 19.
[7] Canon 113, *The Constitutions and Canons of the Church of
England* (Oxford: Clarendon Press, 1825), p. 36.
[8] J. Edward Vaux, *Church Folklore* (London: Griffith, 1894),
p. 192.
[9] William A. Jarvis, "A Cousin of John Keats," *Keats-Shelley
Memorial Bulletin*, 14 (1963), 39.

the street in front of St. Botolph's Church and lifting her skirts to attract the eye of a nearby grocer.[10] A more serious indication of neglect of religious duty is the fact that her three youngest sons were all baptized at once—in one swoop, as it were—when the youngest of them (Edward, who died in infancy) was six months old.[11] A rubric in the Prayer Book advises that children ought to be christened within a week or two after birth. While practice in this matter had become somewhat lax in the period being discussed, Mrs. Keats's having deferred the baptism of her son George until he was four years old seems to indicate more than ordinary laxity.

It may be true, as George Yost suggests,[12] that Keats's fondness for religious imagery derives from early training at home, but it is impossible to guess at the quantity and quality of this religious instruction. We may assume there was some Bible reading (the book was often used as a primer when children were learning to read) and the usual parent-to-child talk about God, angels, and devils, and the different prospects of good and bad boys in the afterlife. At any rate, when Keats arrived at what the Church calls the age of reason and when he might have begun asking more sophisticated questions about religion, circumstances conspired to place him under the care of his grandmother.

Mrs. Jennings' home would have provided a more explicitly Christian environment for the Keats children than their parents' busy household. Keats's sonnet on his grandmother's death (about which more will be said later) was the closest thing to a "devotional" poem he ever wrote, and reflects the religious piety he evidently associated with her memory. As the widow of an active Churchman she would have been in the habit of regular attendance at Sunday services, and it is likely that she brought her grandchildren

[10] KC, I, 303.
[11] Marie Adami, Fanny Keats (London: Murray, 1937), p. 14.
[12] "Keats's Early Religious Phraseology," Studies in Philology, 59 (1962), 579.

with her each week to hear the sermon at the nearby Church of All Saints in Edmonton. There may also have been regular morning and evening prayer at home, in which the entire household would have participated.[13]

For an impression of the religious atmosphere in which the Keats children, and other children on their social level, were growing up, it may be useful to glance at a little book that we know John Keats and his sister Fanny read together during the Edmonton period.[14] *Original Poems for Infant Minds*, a collection of verses "by several young persons," was first published in 1804 and went through several editions. The poems, which Keats called "pleasant little things," are mostly of the exemplary tale variety, with titles like "The Idle vs. the Industrious Boy," "The Vulgar Little Lady," "Meddlesome Matty," etc. Some are intended merely to amuse, but they generally convey moral lessons, and a few are overtly religious. The tone of these is not explicitly Christian: there is no direct reference to Jesus Christ and only one to the Bible. The emphasis is rather on a Supreme Being who keeps watch over the doings of children, and rewards or punishes them according to their conduct. The following excerpts will suggest the tone of the book.

A coach and a footman, and gaudy attire,
Can't give true delight to the breast;
To be good is the thing you should chiefly desire,
And then leave to God all the rest.

There is One, who by night just as well as by day,
Can see all you do, and can hear all you say,
From his glorious throne in the sky . . .

For the Great God, who even thro' darkness can look,
Writes down ev'ry crime we commit in his book,
However we think to conceal.

[13] Regular prayers were a common feature of English domestic life at this time. Keats seems to have been familiar with the form of prayer in the Prayer Book. He quotes one of the rubrics in *Letters*, I, 139.
[14] Adami, p. 40. See also *Letters*, I, 155.

And when the great morning of judgment shall rise,
How wide will its blazes be curl'd!
With heat, fervent heat, it shall melt down the skies
And burn up this beautiful world.[15]

Not, perhaps, what we would call pleasant little things, but quite representative of the sort of literature children in Keats's day were invited to read for their souls' health.

Another environment, much more significant than that of his grandmother's home, had begun to affect Keats's religious development in 1804. In that year he was enrolled as a student at the academy of Mr. John Clarke at Enfield. Clarke's academy was the place where Keats came of age as a Christian; it was also the place where he first began to question the value and validity of the faith in which he had been brought up.

The history of the school at Enfield begins with John Collet Ryland, a popular Baptist preacher of the eighteenth century. While the Baptists in general did not share the enthusiasm for higher education that inspired other sects to establish the famous Dissenting Academies, Ryland saw a need for advancing knowledge of science and "polite learning" among his coreligionists. He established his academy first at Warwick in 1750; in 1759 it was transferred to Northampton, and in 1786 it moved at last to Enfield.[16] One of his assistants at Northampton was a young lawyer named John Clarke, who taught classics and other literary subjects. Clarke became engaged to Ryland's stepdaughter, and when the academy moved to Enfield he was put in charge. Ryland lived on in residence there until his death in 1792.

It is difficult to determine to what extent Ryland's personal religious views affected the character of his school. He was a rigid Calvinist and a leading spokesman for that segment of the Baptist community (the "Particular Baptists")

[15] *Original Poems for Infant Minds*, by Several Young Persons (Boston: House, 1808), pp. 12, 34, 129.
[16] Nicholas Hans, *New Trends in Education in the Eighteenth Century* (London: Routledge, 1951), pp. 61f.

which preserved the doctrines of Calvin in their purest form.[17] But the Dissenting Academies generally tended to downplay dogma in order to attract pupils from all ranks of society, and Ryland's school was once described as "a sort of open house to all the vagrant train."[18] The Particular Baptists were known for being more ecumenical in spirit than other religious groups and they were interested in maintaining some form of unity among Christians. So it is possible that the academy was never really a "Baptist school." The fact that John Jennings sent his sons (Keats's uncles) there would seem to indicate that, if there had ever been anything overtly sectarian about the general tone of the education offered, it had lost that coloring when John Clarke assumed the headmastership.

We know almost nothing of the theological convictions of this man who played so important a part in Keats's intellectual development. Because of his friendship with Joseph Priestley and his admiration for Leigh Hunt, it would be easy to assume that his tendencies in religion were liberal. At the same time, it is very difficult to imagine Ryland, who was strictly and sometimes ferociously orthodox, welcoming into his family and turning his school over to anyone with pronounced heterodox views. What we do know with certainty is that Clarke had an openness and generosity of spirit that would have prevented him from imposing his own views, whatever their nature, upon others. We learn from his son's reminiscences that he was on equally friendly terms with Joseph Priestley, the great Unitarian divine, and Alexander Geddes, the Catholic priest and Biblical scholar. During Keats's time at Enfield, instruction in French was given by an *emigré* priest, the Abbé Béliard, who was extremely popular with the students.[19] One has the

[17] A. C. Underwood, *A History of the English Baptists* (London: Baptist Union Publ. Dept., 1947), p. 143.

[18] George Dyer, quoted by E. V. Lucas, *The Life of Charles Lamb* (London: Methuen, 1921), I, 175.

[19] Charles Cowden Clarke, *Recollections of Writers* (1878; rpt. Fontwell, Sussex: Centaur Press, 1969), p. 7.

feeling that whatever religious instruction there was must have been carried on in a spirit of tolerance and open-mindedness. That religious education of some sort was offered at Enfield there can be little doubt. One of Ryland's favorite works on the theory of education was Charles Rollin's *Traité des Études* (1728), which lays down the principle that "Religion should be the thing aimed at in all our endeavors and the end of all our instructions. Though it is not constantly in our mouths, it should be constantly in our minds and never out of sight."[20] An impression of the kind of religious instruction given at Enfield might be gained by looking briefly at *A Catechism for Children and Young Persons*, published by Joseph Priestley in 1781. Whether or not Clarke actually made use of his friend's catechism, his own approach would probably have been similar to that of Priestley, involved as they both were in educating boys from a Christian background for commercial and lower professional careers. Reflecting the utilitarian approach to religion that characterized the age, Priestley states in his introduction that the catechism attempts to include "in a small compass, every thing that revelation contains which can influence the hearts and lives of men, all that is of *practical use*, and, consequently, all that is properly *fundamental* in religion." It includes, he says, "all the truths of christianity, that can greatly influence mens practice; for these are very few, and such as a child may be made to understand." There will, then, be little discussion of complicated doctrines, and nothing controversial—"nothing but what will be acknowledged to belong to common christianity." And so the catechism focuses upon the existence of a Supreme Being, a just God who rewards the good and pun-

20 *Traité des Études*, I, 22. Quoted by Albert Charles Gaudin, *The Educational Views of Charles Rollin* (New York: Columbia University, 1939), p. 18. Ryland recommended Rollin's work in a book he dedicated "to modest and virtuous young tutors in the seats of learning and science," *The Character of the Reverend James Hervey M.A.* (London: Robarts, 1791), p. xii.

ishes the wicked both in this life and in the next, who is basically benevolent but who "can make us die whenever he pleases." As for Jesus Christ, he was "a person whom God sent to teach men their duty, and to persuade and encourage them to practice it." He was put to death by wicked men and then raised by God. Priestley points out that one learns of such things in the Bible, "which we must diligently read and study, for our improvement in knowledge and goodness, in order to fit us for heaven."[21]

The Bible, of course, was the ideal textbook for a course in religion offered to a mixed group of Christians, as long as arbitrary interpretation was avoided. That it was "diligently read and studied" at Enfield can be demonstrated both from Keats's writings and from what we know of John Clarke. Several critics have called attention to Keats's evident familiarity with the Scriptures. One of them, Lloyd Jeffrey, counted ninety-two direct Biblical allusions, thirty-seven in the poems and fifty-five in the letters.[22] Keats's comfortable grasp of scriptural language is revealed particularly, I think, in his habit of paraphrasing a verse from the Bible to fit his own (often humorous) purposes. For example, in an 1817 letter he speaks of "the Bank Note of Faith and Cash of Salvation," a play on Ephesians VI: 16-17. As for Clarke, we know from his son's memoirs that he was deeply interested and involved in the scriptural scholarship of the time. Charles Cowden Clarke recalls:

> He took peculiar interest in the work, much pursued at that time, of Biblical translation, and closely watched the labours of Gilbert Wakefield, the translator of the New Testament; and the eminent surgeon Mason Good—a self-educated classic—who produced a fine version of Job, the result of his Sunday morning's devotion. . . . My father was intimate with the celebrated Roman Catholic writer, Dr. Alexander Geddes, and subscribed to all the

[21] *A Catechism for Children and Young Persons* (London: J. Johnson, 1781), pp. vii-viii.
[22] "Keats and the Bible," *Keats-Shelley Journal*, 10 (1961), 60.

portions of the Bible that Geddes lived to translate. . . .
And such was my father's Biblical zeal that he made a ms.
copy of Bishop Lowth's translation of Isaiah, subjoining
a selection of the most important of the translator's notes
to the text.[23]

Clarke may have caught his enthusiasm for Scripture
studies from Ryland, who had been something of a Bible
scholar himself.[24] It appears that at Enfield there was a tradition of taking the Scriptures seriously.

With regard to religious practice, Keats would have been
encouraged or, perhaps, required to attend services regularly at St. Andrew's, the Enfield parish church nearby.[25]
The seasons of the liturgical year and the cycle of feast days
must have affected life at the academy, as they still did to
some extent in the country at large. Many of the Church's
holy days were observed as holidays in the English schools.
Perhaps the "days of fast and humiliation," proclaimed pe-
riodically during the war years to seek God's pardon for the
sins of the nation, were taken note of at Enfield. But Keats's
most significant personal involvement with the Church
probably came around the year 1809, when he would have
been expected to undergo formal instruction preparatory
to his confirmation.

As far as I am aware, no record of this event in Keats's
life has come down to us. This is not surprising, since records of confirmation were almost never preserved in English parish registers, there being no directive in canon law
requiring it.[26] But despite the lack of solid evidence, there
is no reason to doubt that Keats did in fact go through this

---

[23] *Recollections*, p. 5.
[24] He was the author of *A Key to the Greek New Testament*
(London: Keith, 1777).
[25] Guy Murchie, *The Spirit of Place in Keats* (London: Newman Neame, 1955), p. 17. An interesting description of the church
as it appeared in Keats's time may be found in W. Robinson's *The
History and Antiquities of Enfield* (London: Nichols, 1823).
[26] J. Charles Cox, *The Parish Registers of England* (London:
Methuen, 1910), p. 70.

ceremony, which was a social convention expected of every youth baptized in the Church of England when he or she reached the age of fourteen. There is no evidence of intellectual rebelliousness so early in his life, and his grandmother was still in control. I would like briefly to consider this admittedly obscure moment in Keats's life, because it marks the only time in his life when he was called upon to make a public profession of the Christian faith.

The rubrics concerning confirmation in the Book of Common Prayer instruct that "so soon as children are come to a competent Age, and can say, in their Mother Tongue, the Creed, the Lord's Prayer, and the Ten Commandments; and also can answer to the other Questions of this short Catechism; they shall be brought to the Bishop." In a school situation, it was generally the headmaster's responsibility to catechize those who were to be confirmed.[27] But this practice was not universally followed, and since Clarke was a layman Keats may have been sent to be instructed by the curate at St. Andrew's. The short catechism, or "Instruction to be learned of every person before he be brought to be confirmed by the Bishop," requires the confirmand to recite the Apostle's Creed and the Ten Commandments and to assent to the Church's teaching on Baptism and the Sacrament of the Lord's Supper. It is a fairly comprehensive summation of the central doctrines of the faith. Having demonstrated to the instructor's satisfaction his grasp of these doctrines, Keats would one day have been brought with many other children to a centrally located church, where the Bishop of London would come to perform the ceremony.

The central significance of the rite must have been made clear to Keats during the period of instruction. It was instituted, as the Prayer Book states, "to the end, that children, being now come to the years of discretion, and having learned what their Godfathers and Godmothers promised

[27] S. L. Ollard, "Confirmation in the Anglican Communion," in *Confirmation or the Laying on of Hands* (London: S.P.C.K., 1926), p. 212.

for them in Baptism, they may themselves, with their own mouth and consent, openly before the Church, ratify and confirm the same; and also promise, that by the grace of God they will evermore endeavour themselves faithfully to observe such things, as they, by their own confession, have assented unto." How seriously did the adolescent Keats take this profession of Christian faith and purpose, this mature ratification of promises made for him in his infancy? That he did pay close attention to his catechism lessons may be seen in the apparent facility with which he answered his sister's questions when she herself was about to be confirmed.[28] In the absence of any evidence to the contrary (from Cowden Clarke, for instance) we may assume that Keats went through the formalities in a docile manner, expressing his belief in the doctrines specified and making the pledges he was expected to make. But reciting answers to questions and giving intellectual assent to them involve different mental processes, as anyone who was catechized as a child can attest. We do not know if Keats had yet begun to look with a critical eye at the Church and its teachings. But it was not long after this formal coming of age as a Christian that he began the process of questioning that eventually led him away from the faith of his childhood.

At some point in this period, 1809–1810, a change began to come over the young Keats. Suddenly he became much more interested in the things of the mind. He began to study intently and read voraciously, rising earlier than the other boys and skipping recreation periods to pursue his new enthusiasm. Whatever provoked the change—whether brooding on his mother's death or simply the normal awakening of intellectual curiosity that comes with adolescence —it is possible to identify this period of intense mental activity as the start of the process by which Keats came to

---

[28] *The Letters of John Keats*, ed. H. E. Rollins (Cambridge, Mass.: Harvard Univ. Press, 1958), II, 49ff. Hereafter, all references to Keats's letters will be included in the text.

reject the religious tradition in which he had been brought up. Charles Cowden Clarke describes him at this time, "sitting back on the form, from the table, holding the folio volume of Burnet's 'History of His Own Time' between himself and the table, eating his meal from beyond it. This work," continues Clarke, "and Leigh Hunt's Examiner—which my father took in, and I used to lend to Keats—no doubt laid the foundation of his love of civil and religious liberty."[29]

The influence of Leigh Hunt on the development of Keats's religious views was profound, and much more will be said on this subject later. One cannot be sure from Clarke's statement whether Keats began to read the *Examiner* while he was at Enfield, or only later when he lived at Edmonton and visited Clarke regularly; so we do not know when precisely the influence began to operate. The volumes from 1808 to 1811 have a different character—in terms of religious ideas—from those published later. While the earlier numbers provide considerable food for thought on the subject of "religious liberty," they contain little or nothing to encourage disaffection from the Church of England or from Christianity itself. In the few instances of specifically religious discussion, Hunt comes across as a surprisingly staunch advocate of the Anglican Establishment, which he sees as a "moderate Church," free from the bigotry of its Methodist critics and from the superstition of continental Catholicism. Against "the intolerant disciples of the merciless Calvin, the gloomy Methodists," he defends "the mild spirit of Christianity, and the Church of England Establishment which cherishes it."[30] Before long, the *Examiner*'s views on such things would undergo a marked change, but the first volumes afford scant argument for regarding the paper as a key factor in Keats's initial questioning of his religious inheritance.

More interesting in that regard is the other work mentioned by Clarke as a source of Keats's "love of religious

[29] *Recollections*, p. 124.
[30] *Examiner*, May 15, 1808, p. 301.

liberty," *The History of My Own Time*, by Bishop Gilbert Burnet of Salisbury (1643–1715). This sprawling narrative is not a formal history so much as a running commentary on the events of the turbulent period from 1640 to 1713 by one who was an eyewitness and participant. There is much that is partisan and prejudiced in Burnet's version of what happened in those years, and little artistry in the writing. But it is a racy, colorful account of an exciting era, narrated with gusto and a sense of immediacy that a more careful and detached historian might not be able to match.

As a member of the hierarchy, Burnet was interested mainly in the religious aspects of the history of his time, and ecclesiastical concerns receive a disproportionate amount of attention. Burnet's exposition of his own views on these matters is one of the more interesting facets of the book. The *Dictionary of National Biography* says that Burnet's chief historical importance "lies in the fact that from his entrance upon public life as a mere boy he was the consistent representative of broad church views both in politics and doctrine. Except in two or three instances . . . his voice was ever for toleration and his practice in his diocese was still more emphatically so."

Burnet was a sincerely devout man: he concludes his history with a long, emotional, and rather moving peroration urging upon all men the study and practice of religion. "I am sure there is nothing else can afford any true or complete happiness." But he stressed that religion was not merely a collection of doctrines and forms and customs; rather, it was an interior "spring of a new nature" whose effects were seen most clearly in a man's character and lifestyle. He did not like doctrinal disputes: "I have ever thought, that the true interest of the Christian religion was best consulted, when nice disputing about mysteries was laid aside and forgotten."[31] It is easy to see why Clarke felt that reading Burnet could inspire a love of religious liberty.

[31] Gilbert Burnet, *History of His Own Time*, ed. Martin Joseph Routh (Oxford: Clarendon Press, 1833), VI, 122.

In the heyday of fanaticism Burnet showed remarkable forbearance concerning the theological convictions of others,
and he was a staunch public advocate of toleration. "I think
it is a right due to all men; their thoughts are not in their
own power; they must think of things, as they appear to
them; their consciences are God's; he only knows them, and
he only can change them."[32]

For reasons both political and religious, Burnet was on
bad terms with most of his fellow clergy. In his account of
the endless wrangling over doctrine and discipline that occupied the various religious factions of his time, the Establishment bishops are depicted as particularly intemperate
and self-serving. Burnet was unsparing in his criticism of
the clergy's contentiousness and neglect of duty. He admits
in the preface to the *History* that, out of "zeal for the true
interests of religion," he may have been rather severe upon
the members of his own profession: "Indeed the peevish-
ness, the ill nature, and the ambition of many clergymen,
has sharpened my spirit perhaps too much against them."[33]
It is possible that the hostility that Keats expressed toward
the clergy later in his life derived in part from impressions
he received while reading Burnet.

Possibly the book had other, more profound effects.
Burnet was vehement in his criticism of the abuses that de-
faced the Church in his day. He refers to the twin evils of
plurality and non-residence as "so shameful a profanation
of holy things, that it ought to be treated with detestation
and horror."[34] This profanation and others like it were still
flourishing in Keats's time. Perhaps he began now to take
note of the existence of these anomalies and to look more
critically at the Church that had tolerated them for so long.
With reference to doctrine, too, Keats's thinking could have
been affected by Burnet. In the "Afterword" to the *History*,
the bishop offers the opinion that "requiring subscriptions
to the thirty-nine articles is a great imposition. . . . The
greater part subscribe without ever examining them; and

[32] *Ibid.*, VI, 189.   [33] *Ibid.*, I, 6.   [34] *Ibid.*, VI, 205.

others do it because they must do it, even though they can hardly satisfy their consciences about some things in them."[35] It may be that, reading of the disputes over the articles, Keats was for the first time confronted with the question of his own assent to the doctrines of his Church; perhaps at this time he discovered that he, too, was unable to "satisfy his conscience" about some of them.

Cowden Clarke's impression that Keats's religious and political liberalism originated at around the same time suggests another consideration. Might it not be that his earliest dissatisfaction with the Church was based on political rather than purely religious factors? One need go no further than the Book of Common Prayer to find possible occasions of conflict between his developing political views and those officially purveyed by the Church. He might, for instance, have read Burnet's portrait of the dissolute Charles II, whose cynical negligence of duty and misdirected machinations did such harm to the kingdom he ruled, and then found in the Prayer Book "A Form of Prayer with Thanksgiving to Almighty God, for Having Put an End to the Great Rebellion by the Restitution of the King and Royal Family." Hearing church bells proclaiming this anniversary a few years later, Keats reacted angrily:

> Infatuate Britons, will you still proclaim
> His memory, your direst, foulest shame?
> Nor patriots revere?[36]

One of the patriots who suffered after Charles' restoration was John Milton, whom Keats had probably begun to revere both as poet and statesman while he was at Enfield. What then would his reaction have been to that section of the Prayer Book called "A Form of Prayer with Fasting, to be used yearly on the Thirtieth of January, being the day

---

[35] *Ibid.*, VI, 184.
[36] *The Poetical Works of John Keats*, ed. H. W. Garrod (Oxford: Clarendon Press, 1958), p. 540. This edition will be the source for all quotations of Keats's poetry, unless otherwise noted.

of the martyrdom of the blessed King Charles I," which consistently and rather startlingly parallels the virtues and sufferings of Charles with those of Jesus Christ? One of the invocations contained in this office is worth quoting at length, as an indication of the Prayer Book's politics.

> O Lord, our heavenly Father, who didst not punish us as our sins have deserved, but hast in the midst of judgement remembered mercy; We acknowledge it thine especial favour, that, though for our many and great provocations, thou didst suffer thine anointed blessed King Charles the First, (as on this day) to fall into the hands of violent and blood-thirsty men, and barbarously to be murdered by them; yet thou didst not leave us forever, as sheep without a shepherd; but by thy gracious providence didst miraculously preserve the undoubted Heir of his Crowns, our then gracious Sovereign King Charles the Second, from his bloody enemies, hiding him under the shadow of thy wings, until their tyranny was overpast; and didst bring him back, in thy good appointed time, to sit upon the throne of his Father; and together with the Royal Family didst restore to us our ancient Government in Church and State. For these thy great and unspeakable mercies we render to thee our most humble and unfeigned thanks; beseeching thee still to continue thy gracious protection over the whole Royal Family, and to grant to our gracious Sovereign King George, a long and happy reign over us: So we that are thy people will give thee thanks for ever, and will always be shewing forth thy praise from generation to generation; through Jesus Christ our Lord and Saviour. *Amen.*

It would not be surprising if the "Amen" to such a prayer stuck in Keats's throat.

Taking the Enfield experience as a whole, one can see a double significance for the development of Keats's religious attitudes. On the one hand, the academy provided him with much of his formal grounding in Christian doctrine and his familiarity with the contents of the Bible. On the other, the liberal atmosphere of Clarke's school provided a matrix for his initial questioning of his religious heritage. To what point Keats's Christian faith had developed at Enfield, and to what extent it had then been undermined, are matters of speculation. I have tried simply to indicate the possibilities in both cases, aware that there is little certainty involved. It *is* fairly certain that in the period immediately following his withdrawal from the academy, Keats's ideas on religion quickly began to take form and direction. And the direction they took was away from Christianity.

Keats left Enfield in 1811 and apprenticed himself to Thomas Hammond, a surgeon in practice at nearby Edmonton. We do not have a great deal of solid information about Keats's life during these years of apprenticeship, but we know they were vital in the development of his poetic talents. There is evidence that the period was also very significant for the progress of his thought on religion, and that by the end of it he had left Christian orthodoxy far behind. The evidence is a letter he received from a certain John Spurgin a short time after enrolling at Guy's Hospital in 1815.[37] Spurgin, who had recently left Guy's for Cambridge, could not have known Keats for more than a few weeks, but he had evidently drawn him out on the subject of religion and, being an enthusiastic believer himself, had not been satisfied with the poet's response. Judging by the topics treated in the letter, Keats had not only expressed doubts concerning the Trinity, the divinity of Christ, and other items in the orthodox creed, but had gone on to question the value and importance of religion generally, claiming to be in a "mazy mist" with regard to the entire matter. It is necessary to attempt an explanation of how Keats arrived at this state of mind.

[37] Edward B. Hinckley, "On First Looking into Swedenborg's Philosophy," *Keats-Shelley Journal*, 9 (1960), 15-25. Hinckley's article contains the complete text of the letter.

When he departed from Clarke's academy, Keats was separating himself from the relatively controlled religious environment in which he had lived until that time, and was leaving behind most of the positive orthodox influences that had operated upon him as a youth. Though residing near his grandmother, visiting her frequently until her death in 1814, he lived alone and was to a great extent at liberty to choose the intellectual direction he would follow. Two roads diverged before him in these formative years, two possible life-styles, and they were represented by two men: his guardian, Richard Abbey, and his friend and tutor, Charles Cowden Clarke. Abbey's world was that of the professional businessman; its values were financial comfort and middle-class respectability. It was Abbey's wisdom that had guided Keats's decision to become a small-town apothecary-surgeon. Clarke's world, on the other hand, was that of the London intellectual, and was populated by poets and musicians, philosophers and critics. Whether or not they were conscious of the fact, these men represented opposing forces in a struggle for Keats's soul.

In the matter of religion, too, Abbey and Clarke inhabited different worlds. Like John Jennings, Abbey was an active Churchman. While serving as Keats's guardian, he was busily involved in ecclesiastical affairs at the parish of Walthamstow, holding a succession of offices, including the prestigious post of churchwarden.[38] H. N. Fairchild characterizes Abbey as "a priggish, nasty-minded, bigoted Evangelical."[39] While the adjectives may be appropriate, I do not know what evidence there is for the noun. It is true that Abbey's life-style resembled in several particulars that of many Evangelicals: he was a man of business who commuted to London from the suburbs; he had a religiously motivated interest in ameliorating social problems; he

[38] Joanna Richardson, "New Light on Mr. Abbey," *Keats-Shelley Memorial Bulletin*, 5 (1953), 27.

[39] *Religious Trends in English Poetry*, III (New York: Columbia University Press, 1949), 456.

adopted a puritanical attitude toward amusements and the pleasures of the flesh; and, as was said, he was active in church affairs. His cutting short Keats's education at Enfield and his philistine reaction to the first volume of poems ("hard to understand and good for nothing when it is understood")[40] may indicate that he shared the Evangelicals' prejudice against learning and the arts. Another aspect of his character is revealed in an incident that took place while he was on the committee of the Walthamstow Sunday School. As Joanna Richardson tells it: "Each pupil, on leaving the Sunday School, would come to be presented with a Bible and a prayerbook, and after a year in service returned to be given a guinea. Whether Abbey expected the pupils in the meantime to sell their Bibles one cannot tell, but in 1819, it was unanimously resolved 'on the motion of Mr. Abbey that in future when Children attend to claim the usual reward of One Guinea for having remained in Service in one place for twelve months, they be required to produce to the Committee their Bible and Prayer Book.' "[41] None of this proves that Abbey was a card-carrying Evangelical. Smallness of spirit is not peculiar to any one sect. But whatever the nature of Abbey's religious practice, it does not seem to have been very attractive or appealing. While Keats had many reasons to dislike his guardian, it is not difficult to imagine that the older man's public religiosity might make his overbearing personality even more irritating. Perhaps Aileen Ward is correct in saying that Keats's "private image of orthodoxy may well have been Richard Abbey, the prosperous churchwarden haggling with his Sunday-school pupils over their rightful guinea."[42]

Keats's eventual rejection of Abbey's plans for him and of his entire world-view is attributable in large part to the influence of the other authority figure in his life at this time. To Charles Cowden Clarke, Keats wrote in 1816,

[40] KC, I, 308.　　　　　　　　[41] "New Light," p. 27.
[42] John Keats: The Making of a Poet (New York: Viking Press, 1963), p. 82.

Oh! had I never seen,
Or known your kindness, what might I have been?
What my enjoyments in my youthful years,
Bereft of all that now my life endears?

His tutor at the academy and now his friend, Clarke opened
to Keats the treasures of Spenser, Shakespeare, and Milton,
and presided over his own birth as a poet. During the after-
noons and evenings that Keats, free of his duties at Hammond's dispensary, spent back at Enfield, Clarke would
speak also of music and the theater, describing the plays
and concerts he had been attending in London. They would
discuss current events too, as the conversation turned inevitably to the visits Clarke was paying to the political pris-
oner, Leigh Hunt. If only in connection with Hunt and his
Examiner, their talk would sooner or later come round to
the topic of religion.

Clarke appears to have been a sincerely religious man, as
may be seen in his "Hymn to God," written in the 1820's.

In Thy large temple,—the blue depth of space,—
And on the altar of Thy quiet fields,
(Fit shrine to hold the beauty of Thy love),
Great Spirit! with earnest cheerfulness I place
This off'ring, which a grateful heart now yields,
For all those high and gracious thoughts that rove
O'er all Thy works; for all the rare delights
Of eye and ear,—harmonious forms and strains,
Of deepest breath; for each ensuing spring,
With all its tender leaves and blossoming:
And dainty smells that steam from dropping rains;
For sunlit days, and silent, shining nights,
For youth, and mirth, and health. . . .[43]

But hand in hand with this gentle, serene natural religion went a severely critical attitude toward the Christian

[43] Quoted by Mary Cowden Clarke, *My Long Life* (New York:
Dodd, Mead & Co., 1896), pp. 39f.

faith. The usually tolerant Charles Lamb once commented on Clarke's "horse-insults and indecent obstreperousness against Christianity."[44] Among his favorite authors were Voltaire and Jeremy Bentham; his biographer suggests that when, in 1825, Clarke became a partner in a publishing firm, it was his influence that led to the publication of works like Voltaire's *Dictionnaire Philosophique* and Bentham's *The Church of England Catechism Examined.*[45] As an indication of the tone of the latter work, Bentham accuses the Catechism of "thickly sowing in the mind, at the earliest dawn of reason, the seeds of depravity in every shape." Bentham's anti-Christian works had not yet been published in this period when Clarke was directing Keats's continuing education, but there is good reason to suppose that the works of Voltaire were among the books that Keats borrowed from his friend and that they discussed during their weekly meetings.[46] It is possible to see these conversations with Clarke as originating or, at least, helping to solidify Keats's skepticism concerning Christianity. It is possible, too, to name Voltaire as the major literary influence affecting the evolution of his religious thought during this period.

Breaking upon a young mind, the impact of Voltaire was often overwhelming. He called all things into question and seemed to leave the great icons of the past strewn as rubble in his wake. Coleridge attributed the origin of all the religious doubts that beset him as a youth to his reading the *Dictionnaire Philosophique* (a copy of which Keats owned).[47] In the *Apologia Pro Vita Sua*, Newman wrote: "I recollect copying out some French verses, perhap's Voltaire's, against the immortality of the soul, and saying to

[44] *The Letters of Charles Lamb*, ed. Alfred Ainger (London: Macmillan, 1904), II, 121.

[45] Richard Altick, *The Cowden Clarkes* (London: Oxford Univ. Press, 1948), pp. 52ff.

[46] *KC*, II, 148. Aileen Ward and Stuart Sperry agree that Keats began reading Voltaire at this time. Ward, p. 27; Sperry, "Keats's Skepticism and Voltaire," *Keats-Shelley Journal*, 12 (1963), 75-93.

[47] *KC*, I, 258. See Lawrence Hanson, *The Life of S. T. Coleridge* (London: Allen, 1938), p. 21.

(49)

myself something like 'How dreadful, but how plausible!' "[48]
On these men the effect was transient, but Keats did not live
long enough to have a chance to outgrow it.

Reading Voltaire at this time, Keats would have learned,
among other things, that all theological doctrines, all scripture and tradition, all forms and systems are not only unnecessary for, but pernicious obstacles to, true religion. He
would have been assured that Christianity was based on
shadowy historical facts that were unreliably or fraudulent-
ly reported and on metaphysical premises that intelligent
men could no longer accept, and that its history had been
a long nightmare of cruelty and oppression.[49] He would
have been told that dogmatic religion "is the source of all
the follies and turmoils imaginable; it is the mother of fanaticism and civil discord; it is the enemy of mankind,"[50]
and that the only religion worthy of a thinking man is a
beautifully simple one involving only two propositions,
based not on faith but on reason: that God exists, and that
men must be virtuous. "Now on what dogma do all minds
agree? On the worship of a God and on probity. All the philosophers on earth who had a religion have said at all times:
'There is a God, and men must be just.' This, then, is the
universal religion established in all times and for all men."[51]
Any speculation beyond these simple premises is idle. "The
theist," writes Voltaire, using the name he applied to his
own position, "does not know how God punishes, how he
protects, how he forgives; for he is not rash enough to flatter himself that he knows how God acts; but he knows that
God does act and that he is just. The difficulties in the notion of Providence do not shake him in his faith, because
they are only great difficulties and not disproofs."[52] There

[48] *Apologia Pro Vita Sua*, ed. Charles F. Harrold (New York:
Longmans, Green, 1947), p. 3.
[49] As my source for this sketch of Voltaire's religious ideas I have
used his *Dictionnaire Philosophique*, translated by Peter Gay (New
York: Basic Books, 1962); it is a useful compendium of the author's
thought.
[50] *Dictionnaire*, p. 448.   [51] *Ibid.*, p. 464.
[52] *Ibid.*, p. 479.

would be a time in the future when "difficulties in the notion of Providence" would come upon Keats in full force and reveal the inadequacies in Voltaire's pleasant, reasonable type of natural religion, but now, intoxicated with the light and the atmosphere of the Chamber of Maiden-Thought, he must have delighted in the freshness and newness of the ideas that crowded into his mind.

More important in the long run than specific ideas, however, was a general attitude Keats would have observed in Voltaire—an attitude of cool, quizzical skepticism about almost everything having to do with religion. "Certainly I don't understand any of this; nobody has ever understood any of this, and this is why people have cut one another's throats!"[53] "*Que sais-je?*" is a recurrent refrain, as Voltaire stresses the incapacity of men to arrive at conclusions about the supernatural and the consequent absurdity of all theological speculation and debate. "Whether Jesus was in time or before time, we must be decent men just the same."[54] Although it was not derived solely from his reading of Voltaire, as I shall point out, one finds a similar attitude running through Keats's letters and acting as a kind of censor that breaks in whenever he becomes involved in theological discussion. "You know my ideas about Religion," he writes to Bailey. "I do not think myself more in the right than others. . . . I have not one idea of the truth of any of my speculations" (I, 242f.).

If Keats's reading of Voltaire under Clarke's guidance did not succeed fully in undermining his allegiance to Christianity, perhaps the job was completed through the influence of one of Voltaire's most ardent contemporary admirers, Leigh Hunt. Through his relationship with Clarke, a regular caller at Hunt's prison bower, Keats became completely caught up in the excitement surrounding "the wrong'd Libertas," and followed his deeds and writings eagerly. I mentioned earlier that in its first years of publication the *Examiner*, when it discussed religion at all,

[53] *Ibid.*, p. 93.   [54] *Ibid.*, p. 208.

concerned itself with attacking superstition and fanaticism
(particularly as these qualities were embodied in the
"Methodists") and came forward as a surprisingly ardent
defender of the Establishment. But in 1812, as though to
match in the religious sphere the political recklessness of
the attack on the Prince Regent that led to his imprison-
ment, Hunt suddenly turned his sights on Christianity itself.
The lead editorial for May 3, 1812, entitled "The Catholic
Claims," was devoted in part to a critique of the Thirty-
nine Articles, and what amounted to a retraction of the
paper's earlier defense of the Church.

> It is a fact easily ascertainable by general readers and
> observers, that the Christian faith itself is on the decline
> and has been so these hundred and fifty years past. It is
> true, they who have witnessed the progress of Methodism
> in this country have had their doubts whether some dan-
> ger was not threatened to the church, and have for that
> reason been anxious to stand up in defence of a learned
> and well-tempered establishment; but their fears have
> been pretty generally settled, we believe, by a close look
> at the opinions of the well-informed classes, who have
> evinced of late years an appetite much more delicate than
> voracious in matters of faith, and who begin to suspect
> that a system of philosophic morals,—a love of the gen-
> eral good, founded on a well-educated conscience and a
> trust in the wisdom of Deity, is a much more useful as
> well as noble principle of conduct than any which in-
> volves a dereliction of reason and a shock to humanity.—
> This, we verily believe, is the true state of the spirit of the
> times with regard to the enquiring part of the commu-
> nity, not only in this country, but all over Europe, from
> Italy to Russia.

As though to leave no doubt where he himself stood with
regard to the spirit of the times, Hunt added: "We are not
Christians ourselves: we believe in nothing but God and the

beauty of virtue: and as we make reason and conscience our guides, we make the good of our fellow-creatures our object." For a youth who aspired to become a member of "the enquiring part of the community," and to whom Leigh Hunt was becoming a kind of culture hero, a judgment like this would probably have been enough to solidify any anti-Christian tendencies that had developed from his other reading and associations. Knowing then the kind of intellectual influences operating on Keats during his years of apprenticeship at Edmonton, one is not surprised to find him expressing doubts about Christian doctrine and about religion in general to John Spurgin, a few weeks after enrolling at Guy's Hospital in 1815.

The intellectual atmosphere that Keats began to breathe on his arrival at the Borough School of Medicine (the name given to the combined facilities of Guy's and St. Thomas's Hospitals) would have done little to discourage whatever critical tendencies he brought with him. The London medical schools harbored a strain of skepticism more radical than any he could have found in the writings of Voltaire. Scientists in the latter half of the eighteenth century had gone far beyond that thinker in questioning the traditional view of the nature of things. Voltaire had been an admirer of Newton and subscriber to his notion of the cosmos as a perfect and permanent machine, obviously the creation of a Great Artificer who continued to keep the mechanism working smoothly. Even at his most skeptical, he never doubted the reality of a supernatural order. But the early discoveries of the geologists, which Voltaire refused to take seriously, and new insights in physics and biology caused cracks to appear on the surface of the Newtonian order. Evolution rather than stability began to seem the most significant characteristic of physical phenomena. In d'Holbach's *Système de la Nature*, published in 1770, Necessity replaced Providence as the governing force in the universe, and the natural religion of Voltaire was dismissed as a kind of superstition.[55]

The effect of these new ideas was being felt in the London medical community when Keats arrived on the scene. In a series of lectures delivered in 1816, John Abernethy, Professor of Medicine at the Royal College of Surgeons, felt obliged to attack what he considered pernicious new tendencies in scientific thought. He spoke of those who "feel a repugnance to believe that any thing may originate in causes which they cannot comprehend; and, therefore, probably they are induced to suppose a kind of necessity." In rebuttal he pointed out that "the most intelligent men who have studied the works of nature to the greatest extent, and with the greatest attention, have been convinced that they are the results neither of necessity nor of chance; and, consequently, that intelligence must have operated in ordaining the scheme and order of the universe."[56]

Abernethy's remarks were directed primarily at William Lawrence, Professor of Anatomy and Physiology at the Royal College, who had identified himself with the newest and most radical of contemporary scientific theories. For example, he attacked publicly the traditional view of the spiritual independence (and thus the immortality) of the vital principle in man, on the grounds that this conception involves "suppositions without any ground in observation or experience, the only sources of our information on these subjects."[57] I will quote further from Lawrence's lectures, because they indicate an attitude of mind that was beginning to take hold among English scientists, and because it is quite likely that some of the ideas became known to Keats.

[55] Norman Hampson, *A Cultural History of the Enlightenment* (New York: Pantheon Books, 1968), pp. 93f.

[56] *Physiological Lectures . . . Delivered before the Royal College of Surgeons in the year 1817*, 2nd ed. (London: Longmans, 1822), pp. 323ff.

[57] *An Introduction to Comparative Anatomy and Physiology* (London: Callow, 1816), p. 178.

Life, using the word in its popular and general sense, which at the same time is the only rational and intelligible one, is merely the active state of the animal structure. It includes the notions of sensation, motion, and those ordinary attributes of living beings, which are obvious to common observation. It denotes what is apparent to our senses; and cannot be applied to the offspring of metaphysical subtlety, or immaterial abstractions, without a complete departure from its original acceptation; without obscuring and confusing what is otherwise clear and intelligible.

The close connection between life and respiration has not escaped the notice of ordinary observers; of those who were ignorant of anatomy and physiology. Hence the breath has been popularly deemed the mark of life. . . . The Latin spiritus, or original of our spirit, from spiro to breathe, means merely breath; the same is the case with the Greek *pneuma;* and this is the original sensible object, out of which all the abstractions and fancies, all the verbal sophistry and metaphysical puzzles about spirit have proceeded.[58]

It seems to me that this hypothesis or fiction of a subtle invisible matter, animating the visible texture of animal bodies, and directing their motions, is only an example of that propensity in the human mind, which has led men at all times to account for those phenomena, of which the causes are not obvious, by the mysterious aid of higher and imaginary beings. . . . It may appear unnecessary to disturb those, who are inclined to indulge themselves in these harmless reveries. The belief in them, as in sorcery and witchcraft, is not grounded in reasoning, and therefore has nothing to fear from argument.[59]

[58] *Lectures on Physiology, Zoology, and the Natural History of Man, Delivered at the Royal College of Surgeons* (London: Benbow, 1822), p. 53. These lectures were delivered in 1817.
[59] *An Introduction,* pp. 174, 177.

Even at this early date, 1816–1817, Lawrence was espousing and teaching certain other opinions that, later in the century, would astonish and trouble many outside the scientific community.

A distinguished English naturalist has argued that the fossil elephant bones must belong to some species still existing, because, says he, "Providence maintains and continues every created species; and we have as much assurance, that no races of animals will any more cease, while the earth remaineth, than seed-time and harvest, cold and heat, summer and winter, day and night." Unluckily for the credit of this gentleman's assumed acquaintance with the designs and schemes of Providence, we have the fullest evidence that many species and genera of animals have been annihilated.[60]

The entire or even partial inspiration of the various writings comprehended in the Old Testament has been, and is doubted by many persons, including learned divines, and distinguished oriental and biblical scholars. The account of the creation and of subsequent events, has the allegorical figurative character common to eastern compositions; and it is distinguished among the cosmogonies by a simple grandeur and natural sublimity, as the rest of these writings are by appropriate beauties in their respective parts not inferior to those of any human compositions.

To the grounds of doubt respecting inspiration, which arise from examination of the various narratives, from knowledge of the original and other oriental languages, and from the irreconcilable opposition between the passions and sentiments ascribed to the Deity by Moses, and

[60] *Lectures*, p. 46. This notion of the annihilation of species (which deeply disturbed Tennyson: see *In Memoriam*, lvi) was familiar to Keats: "Parsons will always keep up their Character, but as it is said there are some animals, the Ancients knew, which we do not; let us hope our posterity will miss the black badger with tri-cornered hat" (II, 70).

that religion of peace and love unfolded by the Evangelists, I have only to add, that the representations of all the animals being brought before Adam in the first instance, and subsequently of their being all collected in the ark, if we are to understand them as applied to the living inhabitants of the whole world, are zoologically impossible. . . . If we are to believe that the original creation comprehended only a male and a female of each species, or that one pair only was rescued from an universal deluge, the contradictions are again increased. The carnivorous animals must have soon perished with hunger, or have annihilated most of the other species.

Such an assumption, in short, is at variance with all our knowledge of living nature. Why should we embrace an hypothesis so full of contradictions?—to give to an allegory a literal construction, and the character of revelation.[61]

These heretical assertions did not go unchallenged. Lawrence's 1816 lectures provoked a heated controversy that persisted, within and without the medical community, for several years. Abernethy publicly denounced Lawrence and the French scientists whose theories he embraced as "a band of modern skeptics,"[62] and urged his colleagues to repudiate the new and dangerous ideas. "We should not . . . suffer crude speculations to go forth, bearing the seeming stamp of medical authority, when they are contrary to the sentiments of the bulk of the profession, derogatory to its

[61] *Lectures*, pp. 215f., 220.

[62] Lecturing at the Royal College in 1817, Lawrence denied knowing anything of a band of skeptics, but he clearly revealed his own attitude toward religion in such statements as the following. Speaking of religious persecution, he said: "The increasing light of reason has destroyed many of these remnants of ignorance and barbarism; but much remains to be done, before the final accomplishment of the grand purpose, which, however delayed, cannot be ultimately defeated; I mean the complete emancipation of the mind, the destruction of all creeds and articles of faith, and the establishment of full freedom of opinion and belief." *Lectures*, p. 84.

character, and injurious to society."[63] Lawrence answered with ridicule, employing (according to Abernethy's biographer) abuse and invective "as scarcely to be paralleled in the whole history of literary or scientific controversy."[64] Churchmen soon became involved in the dispute, accusing Lawrence and the entire Royal College, which had refused to censure him, of espousing opinions leading to "practical atheism" and of undermining the faith of medical students. As Thomas Rennell of Cambridge University complained: "The volume [Lawrence's published lectures] does not appear as the work of a private individual, but as the production of a Professor in the Royal College of Surgeons, recited in their school and sanctioned by their authority. As such it is in the hands of every student in the metropolis, and as I have lately understood, it has had its full share in the formation of their opinions."[65]

Rennell seemed to feel that medical students were particularly susceptible to being infected with heterodox opinions. In an earlier attack on Lawrence's 1816 volume, he wrote:

> By far the larger part of those who look up to Mr. Lawrence for instruction, as far as intellect is concerned, have received no education at all. At the age of fourteen all general instruction has in their case been concluded, and their views have been unceasingly directed to the study and practice of their future profession. The superiority which they feel from an early initiation in the mysteries of a science so important in its object, and so general in its application, naturally enough engenders that pertness and conceit which are the surest obstacles to any advancement in the paths of general knowledge. From

[63] *Physiological Lectures*, pp. 333f.

[64] George Macilwain, *Memoirs of John Abernethy F.R.S., With a View of his Lectures, Writings, and Character* (New York: Harper, 1853), p. 220.

[65] *Remarks on Skepticism, especially as it is connected with Organization and Life* (London: Rivington, 1819), p. 64.

dwelling again so minutely and so anxiously upon secondary causes, they rapidly contract the range of their intellect, till they finally lose every idea of the great first Cause of all things. Forgetting then the existence of a first cause, they endeavor to account for all *phenomena* from the action of secondary causes alone; the more accurately they observe, and the more deeply they investigate, the more surely they puzzle and perplex their understandings; till at last their embarrassments conclude in a state of general scepticism. . . . This we take to be the general process of infidelity in the minds of the young; in the medical profession, indeed, the Lecturer has further opportunities of engrafting it upon the minds of his pupils by a sagacious sarcasm or two in the dissecting room, upon his disappointment in not finding the soul, &c. &c.[66]

While this description of the typical medical student may not fit Keats in all its particulars, we know that George Felton Mathew, a close friend at this time, considered him "of the skeptical and republican school. An advocate for the innovations which were making progress in his time. A faultfinder with everything established."[67] Although he was not one of Lawrence's pupils, the new ideas being debated in the London medical community must have become known to him. At the time of Lawrence's first lectures Keats was living with other medical students, and exposed to the kind of professional gossip in which novices in any field like to indulge. It was a common practice for students at one medical school to attend courses at another, and young men from the Borough School were often seen at John Abernethy's lectures across the river.[68] (That Keats knew of Abernethy is certain; his name appears in the poet's physiology notebook.)[69] It does not seem implausible that these ideas had an influence on Keats's later uncertainty with re-

[66] *British Critic*, 8 (July, 1817), pp. 64-65.
[67] *KC*, II, 185f.   [68] Macilwain, p. 198.
[69] *John Keats's Anatomical and Physiological Note Book*, ed. M. B. Forman (London: Oxford Univ. Press, 1934), p. 26.

gard to the immortality of the soul and his inability to accept the Bible as the inspired word of God.

It is clear that the intellectual milieu in which Keats lived during his year at Guy's Hospital would certainly have countenanced if not encouraged free thinking on religious matters, as well as the sort of man-of-the-world irreverence expressed in the doggerel verse he scrawled in the notebook of a fellow student:

> Give me women, wine and snuff
> Until I cry out "hold, enough!"
> You may do so sans objection
> Till the day of resurrection;
> For bless my beard they aye shall be
> My beloved Trinity.

But there was another and deeper current in this mental environment that seems to have had a far more profound effect on Keats than simple encouragement of heterodoxy or irreligion. It was a general attitude toward knowledge and the proper objects of knowledge that pervaded the medical profession at this time. To understand it some historical background is necessary.

Keats began his studies at the Borough School in the midst of a very exciting period in the history of medicine— a period often referred to as the dawn of modern medical science.[70] Encouraged by the spirit of a revolutionary age, medicine was finally beginning to break free of the shackles placed upon it by various philosophical and theological systems, and adopting as its mode of inquiry what we now call the scientific method. Throughout the medical community of Western Europe there was a sense of emancipation, of discovery, of finally having got onto the right track after a century of false starts and misdirected energies.

[70] See Albert H. Buck, *The Dawn of Modern Medicine* (New Haven: Yale Univ. Press, 1920); and Richard Harrison Shryock, *The Development of Modern Medicine* (New York: Knopf, 1947). To the latter work I am indebted for much of the information used in the following discussion.

The eighteenth century had not been a prosperous time for medicine. The direction pointed to by pioneers like Harvey was left unpursued, as medical men became more interested in synthesis than in analysis. If Newton could so easily systematize and codify the laws that controlled the universe, they reasoned, why could not the laws governing the human body be reduced to a few basic principles? The premature attempts to impose symmetry upon the enormously complex phenomena connected with human health and sickness led, inevitably, to many absurdities. An example is Brunonianism, named for Dr. John Brown, who theorized that all diseases could be divided into two categories: those produced by too much bodily excitement, and those resulting from too little. For the first condition opium was prescribed; for the second, alcohol. There were many such attempts at systematizing disease, most of them products of the study or the library rather than of the hospital ward, and almost none of them withstood the test of experience. Toward the end of the century there occurred the inevitable reaction against speculative system-making, and a general trend back to critical empiricism. In London, the surgeon John Hunter, who devoted less time to reading than to observing at the bedside and at the dissecting table, almost singlehandedly transformed surgery into a respectable experimental science. Hunter's empirical approach to pathology was rejected by his contemporaries but eagerly embraced by his students, among whom were John Abernethy and Astley Cooper, and it became the foundation of surgical practice in the early nineteenth century.

It is not surprising that the homeland of Bacon and Locke should provide a hospitable milieu for scientific empiricism, but the trend can be observed even more clearly in France. Around 1795 there appeared in Paris a group of young medical men, led by Xavier Bichat, whose methods and general outlook were much more objective and critical than those of their predecessors. Their approach was similar to, and greatly influenced by, the radical empiricism of a group of philosophers and scientists known as the *Idéologues*.[71] *Idéologie* was an epistemological method rather than a philosophic system: actually, it was intended to replace systems. The method was characterized by a concern for careful observation of facts and a reluctance to go beyond such empirical evidence in formulating theories. Any supposition or speculation not grounded firmly in demonstrable fact was suspect. The *Idéologues* were suspicious too of abstract or general ideas and tried whenever possible to simplify them, breaking them down into the original perceptions from which they had been derived. If it was found impossible to reduce a thought into verifiable sensations, there was no alternative but to reject it and suspend judgment on the matter entirely, rather than attempt to explain what was not experientially known. One important consequence of such an attitude should be noted here: radical empiricism of this sort leads almost necessarily to a confrontation with religion. On the basis of what cluster of sensations could one arrive at the idea of the Trinity, for example? The Church in France quickly and correctly recognized *Idéologie* as an enemy.

This, then, was the philosophic underpinning of modern medicine as it developed in Napoleonic France. When, after 1814, channels of communication were reopened between the scientific communities of France and England, these ideas spread to the London medical schools. I pointed out earlier that William Lawrence of the Royal College adopted many of the advanced theories of his French colleagues. He seems to have shared as well their epistemological tendencies. In his discussion of the soul in the 1816 lectures he said:

> I only oppose such hypotheses, when they are adduced with the array of philosophical deduction, because they

71 See George Boas, *French Philosophies of the Romantic Period* (New York: Russell & Russell, 1964); and George Rosen, "The Philosophy of Ideology and the Emergence of Modern Medicine in France," *Bulletin of the History of Medicine*, xx (1946), 329-39.

involve suppositions without any ground in observation or experience, the only sources of our information on these subjects. I repeat to you that the science of physiology, in its proper acceptation, is made up of the facts, which we learn by observation and experiment on living beings, or on those which have lived; of the comparison of these with each other; of the analogies which such comparison may discover, and the general laws to which it may lead. So long as we proceed in this path, every step is secure; when we endeavor to advance beyond its termination, we wander without any guide or direction, and are liable to be bewildered at every moment.[72]

Again and again in his lectures Lawrence emphasized this point: "Experience is our only safe guide, and inductions from numerous facts the only sure support of our reasonings." In his case, scientific empiricism went hand in hand with religious skepticism. How common this association was among London medical men at the time would be difficult to determine. Abernethy liked to think that Lawrence and his followers were atypical. At any rate, the combination of empiricism and skepticism appears again in Keats's teacher and guide, Astley Cooper.

Cooper was the most famous surgeon of his time, and the idol of the students at the Borough School. His lectures were always crowded, and while making his rounds of the hospital wards he was generally followed by a multitude of disciples, jostling each other to get close to him. He appears to have taken a personal interest in Keats,[73] who regularly attended and took careful notes at Cooper's course in physiology. As a young man, Cooper had acquired a reputation for political and religious radicalism; he avowed his Jacobin ideas openly and, like Wordsworth, visited Paris in 1792 to see the Revolution at firsthand. He was a close associate of the radical (and atheist) Thelwall, who exercised what Cooper's biographer describes as "a serious influence" over

[72] *An Introduction*, pp. 178f.   [73] *KC*, II, 207n.

the mind of the young surgeon. It was said that he used to join with his radical friends in ridiculing religion.[74]

A contemporary judgment, made not long before his death, said of Astley Cooper: "His general influence on the practice of surgery in this country, has, perhaps, been most evident in the great share he has had in establishing pure induction as the only sure means of a just diagnosis. . . ."[75] Cooper constantly urged upon his students the importance of original observation, and warned of the dangers inherent in hypothesis and speculation not based firmly on demonstrable fact. Hypothesis, he said, was an *ignis fatuus*, sure to mislead any who followed it. "Young medical men find it so much easier a task to speculate than to observe, that they are too apt to be pleased with some sweeping theory, which saves them the trouble of observing the processes of nature. Nothing is known in our profession by guess, and I do not believe, that, from the first dawn of medical science to the present moment, a single correct idea has ever emanated from conjecture alone."[76] I think we can see here another source of Keats's distrust of "speculation" and certain other related thought processes. Compare the last sentence of Cooper's remark just quoted with the following statement of his pupil: "I have never yet been able to perceive how any thing can be known for truth by consequitive reasoning" (*Letters*, I, 185). "Conjecture" and "consequitive reasoning" have this in common: both are mental processes that occur independently of direct sensory perception. It is doubtful that Cooper would have gone along with Keats in considering the imagination a more reliable guide to some kinds of truth than abstract reasoning, but he would have understood and admired the kind of intellectual restraint expressed in remarks like: "I have not one idea of the truth of any of my speculations" (*Letters*, I, 243). Keats's suspicion of thoughts not grounded in sensation

[74] Bransby Blake Cooper, *The Life of Sir Astley Cooper, bart* (London: Parker, 1843), I, 95, 249f.
[75] *Ibid.*, II, 467.   [76] *Ibid.*, II, 53.

might be explained in other ways, without reference to his experience in medical school. But his attitude becomes easier to understand when one recalls that he lived for many months in an intellectual atmosphere that harbored a peculiar prejudice against abstract theorizing, and under the tutelage of a man who never lost an opportunity to impress upon his students the basic lesson, "Don't speculate. Observe!" And one cannot but notice the medical flavor of one of Keats's remarks apropos the subject: "Axioms in philosophy are not axioms until they are proved upon our pulses" (*Letters*, I, 279).

There is another element in Keats's later thought that can, I believe, be linked with his medical school experience. A necessary corollary of the rejection of all theory not based on observation is a willingness to accept uncertainty when there is not sufficient data at hand for an inductive conclusion. A true empiricist must learn to discipline his mind, forcing it at times to rest content with less than complete certitude. Such acceptance of, or at least patience with, incomplete knowledge can be seen in the following words of a physician who, like Keats, attended a London medical school in 1816. "Nothing shows the real tendencies of mind more than its restless desire to arrive at *some* conclusion, some tangible evidence of its highest functions. It is the impulse of this instinct—the ungoverned abuse of a high faculty, impatient for illegitimate fruition, which lies at the bottom of much false reasoning, and which blinds men, even of great power, to obstacles which are luminously evident to the most ordinary capacity."[77] One cannot help noticing the resemblance to Keats's description of Negative Capability, the ability to be "in uncertainties, Mysteries, doubts, without any irritable reaching after fact & reason," and to his criticism of Coleridge for being "incapable of remaining content with half knowledge." One thinks too of his observation that "Dilke will never come at a truth as long as he lives; because he is always trying at it" (*Letters*,

[77] Macilwain, p. 170.

I, 193f. and II, 213). Keats said that the concept of Negative Capability came to him after "several things dovetailed" in his mind. It seems not unlikely that one of these things was the memory of his medical training.

I will speak later of a particularly interesting connection between Negative Capability and Keats's attitude toward religious belief. Here I would simply point out what is perhaps an obvious consequence of an attitude toward knowledge such as the medical schools propounded and Keats shared. I said earlier, in connection with *Idéologie*, that strict empiricism places one almost necessarily on a collision course with theology. The father of modern scientific empiricism, Francis Bacon, saw from the beginning this potential for conflict with religion,[78] but because of the piety of most English scientists and the enormous ability of English theologians to adapt and compromise, the confrontation was put off until the nineteenth century. It was not until the Victorian period that a majority of English scientists abandoned the attempt to accommodate religion and decided to go their own way. At that time the word "agnostic" was coined to describe a man's state of mind when there simply did not seem to be sufficient evidence at hand to warrant any conclusion on the fundamental questions of religion. But the Victorian conflict between faith and science had its roots in the developments we have been noting in the early years of the century. And the intellectual attitude that many scientists would take toward religion later on was already present in the time of Keats. Once again I quote William Lawrence of the Royal College: "The theological doctrine of the soul, and its separate existence, has nothing to do with this physiological question, but rests on a species of proof altogether different. These sublime dogmas could never have been brought to light by the labors of the anatomist and physiologist. An immaterial and spiritual being could not have been discovered amid the blood and filth of

[78] Basil Willey, *The Seventeenth Century Background* (New York: Columbia Univ. Press, 1958), pp. 24-40.

the dissecting-room."[79] While unable to resist an ironic reference to "sublime dogmas," Lawrence was attempting to draw a clear line between his own realm of knowledge and what lies beyond it. He would not have known the word, but he was taking an agnostic position.

Keats never went quite so far as some contemporary scientists in questioning the basic premises of religion. As we shall see, he never abandoned the belief that a Supreme Intelligence governed the universe and, though shaken by doubts, he ardently desired to believe in a spiritual principle that would survive the death of the body. But with regard to other religious doctrines he cultivated an attitude closely resembling what we would call agnosticism. As a general rule, "when retired from bickering and in a proper philosophical temper" (*Letters*, 1, 243), he did not deny the validity or worth of particular tenets so much as his own ability to come to a satisfactory conclusion about them one way or another. He was much more tolerant than many of his friends, much more considerate of the religious sensibilities of others. His diffidence in these matters explains his ability to remain on friendly terms with men who quarreled bitterly with each other over religion. Though he was not able to sustain it throughout his life, this intellectual equipoise, which sometimes had the nature of ambivalence, this ability to remain cooly noncommittal in the midst of religious arguments, this attempt at critical detachment from transcendental preoccupation, may have been the most important thing Keats derived from his experience at Guy's Hospital.

Throughout the preceding discussion of Keats's time at the Borough School, I have been aware that an objection might be raised to the effect that he did not really pay a great deal of attention to the study of medicine, his thoughts at the time being monopolized by poetry. We have the testimony of Henry Stephens, a medical student who

[79] *Lectures*, p. 7.

lived with Keats, that the poet did not take his work at the hospital very seriously. "He attended Lectures and went through the usual routine, but he had no desire to excel in that pursuit, In fact Medical Knowledge was beneath his attention. . . . Poetry was to his mind the zenith of all his Aspirations—The only thing worthy the attention of superior minds—So he thought—All other pursuits were mean & tame."[80] But Stephens' recollections, written in 1847, should be weighed against other evidence. That Keats paid close attention at least to Astley Cooper's lectures may be seen in the careful notes he took. That he himself thought he was devoting a considerable amount of time to his studies and other duties is reflected in his complaint, in the "Epistle to George Felton Mathew," that he had little time for poetry: "Far different cares / Beckon me sternly from soft 'Lydian airs,' / And hold my faculties so long in thrall. . . ." Cowden Clarke records that at the end of his formal studies, when he appeared before the Court of Examiners of the Society of Apothecaries, "he displayed an amount of acquirement which surprised his fellow students, who had scarcely any other association with him than that of a cheerful, crochety rhymester."[81] The truth of the matter seems to be that Keats was a more serious medical student than his contemporaries suspected. Still, there is no doubt that poetry was at this time becoming more and more the center of his life and the focal point of his intellectual endeavor, and this study must now begin taking that aspect of his life into account.

Among the poems written by Keats up until the autumn of 1816, one is of particular interest here, since it deals explicitly with a religious theme. It was written during the Edmonton period, and was apparently inspired by the death of the poet's grandmother. Alice Jennings was buried at St. Stephen's Church, Coleman Street (where her husband had served as churchwarden), on December 19, 1814. A few days after her death Keats wrote the following lines:

[80] *KC*, II, 208.   [81] *Recollections*, pp. 131f.

As from the darkening gloom a silver dove
  Upsoars, and darts into the Eastern light,
  On pinions that naught moves but pure delight,
So fled thy soul into the realms above,
Regions of peace and everlasting love;
  Where happy spirits, crown'd with circlets bright
  Of starry beam, and gloriously bedight,
Taste the high joy none but the blest can prove.
There thou or joinest the immortal quire
  In melodies that even Heaven fair
Fill with superior bliss, or, at desire
  Of the omnipotent Father, cleavest the air
On holy message sent—What pleasure's higher?
  Wherefore does any grief our joy impair?

From the initial affirmation of the soul's immortality to the
final suggestion that joy and not sorrow is the proper emotional reaction to death, the sonnet seems, at first glance,
authentically Christian in tone. The description of the
heavenly state seems to derive in equal parts from Milton
and the Book of Revelation. Yet when the lines are examined closely, two basic doctrines can be discerned through
the imagery—personal immortality and the existence of a
benevolent Deity—doctrines quite in line with the sort of
natural religion Keats was beginning to adopt during his
years at Edmonton. There is, in fact, nothing in the poem
that Voltaire in a tolerant mood would not have accepted.[82]

[82] One possible "source" for the poem that I do not believe has
been suggested by any critic is contained in a work I mentioned earlier,
Original Poems for Infant Minds, which we know the Keats children read while living with their grandmother at Edmonton. The
lines are worth quoting, if only to show the extent by which Keats's
sonnet transcends the level of some contemporary religious verse:

> But as from the silence and gloom,
> Another gay morning shall rise,
> So, bursting awake from the tomb,
> We shall mount far away to the skies.
> And those, who with meekness and pray'r,
> In the paths of religion have trod,
> Shall worship all glorious there,
> Among the arch-angels of God. (p. 94)

The poem on his grandmother's death is the most interesting of Keats's early productions for direct statement on religious themes, but almost all the early verse is noteworthy for incidental use of religious imagery. George Yost has done an interesting study of Keats's early religious phraseology and found an impressive quantity of such imagery, some of it classical or pagan and some unspecific ("prayer," "worship," etc.), but most of it clearly Christian.[83] Yost concludes that Keats very early in life must have had a great deal of interest in the Christian religion. This may be true, but it is well to remember that Keats's poetry in this period is largely imitative and derivative, and that this applies to words as well as to ideas. Reading Spenser and Milton and much romance literature with an eye toward imitation would tend to add many words like "angel" and "nun" and "chapel" and "cross" to a poet's vocabulary. Later on, when Keats is in more complete control of his art, his choice of imagery will be a more reliable indication of his interior state of mind.

Keats may be said to have come of age as a poet in October, 1816, when he wrote the sonnet, "On First Looking into Chapman's Homer." That same month marks a turning point in his religious life as well, for it was then that Charles Cowden Clarke introduced his young friend to Leigh Hunt. Fortunately, from this point on we begin to have more solid evidence on which to base a study of Keats's religious development. It is at this time that the letters begin. The first one of any importance (other than the early verse epistles) is that in which Keats accepts Clarke's invitation to meet Hunt, predicting better than he knew the significance of that event: "I can now devote any time you may mention to the pleasure of seeing Mr. Hunt—'t will be an Era in my existence" (I, 113).

[83] "Keats's Early Religious Phraseology," p. 581.

CHAPTER TWO

Leigh Hunt and His Circle

A s Keats had anticipated, his introduction to Leigh Hunt marked the beginning of a new era in his existence. Hunt was the first poet of any eminence he had met, and the older man's sympathy, encouragement, and advice were invaluable to him at this stage of his own poetic development. Moreover, Hunt introduced Keats to a new and exciting world of culture. His personal charm and generosity, and his position as editor of a popular liberal newspaper, had attracted into his immediate circle of acquaintance many of the brightest, most talented, most creative men of the day. For the first time, Keats was associating on familiar terms with men who lived by their imaginations.

What is more significant in the perspective of this study, Hunt ushered Keats into an environment where religion was a subject of intense interest and a topic of frequent lively discussion. Every major tendency in English religious life was represented in the Hunt circle, from enthusiastic piety to skeptical irreverence. Every important shade of opinion in the theological spectrum was reflected—Agnostic, Deist, Unitarian, and orthodox Christian. Benjamin Bailey was mistaken when, looking back on this period after Keats's death, he suggested that the young poet's store of religious knowledge was not increased by his association with Hunt and his friends.[1] If Keats's theological education needed completion he could not have come to a better school; at least he could not have found one with a more diverse faculty. The religious debates into which these men threw themselves with enthusiasm provided Keats with an opportunity to acquire a great deal of knowledge concerning the content and the viability of various creeds.

[1] *KC*, II, 292.

Of all the new acquaintances Keats made in the autumn of 1816, none had a more profound effect on his religious development than Hunt himself. After the poet's death, those of his friends who were Christians agreed on the importance of Hunt's role, but felt that his influence had been largely negative. They believed with Haydon that, in the matter of religion at least, Hunt had been "the great unhinger of his best dispositions."[2] Yet when all the evidence is weighed, one is not forced necessarily to that conclusion. Keats's estrangement from Christianity began long before he came into personal contact with Hunt. A year earlier he had confessed to serious doubts concerning such central doctrines as the Trinity and the divinity of Christ, telling John Spurgin that he was in a "mazy mist" on many points of orthodox belief. Hunt's influence may be seen as positive in this respect at least: he, along with his friends, forced Keats to come to grips with the central questions of religion, to clarify his own hazy ideas, to weigh doctrines and to decide for himself whether they were worthy of belief. The fact that at the end of this winnowing process Keats was closer to Hunt's point of view than to that of the Church of England may be regarded as unfortunate from a Christian standpoint. But Hunt's views did constitute a coherent religious faith, and there is no assurance that Keats would have constructed a fuller or richer one—or a more orthodox one—on his own. Indeed, there is some evidence that Hunt inspired in the young poet deeper sentiments of religious piety than he had felt before. To understand more fully the important influence of this man on Keats, some detailed knowledge of his own religious attitudes is necessary.

"No man ever had a more abiding sense of religion," said Thornton Hunt of his father.[3] Though metaphysics interested him only slightly, he was deeply concerned with the

[2] *The Diary of Benjamin Robert Haydon*, ed. Willard B. Pope (Cambridge, Mass.: Harvard Univ. Press, 1960-1963), II, 317.
[3] Quoted by Louis Landré, *Leigh Hunt* (Paris: Société d'Édition "Les Belles Lettres," 1936), II, 58.

moral aspects and consequences of religious faith. "It is much easier," he once remarked, "to prate darkly about mysterious and spiritual matters, and of another world, than to dilate sensibly on our social duties, and show people the right way to be useful and happy in this."[4] To "show people the right way" in religion was for Leigh Hunt a lifelong preoccupation. Believing that orthodox Christianity had throughout history been more of a bane than a blessing to mankind, he devoted himself to formulating a creed that would be more salutary in its effects. He was at one time willing to identify this faith with Deism, but only if that word was understood to mean "the practical and purely theistical part of the Christian doctrine."[5] This is a good example of Hunt's ambivalent attitude toward Christianity. He could not bring himself to bend the knee at the same shrine with Methodists and Catholics, but was reluctant to relinquish title to Christianity completely. He spent a good deal of time trying to decide and explain just how much of a Christian he was, and his views on the matter seemed to change with the seasons. At one moment he was the mocking skeptic, disciple of Voltaire and enemy of all churches. At the next, he would revert to a kind of sentimental Unitarianism (the faith in which he had been brought up) and begin "sighing for some good old country church . . . breathing nothing but the peace and love befitting the Sermon on the Mount."[6] "Damn it!" cried the more consistently skeptical William Hazlitt, "It's like a rash that comes out every year on him."[7]

Hunt always revered the person of Jesus, but preferred to think of him "not as he is seen through the dark and dreary mists of some of his followers, with inhuman doctrines and everlasting denouncements; but as he is repre-

---

[4] *Examiner*, March 1, 1818, p. 138.
[5] *Ibid.*, October 24, 1819, p. 675.
[6] *The Autobiography of Leigh Hunt*, ed. J. E. Morpurgo (London: Cresset Press, 1948), p. 178.
[7] Quoted by Herschel Baker, *William Hazlitt* (Cambridge, Mass.: Harvard Univ. Press, 1962), p. 30.

sented to us through his affection for John and Mary Magdalen, and through the amiable religion of the apostle James."[8] For most of the contemporary churches and sects who claimed to preach the religion of Christ, Hunt had little use. "If there were no alternative between blank Atheism and Christianity, and Christianity were such as it is represented to be, and demanded to be believed, then we should be Atheists at once in the blankest sense of the word."[9]

Of course, Hunt thought he had found an "alternative." The content of this creed which stood between atheism and Christianity was not formulated in an organized fashion until much later in his life—in *The Religion of the Heart* (1853)—but its basic tenets are stated clearly enough in his early writings. Much if not most of his theology is suggested in the following hymn, which Hunt composed in 1817.

> To the Spirit great and good,
> Felt, although not understood,—
> By whose breath, and in whose eyes,
> The green earth rolls in the blue skies,—
> Who we know, from things that bless,
> Must delight in loveliness;
> And who, therefore, we believe,
> Means us well in things that grieve,—
> Gratitude! Gratitude!
> Heav'n be praised as heavenly should
> Not with slavery, or with fears,
> But with a face as toward a friend, and with
> thin sparkling tears.[10]

For Hunt the heart, and not the head, is the center and source of religious consciousness. "God has written his religion in the heart, for growing wisdom to read perfectly,

---

[8] *Examiner*, November 30, 1817, p. 754.
[9] *Ibid.*, October 24, 1819, p. 676.
[10] *The Poetical Works of Leigh Hunt*, ed. H. S. Milford (London: Oxford Univ. Press, 1923), p. 381. On March 26, 1817, Keats apparently joined in singing the hymn (*Letters*, I, 127).

and time to make triumphant."[11] God's reality is felt even when his nature is not understood. If one would attempt to understand him, the feelings of the heart are a much more dependable guide than the intellect. Human reason has too often arrived at erroneous and even monstrous conceptions of the Divinity. If we consult our hearts, we learn that God is above all things benevolent and loving. We learn this also by studying the beauty of his creation. Hunt shared the "cheerful faith" that Wordsworth expressed in "Tintern Abbey," "that all which we behold is full of blessings." The existence of evil was never much of a theological problem for Hunt. He liked to point out that the evil in the world is far outweighed by the good and is gradually being diminished further through the efforts of benevolent men. As for ills that appear irremediable, they are part of a mystery the meaning of which will be cleared up for us when our lives are over.

Hunt had no doubt that all men were destined to happiness in an afterlife, though he preferred to describe his feelings on the matter as hopeful rather than certain. He was suspicious of certainty, since it so often went hand in hand with "barbarous" conceptions of the hereafter. From his parents, who were among the first Universalists, he had acquired a profound abhorrence of the very idea of Hell, and he never lost an opportunity to show contempt for those who preached the doctrine. "We like, and admire, and love, the aspirations after immortality and heaven, as much as any human being can do; but we would rather put up with the meanest, shortest, and most earthy existence imaginable, or go through a perpetual round of such existences, than entertain those hopes upon the terms on which the *faith of Christianity* offers them. The idea of fifty millions of heavens would be no heavenly idea to us, if we thought that one single fellow creature were to suffer eternal punishment."[12] Since there is nothing to fear from God, either

[11] *The Religion of the Heart* (London: John Chapman, 1853), p. 1.
[12] *Examiner*, October 24, 1819, p. 677.

in this world or in the next, the attitude of a worshipper should not be timid or slavish in any way. The "Great Beneficence" does not require abasement of mind or body. Nor does he demand elaborate ceremony and ritual. "The praise which God requires from creatures no greater than ourselves, is to love one another; to delight ourselves in his works; to advance in knowledge; and to thank him, when we are moved to do so, from the bottom of our hearts."[13]

"Our religion begins where the love of disputation ends," wrote Hunt in 1853.[14] But by that time his battles were behind him, and he felt that many victories had been won. Earlier, amid the heat and smoke of his prolonged conflict with the political and religious establishment, it was not always easy to distinguish his religion from his love of disputation. While most of the spokesmen for the Christian churches were lining up on the side of reaction and repression, he found it hard to cultivate placidity or even charity. His most characteristic religious attitude during the years of his association with Keats was, by necessity, critical rather than constructive. "Bigotry itself must be destroyed; religious dogmatism must be destroyed. Foolish and violent men must no longer be suffered to palm their bad and vindictive passions on Heaven; nor must the Divine Being be supposed capable of acting upon the most half-witted and savage principles."[15]

For a moment, in 1812, it had seemed to Hunt that the progress of human thought was ushering in a new religious consciousness, that Europe was about to embrace a purer, more enlightened, and more tolerant faith. But with the end of the war, his optimism was gradually undermined as, one by one, the old idols were returned to their pedestals. Not only was the Pope restored to his throne and Catholicism reestablished in France, but the Inquisition itself, symbol of superstition and intolerance, was reinstituted in Spain.

[13] *The Religion of the Heart*, p. 56.
[14] *Ibid.*, p. 218.
[15] *Examiner*, September 6, 1818, p. 563.

"Monks with their mummeries begin to parade the streets again," Hunt lamented. "The age seems fairly sliding back into old times."[16] There were even darker examples of religious atavism. At the end of 1815 Hunt received word that a massacre of Protestants had taken place in the south of France shortly after Waterloo. This apparent reemergence of the spirit of St. Bartholomew's Day seems genuinely to have frightened him. "And this, we suppose, is to be the concluding argument in the list of all we have heard of late years against *Philosophy*! against that love of wisdom, which, if it shares the fate of all earthly things and is not secure from perversion, is at last the only thing to prevent greater perversions,—the only thing to render men really devout and charitable, by teaching them to think the best of their Maker and the humblest of themselves, and not to contradict either by pretending to the exclusive knowledge of his intentions or enjoyment of his favour."[17] The philosopher's fears and suspicions were hardly allayed by the formation of the Holy Alliance in 1816, when the monarchs of Russia, Prussia, and Austria proclaimed themselves "defenders of the Christian religion, as a united Christian family." "The sole effect of this Treaty," wrote Hunt, "will be to bring into additional doubt the further utility of what it preaches . . . and to assist that spirit of anti-dogmatism in religious matters, which has so widely gone forth in these times."[18]

With every new manifestation of the counterrevolutionary spirit in religion, Hunt's hostility to organized Christianity grew, and his state of mind was reflected in his newspaper. Throughout 1816, the *Examiner* eagerly called attention to any bit of hypocrisy or absurdity that might serve to discredit the religious community. On September 8, for instance, there was the story of a poor widow who had been driven from her home and means of livelihood by

[16] *Ibid.*, December 10, 1815, p. 786.
[17] *Ibid.*
[18] *Examiner*, February 11, 1816, p. 83.

new landlords—who happened to be the Committee of the British and Foreign Bible Society. On September 22, it was revealed that many victims of the current economic depression were being deprived of relief on account of a dispute between the regular and dissenting clergy over distribution of funds. These are small scandals, but in the autumn of 1816—when Keats first joined the Hampstead set—Leigh Hunt had his eye sharpened and his scalpel ready to detect and lay bare any manifestation of pathology in the Christian body. By coincidence, just at this time, fate delivered into his hands an ideal subject, in the person of Benjamin Robert Haydon.

Hunt and Haydon had been acquainted for some time, and religious squabbling was not a new thing with them. "I have known Hunt now 10 years," wrote the painter in 1817, "during which we have scarcely ever met without a contest about Christianity."[19] But in October, 1816, propinquity seems to have raised their running argument to new levels of intensity and bitterness. Haydon was spending a few weeks at Hampstead for the benefit of his eyes, and he passed a good deal of the time in Hunt's company. Two such proud, sensitive, and assertive men might have struck sparks from each other even if they thought alike on most things. As it was, they disagreed profoundly on a subject that was very close to the heart of each. Hunt was spoiling for a fight about Christianity at this time, and in Haydon he found someone more than willing to knock the chip from his shoulder. Keats arrived on the scene just as the battle was getting under way.

To describe Haydon as a devout Christian does not adequately convey a sense of the quality of his faith. There was something of the crusader about him, something of Roland confronting the Paynims at Roncevaux. He tended to see himself as a heroic figure, engaged in mental fight with God's enemies. Reading his diary, one sometimes gets

[19] *Diary*, II, 80.

the feeling that religion was the real center of his life and consciousness, and that art was relegated to a secondary, ancillary position. He saw God as the source of his powers and the glory of God as the final purpose of his work. His journals are filled with lengthy, passionate prayers to the Almighty, mingling adoration and praise with pointed petitions for assistance in his earthly projects.

O God have mercy on me, strengthen every virtuous wish, & grant me success in all my schemes, as far as thou knowest them to be purely beneficial to the cause of intellect and virtue, and thy Divine Religion. Amen with all my soul.

Bless me throughout the year to come, as thou hast blest me throughout the year past—grant me kind friends, grant me extrication from all coming difficulties, and grant I may really & truly at last bring my Picture to a grand and a magnificent conclusion—save it from danger & accident & fire & grant it may have that effect on the taste of my country, I have always wished to excite, so that the future prospect of historical painters may be less strewn with difficulties than it has hitherto been—Grant these things for Jesus Christ's sake. Amen with all my soul.[20]

O God, grant I may come in with a sweep and compleat my triumph by bringing my Present Picture to a glorious & magnificent conclusion. Let me present to the World a new head of my sacred Saviour, let me be the founder of a great School, let me raise my glorious Country to a great name in Art, and I'll take wing to a purer sphere huzzaing! Let me advance the morals & pious feelings of mankind and contribute by my divine Art to illustrate the pure principles of Christianity, and I'll bow with a glow of gratitude.[21]

Haydon was a man of great faith. He knew what he needed from God and did not hesitate to be specific. He prayed for

[20] *Ibid.*, p. 181.   [21] *Ibid.*, p. 76.

the health of his eyes, he prayed that the public would like and buy his pictures, he prayed for relief in his recurrent "pecuniary emergencies," and he prayed for enlightenment and assistance in his arguments with "the Deists," among whom he numbered Hunt and his friends.

Haydon's highly emotional religion was grounded, he thought, firmly on rational foundations. His belief in God was based on the argument from design; his faith in Christ, on the traditional "evidences" of prophecy-fulfillment and miracle.[22] The viability of his religion was demonstrated conclusively, he felt, by its role in history and human endeavor. "Take the Mosaic & Xtian Dispensations as a whole, connected with their prophecies, their laws, their morals, the state of the Jews, their influence on all the intellectual part of the World, the Conviction that the greatest & best part of men have believed, & conviction of the delight & calmness of Believers with the haunting doubt of Deists, the abolition of African Slavery, the institution of Charities & Hospitals, & all this amelioration of human Conditions, and then say if a clear headed capacity is not inclined to bow in awful adoration."[23] When involved in discussion with an adversary who, he felt, was honestly seeking the truth, Haydon could argue his beliefs intelligently and skillfully, conceding points and accepting qualifications within certain limits. But when he thought he was being baited, and especially when Hunt indulged in his "unfeeling, heartless, and brutal ridicule of Christ and his divine doctrine,"[24] he tended to abandon reason in favor of vituperation and *ad hominem* abuse. This happened more than once during the protracted religious debate that occupied the Hunt circle during the fall and winter of 1816–1817.

Hunt and Haydon were the main protagonists in that struggle, but there were others besides Keats who were

[22] *Ibid.*, pp. 158f., 240.   [23] *Ibid.*, p. 165.
[24] *Ibid.*, p. 56.

present as spectators and participants. Since their presence contributed to and colored the religious milieu by which Keats was influenced during these months, it will be useful to delineate briefly the religious sentiments of some of them.

More formidable in his person and powers than either Hunt or Haydon was William Hazlitt. Keats had admired Hazlitt's writings in the *Examiner* long before meeting him at Hunt's, and his respect and admiration endured throughout his life. Keats was to have second thoughts about many of his early acquaintances, but "Hazlitt's depth of Taste" remained one of the "things to rejoice at in this Age" (*Letters*, I, 203). He never became as intimate with Hazlitt as he did with some of the others, but even from a distance the critic exercised a profound influence on Keats's developing philosophy of art. His influence on the poet's religious views is not so easy to determine, partly because his own ideas on the subject are somewhat obscure.

Hazlitt can be described as a skeptic if it is understood that his skepticism was detached and non-partisan, detecting flaws in the arguments of non-believer and believer alike. In the tradition of empiricism, he refused to go any further in his beliefs than his empirical method would take him. He saw the business of the mind as twofold: "to receive impressions and to perceive their relations."[25] Beyond this there could be no certainty. Thus we find him expressing an agnostic attitude on the most basic premises of religion. Even regarding the immortality of the soul, belief in which was so important to Hunt, Hazlitt expressed doubt. "There was a time when we were not: this gives us no concern—why then should it trouble us that a time will come when we shall cease to be? . . . To die is only to be as we were before we were born."[26]

Haydon once bestowed high praise on Hazlitt by charac-

[25] Baker, p. 189.
[26] *Complete Works of William Hazlitt*, ed. P. P. Howe (London: Dent, 1930-1934), VIII, 322.

(81)

terizing him as the only skeptic he knew who would discuss religion "with the gravity such a question demanded."[27] Hazlitt saw the flaws and failures of Christianity but recognized its tremendous contribution to European civilization. He acknowledged the beauty and ethical value of the Bible and deeply admired the person of Jesus. He became irritated when non-believers treated the Christian system with gratuitous disdain. "We certainly are not going to recommend the establishment of articles of faith, or implicit assent to them, as favourable to the progress of philosophy; but neither has the spirit of opposition to them this tendency, as far as it relates to its immediate effects, however useful it may be in its remote consequences. The spirit of controversy substitutes the irritation of personal feelings for the independent exertion of the understanding."[28] He once remarked that he "liked an interest in something (a wafer or a crucifix) better than an interest in nothing."[29] Hazlitt was a dedicated enemy to hypocrisy and cant in all its forms, but he admired sincerity wherever he saw it. He was more tolerant than Hunt of religious men who did not live up to their ideals. "He is a hypocrite who professes what he does not believe; not he who does not practice all he wishes or approves. . . . The hypocrisy of priests has been a butt for ridicule in all ages; but I am not sure that there has not been more wit than philosophy in it."[30]

In his *Conversations with James Northcote,* Hazlitt speaks more than once of the intolerance of unbelievers. In one passage, he illustrates his point with an anecdote that may have particular relevance to this study.

I said that skeptics and philosophical unbelievers appeared to me to have just as little liberality or enlargement of view as the most bigoted fanatic. They could not bear to make the least concession to the opposite side. . . .

[27] *The Autobiography and Memoirs of Benjamin Robert Haydon,* ed. Tom Taylor (London: Davies, 1926), I, 255.
[28] *Complete Works,* IV, 48.
[29] *Ibid.,* XI, 231.   [30] *Ibid.,* XVII, 345f.

I had once, I said, given great offence to a knot of persons of this description, by contending that Jacob's Dream was finer than any thing in Shakespeare; and that Hamlet would bear no comparison with, at least, one character in the New Testament. A young poet had said on this occasion, he did not like the Bible, because there was nothing about flowers in it, and I asked him if he had forgot that passage, "Behold the lilies of the field," &c?[31]

There is no evidence that Hazlitt was speaking of the Hunt circle or that the young poet was Keats. But the sentiment would not be uncharacteristic of the poet who, in "Written in Disgust of Vulgar Superstition," predicted that when Christianity has passed away "fresh flowers will grow" in its place.

Hazlitt's tolerance was the logical consequence of his uncompromising skepticism. One might criticize the social effects of a particular creed or the motivation of some of its adherents, but the truth or falsity of its metaphysical assertions were beyond knowing. In this attitude, what Elizabeth Schneider calls his "willingness to remain in ignorance or uncertainty of ultimate reality,"[32] one can see the possibility of an influence on Keats. Leigh Hunt, for all his criticism of traditional faiths, could not live without religion. Hazlitt apparently could. This capability (one might say this negative capability) in a man whose intellect he profoundly respected must have made Keats ponder.

Of all the new acquaintances Keats made in 1816, John Reynolds was perhaps closest to his heart. The two young poets came to know and understand each other intimately and confided to one another their deepest hopes and fears. We know that Keats liked to share metaphysical speculations with Reynolds (*Letters*, I, 246), and it can be assumed that their relationship played a part in the development of the former's religious attitudes.

[31] *Ibid.*, XI, 245f.
[32] *The Aesthetics of William Hazlitt* (Philadelphia: Univ. of Pennsylvania Press, 1933), p. 22.

"Religion should be dressed in smiles, not frowns;—it should raise and bless the soul, not depress and confound it."[33] These words, which appeared in a series of articles (Keats pronounced them "very capital") on contemporary styles of preaching, might identify their author as a disciple of Leigh Hunt. But, although he eventually became a Unitarian,[34] Reynolds in these early years seems to have considered himself still a member of the Church of England. He was embarrassed by abuses in the Church and devoted much energy to exposing them and demanding reform. "We are far from being among those who do not love the Established Church," he wrote in 1818. "We only hold ourselves against those who abuse it, under the cloak of petitioning for its safety. . . . We wish from our heart of hearts that the Clergy had no stains upon their cloth,—that they were as worthy of the cause as it merits, or we could wish them to be."[35] In another article, published in 1821, he condemned the clerical practice of buying ready-made manuscript sermons as a "gross infringement of the candour and decency of the church."[36] Even late in life, when he seems to have abandoned the Establishment, he did not lose his capacity for indignation at ecclesiastical abuses. In 1847 he condemned the practice of charging admission at the door of cathedrals as "a disgrace to religious edifices, a desecration of religion itself, and a black national dishonour."[37] In John Reynolds we see another member of the Hunt circle for whom religion was a matter of serious concern.

Joseph Severn was not a regular member of the Hampstead coterie, but since his friendship with Keats began to grow in this period he deserves a word here. William Sharp

[33] Selected Prose of John Hamilton Reynolds, ed. Leonidas M. Jones (Cambridge, Mass.: Harvard Univ. Press, 1966), p. 219.

[34] The Works of Lord Byron, Letters and Journals, ed. Rowland E. Prothero (London: Murray, 1898-1901; rpt. New York: Octagon Books, 1966), III, 46n.

[35] Selected Prose, pp. 212, 215f.

[36] London Magazine, 4 (November, 1821), 516.

[37] New Monthly Magazine, 79 (February, 1847), 164.

speaks of Severn's "enthusiastic sentiment for the Christian faith,"[38] and, as long as "enthusiastic" is understood in its more modern sense, the word is accurate (he had no use for the Methodists and said of them, "It is wonderful how people can pray themselves out of their little wits").[39] What he called his "little but honest religious faith" was very important to him. It may, in fact, be one reason why he never became a regular habitué of Hunt's cottage. In 1820, he wrote to William Haslam: "Keats has been for some time at Leigh Hunts on account of the attention he requires—most certain his body cannot be in better hands—but for his soul—— altho' I can see in Keats such a deep thinking—determined —silent spirit—that I am doing him the greatest injustice to suppose for a moment that such a man as L——H—— can ever taint him with his principles *now*—or even school him with his learning."[40] On one occasion when Severn did appear at Hampstead, he became involved in a religious argument with Shelley.[41] He later blamed Shelley, almost certainly without cause, for undermining Keats's faith, accusing him of being "one of those friends who had most helped to take away the means of hope from Keats, when despair was so shortly to kill him."[42] During those last dreadful days of Keats's life, Severn's religious influence bore strongly upon the poet. His memories of Keats's final acts are not always totally reliable, but he does not tax our credence too much when he reports that the dying poet was impressed by the quiet piety that inspired his friend's dutifulness. " 'Severn,' he said to me one day, 'I now understand how you can bear all this—'tis your Christian faith.' "[43]

Keats met other men at Hampstead in 1816, but the ones I have mentioned emerged as the most influential in his life, and they serve to indicate the wide range of religious opin-

[38] *The Life and Letters of Joseph Severn* (New York: Scribner, 1892), p. 118.
[39] *The Letters of Charles Armitage Brown*, ed. Jack Stillinger (Cambridge, Mass.: Harvard Univ. Press, 1966), p. 122.
[40] *KC*, I, 122.   [41] See p. 93.   [42] Sharp, p. 117.
[43] *Ibid.*, p. 85.

ion that was represented in Hunt's circle of acquaintance. Given such diversity of opinion among strong-minded men, conflict was inevitable. In the winter of 1816–1817, religious conflict became a major preoccupation of the Hunt circle.

Thanks to Haydon, we do not have to guess at the content and character of these discussions. He recorded many of them in his diary, congratulating himself on the arguments he had used and dissecting those of his opponents. Although he may have had a tendency to enrich his part of the dialogue with ideas that came to him later, blending what he actually said with what he would have said had he thought of it, his accounts are nonetheless informative as well as entertaining. He wrote with gusto and with an eye for detail, as in the wonderfully evocative passage that follows:

> It was singular to watch the fiend that had seized Hunt's soul trying with the most accomplished artifices to catch those of his friends. Often, when all discussion had ceased and the wine had gone freely round—when long talk of poetry and painting had, as it were, opened our hearts—*Hunt* would suddenly (touching my arm with the most friendly pressure) show me a passage in the Bible and Testament, and say, as if appealing to my superiority of understanding, "Haydon, do you believe this?" "Yes," I would instantly answer, with a look he will remember. He would then get up, close the book, and ejaculate, "By Heavens, is it possible!" This was another mode of appeal to my vanity. He would then look out the window with an affected indifference, as if he pitied my shallow mind; and going jauntily to the piano, strike up *"Cosi fan tutti,"* or "Addio il mio cuore," with a "Ring the bell for tea."[44]

Here is Hunt's personality, and the tone and atmosphere of his parlor, sketched quickly and adeptly by the pen of an artist. One can easily visualize Keats in this scene, sitting

[44] *Autobiography*, I, 255.

and quietly observing his two new friends engaged in their ceaseless battle of wits and texts.

The particular occasion for the first round of arguments seems to have been Haydon's announcement that he was going to include Voltaire in his new painting of Christ's Triumphal Entry into Jerusalem, and depict him as a sneering skeptic, in invidious contrast with Newton and Wordsworth as men of faith. Haydon appears to have been reading Voltaire for the first time,[45] and he devotes long passages in his diary to exposing inconsistencies in the Frenchman's critique of Christianity. He concludes that "Voltaire was the worst of hypocrites because under the mask of impartiality, he was the most maliciously prejudiced of any human being."[46] To Hunt, who venerated Voltaire as a Christian might venerate his patron saint, Haydon's intention smacked of sacrilege. "It is amusing," the painter wrote, "to see the extreme sensitiveness of Voltaire's admirers to anything that may hurt his Dignity. Ridicule Voltaire, and he is an ill used, amiable, benevolent being, but ridicule St. Paul or St. Peter or the Virgin or the Saviour, and you are a man of enlarged views, who looks beyond your time, who has had strength to shake off the prejudices of education. . . . My resolution to put in Voltaire's head into my Picture seems to have brought up all Hunt's bile & morbidity."[47]

The argument over Voltaire's character led to a larger debate, which continued for months, on whether the great geniuses of the past were liberal or traditional in matters of religion. "Hunt says the Poets have all gone before their age in Religious matter. I deny it. If to believe the established Religion is not to be before the age, Homer was not before it, nor Hesiod, nor Virgil, nor Dante, Ariosto, Tasso, Chaucer, Milton, Camoens, or Petrarch, nor Shakespeare."[48] Hunt liked to think that most of the great men in history were crypto-Deists and rebels against religious orthodoxy. It did not concern him that the evidence pointed the other

[45] *Diary*, II, 58.   [46] *Ibid.*, p. 61.   [47] *Ibid.*, pp. 55, 80f.
[48] *Ibid.*, p. 57.

way; he believed what it pleased him to believe, what his "heart" told him must be true. This cavalier unconcern with facts infuriated Haydon.

Specimen of my Friend Leigh Hunt's candid method of argument relating to Christianity.

Hunt—Haydon, you will never be as great a Painter as Raphael if you believe in Christianity.

Haydon—But unfortunately for you, Raphael was a Christian.

Hunt—Not a jot of it.

Haydon—But I tell you he was. He left a sum for masses to be said for his Soul, & he painted sacred subjects by which he hoped to influence the minds as much as if he had written.

Hunt—Ah, but he did not believe in them.

Haydon—What argument is this? I tell you two facts, and you deny the consequence to be fairly deduced, not by two opposite facts, but by "not a jot of it" & "he did not believe it."

And this was said with that jaunty air of coxcombry which it is impossible to describe, the voice filled the mouth first and then came out, steeped with conceit & burly insolence which it was out of my power to tell, & then every body smiled, and thought what Hunt said was very conclusive.[49]

We do not know whether Keats was one of those who took Hunt's part on this occasion. In 1818 he revealed a much sounder historical sense than Hunt's when in an analysis of Milton's Protestantism he theorized that "a mighty providence subdues the mightiest Minds to the service of the time being, whether it be in human Knowledge or Religion" (*Letters*, I, 282). But there was another dispute in which Keats would probably have agreed with Hunt. Severn recalls hearing Keats talk about the Greek spirit, "the Religion of the Beautiful, the Religion of Joy, as he

[49] *Ibid.*, pp. 86f.

used to call it."[50] This remark takes on special significance in the context of an argument between Hunt and Haydon over the relative merits of Christianity and classical paganism.

On November 5, 1816, Haydon wrote: "Leigh Hunt says he prefers infinitely the beauties of Pagan Mythology to the gloomy repentance of the Christians."[51] The painter does not describe his opponent's idea any further before writing his rebuttal, but we can get an idea of Hunt's argument from an article he wrote the previous year:

> The Christian mythology personifies Death by an animated skeleton;—the Pagan did it by the figure of a pale but beautiful female, or with a reconcilement still more agreeable, by that of a butterfly escaped from its chrysalis. This was death, and the life that followed it, at once, —the soul freed from the body, and fluttering in the fresh air of Heaven. . . . Even the absurd parts of the Greek Mythology are less painfully absurd than those of any other; because, generally speaking, they are on the chearful side instead of the gloomy. We would rather have a Deity, who fell in love with the beautiful creatures of his own making, than one, who would consign nine hundred out of a thousand to destruction for not believing ill of him.[52]

"No man feels more acutely than myself the poetical beauties of the Pagan mythology," said Haydon in answer.

> Apollo, with his fresh cheek & God like beauty, rising like a gossamer from out a laurel grove, heated with love, after having panted on the bosom of some wandering nymph, is rich, beaming, rapturous! But these are beauties fit for those who live in perpetual enjoyment of immortality, without a care or a grief or a want. But what consolation to the poor, what relief to the widow & the

[50] Sharp, p. 29.   [51] *Diary*, II, 68.
[52] *Examiner*, November 12, 1815, pp. 731f.

orphan, to the sick, or the oppressed? Could the minds of such beings turn for assistance to a thoughtless & beautiful youth, warm with love & wine, just rising from having debauched a girl? Christianity is a religion adapted to give relief to the wretched & hope to the good, and Christ having suffered is a bond of sympathy between man & his Saviour that nothing in any other religion before or after affords.[53]

When conversation in the Hunt circle came round to "gloominess" in religion, a debate on the doctrine of Hell was not far off. It was difficult at this point in history to discuss Christianity at all without coming to terms with the notion of eternal punishment. The rise of Methodism and Evangelicalism, with their emphasis on sin and guilt, made damnation a popular subject among preachers, whose sermons would depict in lurid detail the eternal tortures awaiting unrepentant sinners. The doctrine, which receives little attention in the New Testament, was regarded by many in this period as close to the essential core of the faith. Certainly Hunt seemed incapable of discussing Christianity without mentioning eternal punishment. The doctrine defined Christianity in his eyes, since it said much about the nature of the God Christians believed in. That a man on his deathbed, he said, "should be frightened at God, and regard him, not as an all-wise and good Being who would not have made him for ultimate wretchedness, but as a capricious despot who values opinion and flattery more than anything else, and will condemn his creatures to eternal tortures if they do not fall prostrate before him in horror of mind, and pay him the absurdest and most degrading of human compliments,—are slavish and horrible doctrines, which thousands are now sick of, and the world will be infinitely more truly pious, kind, and happy, when they are altogether exploded."[54]

[53] *Diary*, ii, 67.
[54] *Examiner*, January 18, 1818, p. 38.

Although he worried about the "probable damnation" of his unbelieving friends,[55] Haydon had no intellectual difficulties with the doctrine of Hell. "Why may there not be punishment hereafter as well as punishment here? You may as well argue there is no God because we see the innocent suffer, as that Xtianity cannot be of Divine Origin because the guilty are threatened with punishment hereafter."[56] He believed that Hunt's critique of Christianity was not intellectually disinterested, but inspired by personal dread of the doctrines relating to the afterlife. "In an argument with Leigh Hunt, he said he was convinced people believed Xtianity under the influence of terror, & I am thoroughly convinced that his sensitive imagination is alarmed at the probability of being roasted or pitchforked or punished. Rather than acquiesce in the beauty of its doctrines as to virtue, gives the whole up that he might not be harrassed by the apprehension of future torment in case of Sin. He disbelieves in it from terror, I am convinced, but I will defy any terror to alarm me into disbelief of anything, & this I can say with a clear conscience."[57]

Haydon's reference to the probability of Hunt's being pitchforked in the hereafter shows how easily their disputes could descend to an unpleasant, personal level. They both realized that the arguments were getting out of hand and at the end of October agreed to call a truce.[58] This moratorium did not last long. It was shattered by the appearance on the scene, in December, of Percy Bysshe Shelley. The author of *The Necessity of Atheism* and *Queen Mab* was not used to keeping his religious sentiments to himself. He was not the sort of man to allow polite convention or formal armistices to hinder him from asserting his views, and Hunt was unable or unwilling to prevent a clash between him and Haydon. The confrontation came in January, 1817, when Haydon was invited or, perhaps more accurately, lured to

[55] *Diary*, II, 80. [56] *Ibid.*, p. 58. [57] *Ibid.*, p. 57.
[58] *Ibid.*, p. 62.

meet Shelley. The painter has left a vivid account of the meeting:[59]

> I went a little after the time, and seated myself in the place kept for me at the table, right opposite Shelley himself, as I was told after, for I did not then know what hectic, spare, weakly yet intellectual-looking creature it was, carving a bit of brocoli or cabbage on his plate, as if it had been the substantial wing of a chicken. [Hunt] and his wife and her sister, Keats, Horace Smith, and myself made up the party.
>
> In a few minutes Shelley opened the conversation by saying in the most feminine and gentle voice, "As to that detestable religion, the Christian—" I looked astounded, but casting a glance round the table easily saw by [Hunt's] expression of ecstasy and the women's simper, I was to be set at that evening *vi et armis*. No reply, however, was made to this sally during dinner, but when the dessert came and the servant was gone, to it we went like fiends. ——and——were deists. I felt exactly like a stag at bay and resolved to gore without mercy. Shelley said the Mosaic and Christian dispensations were inconsistent. I swore they were not, and that the Ten Commandments had been the foundation of all the codes of law in the earth. Shelley denied it. ——backed him. I affirmed they were—neither of us using an atom of logic.

There followed an argument on whether Shakespeare was a Christian, involving a barrage of texts, and then the discussion dissipated into exchanges of personal abuse. As he concludes his account of the confrontation, Haydon makes a point of remarking that Keats said nothing during the course of the argument. The best explanation for this silence would seem to be Keats's concern for Haydon's feelings: they had become very close friends by this time and

[59] *Autobiography*, I, 253f. In T. Taylor's edition, some of the names are blanked out; I have supplied them where the identities are obvious.

Keats knew that despite his gruff exterior the painter was easily hurt. But on another occasion very like this one, Keats did take the part of a Christian friend in an argument with Shelley.

This time the protagonist was Joseph Severn. As the artist recalled later:

> Shelley, in our first interview, went out of his way to attack me on my Christian creed. He repeated to Leigh Hunt the plan of a poem he was about to write, being a comparison of the Blessed Saviour with a mountebank, whose tricks he identified with the miracles. I was shocked and disturbed, and breaking in upon his offensive detail, I exclaimed, "That the fact of the greatest men having been Christians during the Christian period placed the religion far above such low ridicule." Shelley immediately denied this fact, and we at once began enumerating on our fingers the great men who were Christians, and the few who were not. When we got to Shakespeare he attempted to deny the great poet's belief, and quoted the sailor in "Measure for Measure." My counter quotations were from the utterances of Portia, Hamlet, Isabella, and numerous others; so that Leigh Hunt and Keats declared I had the best of the argument —whereupon Shelley declared that he would study the subject and write an essay upon it.[60]

In a letter to R. M. Milnes in 1848, Severn gave another account of this confrontation, more interesting for the light it casts on the relationship between the two poets. "I dont know that I ever told you of a singular argument with Shelly about the Christian religion in which Keats continually to the annoyance of Shelly declared I had the advantage—I have often thought it was an interesting example of his generosity and love of justice—Shelly was so piqued not at my argument but at Keats triumphing over him that he declared he would write a pamphlet of his argument."[61]

[60] Sharp, pp. 116f.   [61] *KC*, II, 233f.

Severn was right, I think, in attributing Keats's support in this instance to his "generosity and love of justice" (although he may have derived more than a little satisfaction from the young artist's victory over Shelley, whose assertiveness could become irritating). That it did not stem from any love of Christianity can be demonstrated from a poem Keats wrote at about this time—the most explicit statement of religious opinion he ever put into verse. I refer to the sonnet "Written in Disgust of Vulgar Superstition." Because it deals so directly with the subject of religion, the poem demands close attention here—more attention, perhaps, than it merits on the ground of poetic quality alone.

On Sunday evening, December 22, 1816, Keats was sitting with his brothers in their London lodgings, when the sound of church bells broke in upon his consciousness.[62] On the back of an old letter he began putting together some verses. He wrote quickly and easily—the manuscript shows few revisions—and in fifteen minutes the following sonnet was completed.

> The church bells toll a melancholy round,
>   Calling the people to some other prayers,
>   Some other gloominess, more dreadful cares,
> More hearkening to the sermon's horrid sound.
> Surely the mind of man is closely bound
>   In some black spell; seeing that each one tears
>   Himself from fireside joys, and Lydian airs,
> And converse high of those with glory crown'd.
> Still, still they toll, and I should feel a damp,—
>   A chill as from a tomb, did I not know
> That they are dying like an outburnt lamp;
>   That 'tis their sighing, wailing ere they go
>   Into oblivion;—that fresh flowers will grow,
> And many glories of immortal stamp.

[62] For another version of the circumstances surrounding the composition of the poem, see Charles Cowden Clarke's remarks in *KC*, II, 154.

What do these hastily penned lines tell us about Keats's religious dispositions at the end of 1816? They appear to indicate that he looked upon religion—the religion practiced in London churches—as a thing of gloom and dread. They show further that he believed this dreary religion was in its last days, that it would soon disappear from the earth and be replaced by something new, something more beautiful and more glorious. To understand these statements more fully, and to form a proper estimate of their significance as evidence of Keats's considered views, one must have a sense of the intellectual milieu that influenced them.

Without this sense of context, one might at first be puzzled by the description of church-religion as a thing of "gloominess" and "dreadful cares." This might be an apt description of the Evangelical style of religion, but Keats does not seem to limit his criticism to one tradition or sect. Despite Aileen Ward's assertion that the anti-Christian sentiment of the poem was rooted deep in Keats's past,[63] one can see little in the poet's upbringing that would have provoked this sweeping indictment of Christianity as a gloomy, melancholy, dreadful faith. Certainly the liberal environment of John Clarke's academy, where Keats acquired much of his early religious knowledge, could not have had such associations for him.[64] It is possible that his sentiments were influenced by the personality of Richard Abbey, who was attempting at this time to tear Keats away from "Lydian airs" and bring him into the world of business. But

[63] *John Keats: The Making of a Poet* (New York: Viking Press, 1963), p. 82.

[64] Even the rigorously Calvinist founder of the school, John Collet Ryland, disapproved of making religion a melancholy business. "All gloominess and hard thoughts of Christ are exceedingly disgustful to him: every thing dark, desponding, and melancholy, is very injurious to the character and religion of the Lord; for it makes an odious representation of him to the world; it hardens the hearts of the wicked; it gives great advantage to the devil; it terrifies enquiring souls, and most horribly misrepresents the lovely, beautiful, and generous dispositions of our dear redeemer." *Contemplations on the Divinity of Christ*, Vol. III (Northampton: T. Dicey, 1782), pp. 257f.

if one is looking for a personal influence that might have encouraged the attitudes expressed in Keats's poem, a much more likely choice is Leigh Hunt.

Haydon criticized Hunt for "seeing only the gloomy prospects of damnation in believing Christianity,"[65] and he had good grounds for his charge. Hunt felt that most of those who embraced the Christian faith did so under the influence of terror. He saw the primary object of Christian worship as an attempt to placate and stave off the wrath of a cruel and capricious Deity. A few weeks before Keats wrote his sonnet, Hunt had remarked in the *Examiner*: "Many Europeans will start with indignation at being told that the Divine Being is really wise and kind, and does not burn his creatures to all eternity. The worship of Moloch is still the greatest on earth under various names; but we believe it to be fast going down; nor will Mahometanism, nor Methodism . . . save it from vanishing away before a rising and genial knowledge which shall dissipate it as morning does the goblins."[66] One can see a connection between the final remark and the sestet of Keats's sonnet, in which the bells (and the religion they proclaim) are dying like a burnt-out lamp, sighing and wailing as they go into oblivion. Except in some bad moments when Europe appeared to be backsliding into old habits of belief, Hunt was confident that the world was outgrowing Christianity and would soon embrace a purer, more philosophical faith. If he (and Keats) had needed any encouragement in this view, it was provided by Shelley, who arrived on the scene ten days before the sonnet under consideration was written. In *Queen Mab*, the fairy addresses Religion ("prolific fiend,/ Who peoplest earth with demons, Hell with men,/And heaven with slaves!") and prophesies its doom:

> But now contempt is mocking thy gray hairs;
> Thou art descending to the darksome grave,

[65] *Diary*, II, 81.
[66] *Examiner*, November 24, 1816, p. 740.

Unhonoured and unpitied, but by those
Whose pride is passing by like thine, and sheds,
Like thine, a glare that fades before the sun
Of truth, and shines but in the dreadful night
That long has lowered above the ruined world.[67]

Considering, then, the company he had been keeping, the
sentiments Keats expressed in "Written in Disgust of Vulgar
Superstition" are not very surprising. There is really rather
little in the thought of the poem that is original—except
perhaps for one element. One of his chief complaints
against church religion is that it distracts people from
"Lydian airs,/And converse high of those with glory
crown'd." He comforts himself with the thought that when
religion dies it will be replaced by "fresh flowers" and
"many glories of immortal stamp." That these glories will
include great poems is suggested by another sonnet of the
same period, "On Receiving a Laurel Crown from Leigh
Hunt," in which the replacing of turbans and crowns by
laurel wreaths leads to "wild surmises/ Of all the many
glories that may be." In this sonnet, Keats sees poets replacing sultans and kings in the esteem of the world. In the
other, it is priests and preachers who are to be displaced.

The title Keats gave to his anti-Christian sonnet must also
be understood in its intellectual context. The term "vulgar
superstition" has a rather more limited meaning today than
it had in the early nineteenth century. We have learned to
look upon the use of dubious relics—flasks of curative water
or oil, and other paraphernalia to which unsophisticated
faith attributes pseudo-magical power—as an aberrance
from the proper nature of religious faith and worship. In
Keats's time it was not so easy to make these distinctions.
Superstition played a major role in the religious life of the
common people, blending so completely with their Christian faith that it was difficult to know where one began and

[67] *The Complete Poetical Works of Percy Bysshe Shelley*, ed.
Thomas Hutchinson (London: Oxford Univ. Press, 1960), pp. 784f.

the other left off. Walking the wards of a public hospital, assisting at the sickbeds of the poor, Keats would have seen religious superstition at its worst—at its most "disgusting." He may have witnessed the use of sweepings from a church floor in an attempt to ease and hasten a lingering death. He may have known that rainwater collected on Holy Thursday was considered efficacious in eye ailments, that bits of stone chipped from statues were ground into powder to be placed on sores, and that dew collected in a churchyard was believed curative in cases of consumption. These practices and others like them were popular in the early nineteenth century.[68] Outside the hospital, too, religious superstition made itself evident. George Turner, a popular prophet who had inherited many of Joanna Southcott's disciples after her death, was inserting large advertisements in the newspapers during December, 1816, announcing that the world would end in the following month. Numbers of people responded by leaving their jobs and throwing away their money.[69] If Keats needed particular inspiration for an attack on religious superstition, there was plenty at hand.

But as I have said, "vulgar superstition" signified more to Keats than aberrations of piety. The phrase was widely used by exponents of natural religion (in its various forms) to describe Christianity itself. In their view, the universe of nature and the moral law inscribed upon the heart clearly proclaimed a great Original, and this was revelation enough to the enlightened, philosophic mind. Attempts to complicate this sublime simplicity were characteristic of darkened intellects. As Voltaire put it, "Almost everything that goes beyond the worship of a supreme Being, and the submission of one's heart to his eternal commands, is superstition."[70] In the salons and coffee houses of eighteenth-century Europe,

[68] J. E. Vaux, *Church Folklore* (London: Griffith, 1894), p. 302.
[69] George R. Balleine, *Past Finding Out: The Tragic Story of Joanna Southcott and Her Successors* (London: S.P.C.K., 1956), pp. 76ff.
[70] *Philosophical Dictionary*, trans. Peter Gay (New York: Basic Books, 1962), p. 473.

the distinction was generally accepted: the proper religious attitude of the intelligent and cultivated was a refined Theism; Christianity was the faith of the vulgar, the unenlightened, the masses. In the early nineteenth century men like Leigh Hunt continued to see the world as divided into these two cultures, confident that the march of mind was gradually swelling the ranks of the first at the expense of the second. Any indication that the trend might be reversing was met with expressions of anger and dismay. And so, when in late 1816 Coleridge's first "Lay Sermon" appeared, it was greeted with pained surprise. Hazlitt's review may be taken as a representative reaction:

> The truth is . . . that the whole of this Sermon is written to sanction the principle of Catholic dictation, and to reprobate that diffusion of free inquiry—that difference of private, and ascendancy of public opinion, which has been the necessary consequence, and the great benefit of the Reformation. . . . Coleridge, or at least those whom he writes to please, . . . would give us back all the abuses of former times, without any of their advantages; and impose upon us, by force or fraud, a complete system of superstition without faith, of despotism without loyalty, of error without enthusiasm, and all the evils, without any of the blessings, of ignorance.[71]

These remarks, which appeared in December, 1816, or similar sentiments expressed in conversation at Hampstead, may well have contributed to the mood in which Keats wrote his poetic expression of disgust with vulgar superstition.

As revealing as that sonnet is, it does not convey a complete sense of Keats's religious disposition at this time. Its largely negative and critical tone must be compared with more positive sentiments expressed in other poems of the period. The following lines, for instance, were also written

[71] *Complete Works*, xvi, 105f.

in the month of December and express a rather different
side of their author's religious consciousness:

> Good Kosciusko, thy great name alone
>   Is a full harvest whence to reap high feeling;
>   It comes upon us like the glorious pealing
> Of the wide spheres—an everlasting tone.
> And now it tells me, that in worlds unknown,
>   The names of heroes, burst from clouds concealing,
>   Are changed to harmonies, for ever stealing
> Through cloudless blue, and round each silver throne.
> It tells me too, that on a happy day,
>   When some good spirit walks upon the earth,
>   Thy name with Alfred's, and the great of yore
>   Gently commingling, gives tremendous birth
> To a loud hymn, that sounds far, far away
>   To where the great God lives for evermore.

To find inspiration for lofty thoughts in the pealing of the
wide spheres rather than in the ringing of church bells is
typical of natural religion. The sonnet contains the two
basic characteristics of that creed: reverence for God (the
fact that Keats uses that word, instead of a more "enlightened" term like Supreme Being or Great Spirit, is interesting) and belief in immortality—in "worlds unknown,"
where the good are rewarded hereafter. More interesting
than the doctrinal content, however, is the aura of piety that
pervades the poem. The emotion as well as the imagery is
religious. This rather surprising devotional tone appears in
another, more important poem of December, 1816—"Sleep
and Poetry," where, listing some of the wonderful effects of
poetry, Keats writes:

> Sometimes it gives a glory to the voice,
> And from the heart up-springs, rejoice! rejoice!
> Sounds which will reach the Framer of all things,
> And die away in ardent mutterings.

No one who once the glorious sun has seen,
And all the clouds, and felt his bosom clean
For his great Maker's presence, but must know
What 'tis I mean, and feel his being glow. (ll. 37-44)

In the presence of such warm expressions of religious feeling, one cannot but conclude that Keats was, at this point in his life, a rather pious young man (the word "pious" is surprising, perhaps, but I think accurate). The testimony of Charles Cowden Clarke reinforces this impression: " 'Every day,' [Keats] once said, was 'Sabbath' to him, as it is to every grateful mind, for blessings momentarily bestowed upon us. . . . Sunday was indeed Keats's 'day of rest,' and I may add, too, of unprofessing, unostentatious gratitude."[72]

The words "rejoice! rejoice!" in the passage quoted above may recall the "Gratitude! Gratitude!" of Leigh Hunt's 1817 "Hymn." Indeed, if an explanation be required for the expressions of religious feeling that appear in Keats's verse at this time, one can cite the influence of Hunt. The older man's piety was genuine and unconcealed. Perhaps because he was conscious of being "reckoned lax in [his] Christian principles" (as Keats phrased it—Letters, II, 14), he was determined to show that piety based on natural religion could be just as real, just as fervent, as that inspired by Christianity. I believe we can learn as much about the religious tone of the Hampstead environment from Keats's devotional effusions as from Haydon's jeremiads. Hunt no doubt encouraged Keats to reject, and for a time even to despise, Christianity. But he also showed him that religion not only could but should be an important part of an intelligent man's life, that some form of faith was necessary. As I suggested earlier, Hunt's religious influence on Keats must be seen, on balance, as positive. In the years to come, when direct expressions of religious faith no longer appear in the poetry, certain ideas and attitudes learned from Hunt will continue to affect Keats's thoughts on the subject of religion.

[72] Recollections of Writers, p. 157.

There is another passage in "Sleep and Poetry" that demands attention here. Immediately following the lines I have quoted referring to the "great Maker's presence," there comes a long, passionate apostrophe in which the religious emotion of the preceding lines is continued, though in a rather different celestial frame of reference.

> O Poesy! for thee I hold my pen
> That am not yet a glorious denizen
> Of thy wide heaven—Should I rather kneel
> Upon some mountain-top until I feel
> A glowing splendour round about me hung,
> And echo back the voice of thine own tongue?
> O Poesy! for thee I grasp my pen
> That am not yet a glorious denizen
> Of thy wide heaven; yet, to my ardent prayer,
> Yield from thy sanctuary some clear air,
> Smooth'd for intoxication by the breath
> Of flowering bays, that I may die a death
> Of luxury, and my young spirit follow
> The morning sun-beams to the great Apollo
> Like a fresh sacrifice.... (ll. 47-61)

What is one to make of this remarkable language? Is it necessary to take the obvious religious imagery as evidence that Keats looked on poetry in a religious light or as a kind of surrogate for religion? I do not believe so. The emotion and the language can be explained, I think, by the situation in which Keats places himself with regard to poetry. Following an old and respectable tradition, he places the source of poetic inspiration "up there"—above him and beyond him. This necessarily leaves him in a state of yearning, of striving, of attempting to reach beyond his grasp. Having decided to depict himself in this posture, he then looks for language that will suit his situation—which is very like the situation of a votary at prayer. The vocabulary of religious devotion is an obvious choice.

One should note that the religious frame of reference of

the invocation to Poesy differs from that of the lines that
precede it in the poem. In this easy shift we see an example
of the ability of Keats's imagination to operate within two
completely different mythic systems—which I will call,
arbitrarily, Theist and Apollonian.[73] He appears to experience no intellectual difficulty, no hesitation or embarrassment, in passing from one to the other. It is clear that for
Keats the two systems are distinct and disparate, one presided over by the "great Maker" and "Framer of all things,"
the other by "the great Apollo." As Keats grew older, he
carefully withheld from his poetry all direct reference to
the first deity, and Apollo seemed to reign supreme. But, of
course, poetry was not the only mental pursuit with which
he was occupied during his lifetime. The "great Maker"
remained real to him always, and there is evidence of a constant, quiet struggle on his part to define the nature of the
relationship in which he and this Maker were involved.

After January, 1817, the intellectual crucible in which
many of Keats's basic religious attitudes took form began
to cool, as some of the men who had made up the Hunt circle when Keats became a member went their separate ways.
Haydon, who had provided most of the heat, could not for-
give Hunt for what he regarded as an ambush on the night
he was invited to meet Shelley. He was tired of being baited
and goaded and resolved never to place himself in that situation again. His indignation at Hunt's behavior was recorded in his diary on January 20:

> Instead of seeing the absurdity of harrassing me by any
> further persecution about my opinion, instead of being
> delicate in regard to my feelings about the characters and
> persons of the founders of Christianity, a delicacy proper
> to be observed even with regard to a man's friends, much

[73] It is a capability he would have noticed in his Renaissance and
Elizabethan masters, who seemed equally at ease with Christian and
Classical story, and moved gracefully and unselfconsciously from
one to the other as it suited their poetic purposes.

more with regard to the authors of a sacred belief, he makes a point of always beginning to say some brutal joke about them. As he has so little regard to my feelings, I will have no longer any regard to his, and as he is totally invulnerable in regard to sacred feelings of any descriptions, with the exception of those regarding his own person—his own person, his own weaknesses, his own follies, shall always be the object of my allusion. There is a man who complains of the persecuting spirit of the Christians, and to be sure he sets a pretty example of forbearance himself, and to be sure *I* set a pretty example of following the Christian dictates in thus trying to wound, but Christ spared not the Pharisees or Priests; on that principle will I no longer have any regard for him.[74]

As though to illustrate how far he is ready to go in criticizing Hunt, he immediately commences a savage attack on the man's habits and morals, accusing him, for example, of "sliming" the body of his sister-in-law with "the sickly pukings of lechery."

Having decided to quit the fleshpots of Hampstead forever, Haydon seems to have resolved to carry away with him as spoils the mind and soul of John Keats. Haydon had taken a great fancy to the young poet and he was determined to rescue him from the artistic as well as the religious influence of Hunt. Hunt and Haydon differed dramatically in their approach to art; it was the difference between the snug warmth of a parlor and a blustering wind, the difference between busts on a mantelpiece and the Elgin Marbles. Haydon's artistic conceptions were heroic, as large and sweeping as his canvases. His taste in painting centered on Michelangelo and Raphael; in literature, on Homer and the Bible, Shakespeare and Milton. What impressed him in art were grandeur and passion, and his robust, masculine approach provided Keats with a much needed counterweight to the more feminine and domestic taste of Leigh Hunt. It was primarily by transforming the poet's under-

[74] *Diary*, II, 81f.

standing of what poetry should be that Haydon succeeded in luring Keats out of the Hampstead milieu. He was in large measure responsible for fertilizing and quickening an egg over which Hunt might have gone on clucking forever.

Haydon's influence was less successful on the religious front, though probably not for lack of effort. If his diary can be used as a basis for determining his intellectual preoccupations during February and March, 1817, he must have thought and talked constantly about religion. The entries during these months are almost entirely devoted to an attack on Voltaire and a personal response to an anti-Christian article in the *Examiner*. We do not know how much pressure he applied to Keats, but during March he thought he observed a change in the poet. "At first," he wrote, "I feared your ardor might lead you to disregard the accumulated wisdom of ages in moral points—but the feelings put forth lately—have delighted my soul—always consider principle of more value than genius—and you are safe" (Keats's *Letters*, I, 124f.). The "feelings put forth lately" might refer to some things Keats said in conversation, but Haydon may also be alluding to some of his friend's poetic utterances. Among those "put forth lately" which could have reassured the painter were "To Kosciusko," which was published in the *Examiner* on February 16, and "To B. R. Haydon"—the second of two sonnets written by Keats after seeing the Elgin Marbles. In this rather conventional, but in one respect unusual, sonnet, Keats refers to Haydon's success in convincing others of the worth and authenticity of the marbles and in persuading the British government to buy them for the nation.

> Haydon! forgive me that I cannot speak
>   Definitively on these mighty things;
>   Forgive me that I have not Eagle's wings—
> That what I want I know not where to seek:
> And think that I would not be over meek
>   In rolling out upfollow'd thunderings,
>   Even to the steep of Heliconian springs,

Were I of ample strength for such a freak—
Think too, that all those numbers should be thine;
Whose else? In this who touch thy vesture's hem?
For when men star'd at what was most divine
With browless idiotism—o'erwise phlegm—
Thou hadst beheld the Hesperean shine
Of their star in the East, and gone to worship them.

The New Testament imagery in the sestet is the clearest
that appears in any of Keats's poems. Nowhere do we find
such explicit reference to Christ as in these allusions to
touching a "vesture's hem" and to the quest of the Magi.
Perhaps Haydon was thinking of this sonnet when he re-
membered later that Keats "had a tendency to Christianity
when he first knew me."[75] But the tendency revealed in "To
B. R. Haydon" is probably no more than that chameleon-
like quality of the poetic character that Keats once described in a letter (I, 387). The "chameleon Poet" might
easily take on a Christian coloring when in the presence of
so strong a personality as Haydon's.

Certainly, no tendency to Christianity can be observed
in the letters Keats wrote during the spring of 1817. On the
contrary, in one of his letters to Haydon we can see him
deliberately parrying the religious advice of his friend. The
letter was written from Devon on May 10 and 11, in answer
to one recently received from the painter. By juxtaposing
passages from the two letters, one can observe Keats's tact-
ful but persistent rejection of Haydon's religious counsel.
For example, Haydon refers to the fact that Keats was feeling depressed by his lack of sustained productivity, and
advises:

Do not give way to forebodings . . . but begin again
where you left off—without hesitation or fear—*Trust in
God* with all your might My dear Keats this dependance
with your own energy will give you strength, & hope, &

75 *Ibid.*, p. 317.

comfort——In all my troubles, & wants, & distresses, here
I found a refuge—from my Soul I declare to you, I never
applied for help or consolation, or strength—but I found
it . . . never despair while there is this path open to you—
by habitual exercise, you will have habitual intercourse,
and constant companionship, and in every want, turn to
the great Star of your hopes with a delightful confidence
which will never be disappointed. (1, 135)

Keats replies, picking up several of Haydon's phrases:

Thank God! I do begin arduously where I leave off, notwithstanding occasional depressions: and I hope for the
support of a High Power while I clime this little eminence and especially in my Years of more momentous
Labor. I remember your saying that you had notions of
a good Genius presiding over you—I have of late had the
same thought. for things which I do half at random are
afterwards confirmed by my judgment in a dozen features of Propriety—Is it too daring to Fancy Shakspeare
this Presider? . . . You tell me never to despair—I wish it
was as easy for me to observe the saying—truth is I have
a horrid Morbidity of Temperament which has shown itself at intervals—it is I have no doubt the greatest Enemy
and stumbling block I have to fear . . . How ever every ill
has its share of good—this very bane would at any time
enable me to look with an obstinate eye on the Devil himself—ay to be as proud of being the lowest of the human
race as Alfred could be in being of the highest. I feel confident I should have been a rebel Angel had the opportunity been mine. (1, 141f.)

Notice how the "High Power" bringing help and support is
transformed by Keats from God into Shakespeare. He resists, or refuses to acknowledge, Haydon's repeated recommendation of prayer for divine aid. Keats's rejection of his
friend's pious advice may be understood in connection with
natural religion's antipathy toward the notion of particular

divine interpositions in the order of the world. Prayer of praise and thanksgiving was considered proper for man (note that Keats is willing to write "Thank God!") but prayer of petition deemed unreasonable. Such an attitude is expressed by the Savoyard Vicar in *Emile*:

> I consider the order of the universe, not to explain it by any futile system, but to revere it without ceasing, to adore the wise Author who reveals himself in it. I hold intercourse with him; I immerse all my powers in his divine essence; I am overwhelmed by his kindness, I bless him and his gifts, but I do not pray to him. What should I ask of him—to change the order of nature, to work miracles on my behalf? Should I, who am bound to love above all things the order which he has established in his wisdom and maintained by his providence, should I desire the disturbance of that order on my own account?[76]

The Manfred-like Prometheanism expressed at the end of the last passage quoted from the letter to Haydon is not so easy to explain. Nothing like it appears again in Keats's writing. Perhaps it is only an example of the kind of "rhodomontade" he fell into occasionally, particularly in conversation with Haydon (I, 414).

There is another exchange in these letters worthy of note. In what must have been an often repeated warning, Haydon cautions Keats against the influence of Hunt. "I love you like my own Brother, beware for God's sake of the delusions and sophistications that is ripping up the talent & respectability of our Friend—he will go out of the World the victim of his own weakness & the dupe of his own self delusions" (I, 135). It is obvious from both the context of this letter and the larger context of Haydon's polemic vocabulary, in which "delusions and sophistications" almost always mean religious errors,[77] that Keats is being warned

[76] Jean Jacques Rousseau, *Emile, or Education*, trans. Barbara Foxley (London: Dent, 1911), p. 257.
[77] See, for example, *Diary*, II, 87, 100.

against Hunt's doctrinal and moral heterodoxy. Yet he seems to miss the point completely and replies with reference to Hunt's *literary* faults. "His self delusions are very lamentable they have inticed him into a Situation which I should be less eager after than that of a galley Slave—what you observe thereon is very true must be in time. Perhaps it is a self delusion to say so—but I think I could not be deceived in the Manner that Hunt is—may I die tomorrow if I am to be. There is no greater Sin after the 7 deadly than to flatter oneself into the idea of being a great Poet" (1, 143). It must have been very frustrating for Haydon to read Keats's reply to his letter and see his religious admonitions being ignored or evaded in almost every particular.

The painter concludes his letter with repetition of his advice against dejection: "God bless you My dear Keats go on, dont despair, collect incidents, study characters, read Shakespeare and trust in Providence" (1, 135). Once again Keats is selective in his response: "I never quite despair and I read Shakspeare—indeed I shall I think never read any other Book much—Now this might lead me into a long Confab but I desist. I am very near Agreeing with Hazlit that Shakspeare is enough for us" (1, 143). Here too he ignores the religious counsel and focuses on the literary, but for the first time he faces rather than avoids the issue. Haydon must have attempted to communicate his enthusiasm for the Bible to Keats and would understand the poet's decision to read no "other Book much" as implying a rejection of Scripture. Keats seems to realize that he has taken an argumentative stance, but he prefers not to pursue the point, conscious that challenging Haydon directly would only provoke a torrent of counterargument. But throughout the letter in a quiet way he has been making it obvious that, with regard to religion, he does not welcome his friend's advice, or share his views.

A much more direct expression of opinion on the religion practiced and preached by Haydon appears in a letter

Keats wrote to Leigh Hunt a day earlier, on May 10. Following upon a reference to paying bills as a "horrid subject" he remarks: "What a horrid one you were upon last Sunday and well you handled it. The last Examiner was a Battering Ram against Christianity—Blasphemy—Tertullian—Erasmus—Sr Philip Sidney. And then the dreadful Petzelians and their expiation by Blood—and do Christians shudder at the same thing in a Newspaper which they attribute to their God in its most aggravated form? What is to be the end of this?" (I, 137.) The occasion for Hunt's use of a battering ram against Christianity was an attempt in Liverpool to prosecute a Unitarian minister for blasphemy. The charges had no basis in law or in fact and the minister was speedily acquitted, but Hunt, ever on the alert for signs of increased repression of liberal opinions, used the incident as an excuse for an editorial on religious intolerance. Warming to the subject, he extended his remarks to an attack on Christianity in general. One editorial became three, the second of which appeared on May 4 and was the subject of Keats's comments. It will be instructive to investigate what Keats thought was a "well handled" critique of Christianity.

Hunt begins with a brief sketch of the etymology and history of the term "blasphemy" (this in reference to the Liverpool trial). He determines that to blaspheme is to attribute to the Supreme Being qualities that in their nature must be reckoned odious by humanity. This definition allows him, harping on a favorite theme, to suggest that belief in the doctrine of eternal punishment is blasphemy. It is in this connection that the references to Tertullian, Erasmus, and Sir Philip Sidney are made. The passage runs as follows:

"You are fond of spectacles," exclaims the stern Tertullian, "expect the greatest of all spectacles, the last and eternal judgment of the universe. How shall I admire, how laugh, how rejoice, how exult, when I behold so many proud Monarchs, and fancied Gods, groaning in the lowest abyss of darkness; so many Magistrates who persecuted the name of the Lord, liquefying in fiercer fires than they ever kindled against the Christians; so many sage philosophers blushing in red hot flames with their *deluded* scholars; so many celebrated poets trembling before the tribunal, not of Minos, but of Christ; so many tragedians more tuneful in the expression of their own sufferings." . . . On the other hand, the gentler Erasmus used to be so moved with the just and charitable wisdom of one of these heathen philosophers, that he confessed he was almost tempted to add his name to the list of the Saints, and exclaim, "Sancte Socrates, ora pro nobis!"—Holy Socrates, pray for us.—The noble Sir Philip Sidney, who when tormented with thirst in his last moments, ordered the cup of water he was about to drink to be given to a dying brother-soldier, was a friend of Giordanus Bruno, a famous sceptic, afterwards burnt on a charge of atheism. And one of the most amiable writers of antiquity, Plutarch, though himself a priest, expressly preferred atheism to that kind of superstition which leads to inhuman notions of the Divinity.[78]

Hunt concludes the editorial by touching on another of his favorite themes, the contrast between paganism and Christianity:

The Christians arose, who by degrees excluded the Jews themselves;—then came religious authority, power, contention; and at last they fell to excluding each other,—a scandal, which has continued with more or less violence ever since. . . . And thus it has happened, that a religion, peculiarly professing charity, has been the most intolerant and sanguinary that ever existed. Dispute and bloodshed on holy accounts were phenomena in the ancient world. It may be said, that these are the abuses of religion, not religion itself: but not to stop and examine

[78] *Examiner*, May 4, 1817, p. 274.

the still more fearfully minute portion of mankind to which this would confine the chance of salvation, the abuses of Paganism led to no such horrors. They were chiefly on the pleasurable side of things, whereas the former were on the painful. They dealt in loves and luxuries, in what resulted from the first laws of nature, and tended to keep humanity alive:—the latter have dealt in angry debates, in intolerance, in gloomy denouncements, in persecutions, in excommunications, in wars and massacres, in what perplexes, outrages, and destroys humanity.

The "dreadful Petzelians" alluded to by Keats did not figure in Hunt's editorial, but were the subject of a news item from Vienna. The article tells of the arrest of a priest named Petzel (actually Poeschel) along with eighty-six of his followers for being involved in a religious cult that practiced human sacrifice. The purpose of the sacrifices, it seems, was the purification of the cult's members from their sins. Referring to this story in a later issue of the *Examiner*, Hunt wrote: "What is this but a bleeding branch of the famous doctrine of the Atonement, which tells us that God was pleased with the vicarious sacrifice of his own agonized Son, as a pain necessary to satisfy his sense of justice?"[79] Keats, too, saw the connection with the doctrine of the Atonement. "And do Christians shudder at the same thing in a Newspaper which they attribute to their God in its most aggravated form?" The comment is interesting, especially since Keats so seldom expressed an opinion on particular religious doctrines. We discover that his rejection of Christianity was based, at least in part, on an objection to its central article of faith—the redemption of mankind by the suffering and death of Jesus Christ. The precise reasons for his objection are revealed later, in his 1819 discussion of the world as a "vale of Soul-making" (II, 101ff.), and will be considered in connection with that letter. For now, I

79 *Ibid.*, September 6, 1818, p. 562.

simply wish to call attention to the fact that Keats's abandonment of his childhood faith involved more than a mere absentminded "drifting away," more than a culturally inspired replacement of one *Weltanschauung* with another more modern and sophisticated. He had, or thought he had, serious intellectual difficulties with important elements of the Christian creed.

Here again one can see the effect of his experience as a member of the Hampstead circle. It can be questioned whether Keats would ever have given much thought to doctrines such as the Atonement if he had not been challenged by the opinions of men like Hunt and Haydon. His congratulating Hunt on the May 4 editorial, which contains a fairly comprehensive summary of its author's chief objections to Christianity, marks him, for the moment, as that man's disciple in religious matters rather than Haydon's. But Keats was already beginning to cut the leading strings that bound him to his early mentors. In the months and years ahead he would make new friends, experience new influences, and be confronted by new questions. The religious consciousness that had been quickened in the winter of 1816 would develop according to a more personal pattern.

CHAPTER THREE

The Challenge of Benjamin Bailey

D URING the period from spring, 1817, through the following winter, most of Keats's mental energy was chan-
neled into the composition of *Endymion*, that ambitious
"trial of invention" by which he hoped to demonstrate, at
least to himself, his competence as a poet. But preoccupation with poetry did not abate the new interest in religion
that had been awakened by his association with Leigh Hunt
and his friends. Keats's letters reveal that he was devoting
a good deal of thought to certain specific religious questions
and, more generally, trying to come to some decision concerning the role religion should play in his life as man and
poet. As he began to outgrow the literary influence of Hunt,
he also appears to have left behind some of the "disgust"
with organized Christianity that Hunt had encouraged.
Keats in this period seems to have been attempting to cultivate a greater degree of intellectual tolerance than he had
observed among the members of the Hampstead set—a
philosophical detachment that would enable him to "enter
into the feelings" of orthodox believers and join with them
in religious discussion and speculation, while at the same
time withholding personal assent or commitment to their
beliefs. Throughout this period of development and matura-
tion, the most significant new factor affecting his religious
attitudes was his close friendship with Benjamin Bailey.

Walter Jackson Bate notes that Bailey "was perhaps the
last of Keats's close personal friends to affect his intellectual
development in an essential formative way."[1] He was introduced to Keats, probably by John Reynolds (who had
known Bailey since 1814), in March or April of 1817. The

[1] *John Keats* (Cambridge, Mass.: Harvard Univ. Press, 1963), p.
196.

two new acquaintances saw much of each other during the following summer, and their mutual affection and respect grew rapidly. An intensely serious young man, Bailey provided just the sort of companionship Keats needed at this time. The youthful poet must have been somewhat dazzled by the bright, if often superficial, intellectual banter of the Hunt circle. Bailey, with his serious and scholarly approach to literary, philosophical, and theological questions, provided a new point of stability in Keats's life, encouraging him to put order into the jumble of impressions he had been receiving since the fall of 1816.

Even his earliest impressions of Bailey must have affected Keats's outlook on the merits of the Christian religion. A student of theology and candidate for Holy Orders, "fully & gravely determined to [his] sacred profession,"[2] Bailey was a more impressive spokesman for orthodoxy than any other of Keats's close acquaintances. It was not difficult to classify Haydon's pugnacious defense of the faith as just one more eccentricity of a very eccentric man. One could not so easily dismiss Bailey's solid, learned, thoughtful advocacy of his beliefs. Nor was it easy to classify him as a typical professional apologist for religion. I have suggested that Keats's prejudice against Christianity was in part political, a reaction against the conservative stance of most Churchmen. Unlike the majority of his colleagues, Bailey was in this period of his life an ardent political liberal.[3] In this and in other matters he impressed those who knew him as a totally admirable young man. In John Reynolds's description of him in 1818, we can read Keats's sentiments also. "We know at this moment of one who is about to enter holy orders, with a heart pure for the truth, and a mind ardent and strong and just. If he has any failings, they are such as bind us closer to him. He is destitute of selfishness, loves his God, and feels for all mankind. . . . He is still

[2] *KC*, II, 291.
[3] Paul Kaufman, "The Leigh-Browne Collection at the Keats Museum," *The Library*, Fifth Series, 17 (1962), p. 215.

young; but ere his days are told, we look to see his name placed with the best, and of a kin with the noblest."[4] Keats was not content to await the future's verdict on Bailey's stature: he already thought him "one of the noblest men alive at the present day" (I, 204).

In the perspective of this study, the month Keats spent with Bailey at Oxford in 1817 emerges as one of the most important in his life. The effect of these weeks on Keats, as Bate describes it, was "an essential, though rapid, moral deepening—moral in the broadest sense of the word."[5] The university was not in session, and the quiet days and evenings provided plenty of opportunity for reading, conversation, and long thoughts. Bailey has left an account of their manner of life together. "He wrote, & I read, sometimes at the same table, & sometimes at separate desks or tables, from breakfast to the time of our going out for exercise,— generally two or three o'clock. . . . When we had finished our studies for the day we took our walk, & sometimes boated on the Isis . . . I knew him at that period of his life, perhaps, as well as any of his friends. There was no reserve of any kind between us. . . . Our conversation rarely or never flagged, during our walks, or boatings, or in the Evenings."[6] Bailey recalled that during these days he and Keats had "much earnest conversation" on the subject of religion.[7] The precise nature of these conversations was not recorded, but we can assume that the discussion centered around Keats's refusal to accept Christianity as the divinely ordained path to salvation. Bailey's probable mode of argument can be learned from a pamphlet he wrote a few months later, which contained the following defense of the doctrine of the Atonement—a doctrine that, as we have seen, Keats explicitly rejected.

[4] *Selected Prose of John Hamilton Reynolds*, ed. Leonidas M. Jones (Cambridge, Mass.; Harvard Univ. Press, 1966), p. 215.
[5] *John Keats*, p. 215.   [6] *KC*, II, 270ff.
[7] *Ibid.*, p. 292.

THE CHALLENGE OF BENJAMIN BAILEY

To those again who object generally that it is not necessary to our salvation that God should have given his only son to suffer on the cross for our redemption, I have but two brief and plain, but, as I think, insuperable answers. The first is rather an admonition: read your Bible intensely; yet simply as a child, bow your mind to its decrees; and if you believe any part of the scheme you must believe the whole; for the sophistication of accepting one part and rejecting another, is, I confess, to my apprehension so vast and so melancholy, that I cannot reflect upon it without extreme commiseration and pain. My second reply shall be more philosophical. If we believe the first pages of our Bible, that man fell by the greatest *evil* spirit, it is impossible in the nature of things, if a particular scheme of redemption be appointed, like the Christian, that he can rise again to his first state of perfection, but by the mediation of the highest *good* spirit. This is God. Good and evil we have seen materially and morally divide the world. The last in its deepest dye can only be effaced by the first.[8]

We cannot, of course, know whether Bailey employed these two "answers" against Keats's objections to Christianity. But there is strong evidence that the poet was reading the Bible attentively at this time. His letters from Oxford, as Bate notes, "are suddenly filled with allusions to the Old Testament."[9] As for Bailey's second, "more philosophical," argument, the problem of evil became a major intellectual concern for Keats in the remaining years of his life. He could not accept the Christian response to the question, and yet he could not totally dismiss Christianity until he had worked out for himself an alternative explanation for the presence of pain and suffering in the world. His conception of the world as a "vale of soul-making" involved, as we shall

[8] *A Discourse Inscribed to the Memory of the Princess Charlotte Augusta* (London: Taylor and Hessey, 1817), pp. 48f.
[9] *John Keats*, p. 218.

see, a direct repudiation of the argument Bailey put forward in the passage quoted above.

If Bailey was trying during these weeks at Oxford to win Keats back to Christianity, his efforts were unsuccessful. He did succeed, however, in softening some of the anti-Christian sentiment Keats had developed under the tutelage of Leigh Hunt. If "one of the noblest men alive" could devote his life to preaching and defending Christianity, it could hardly be looked on as mere "vulgar superstition." Oxford itself may have contributed to rubbing off some of Keats's prejudice. The atmosphere of the university was, if not especially pious, richly ecclesiastical. The new spirit that would produce the Tractarian reform movement was already being felt (John Henry Newman had established residence at Trinity College three months before Keats visited Bailey at Magdalen). The poet spent a good deal of time in the company of clergymen and clergymen-to-be; it is not unlikely that on occasion he attended chapel ceremonies with them.[10] He seems to have become rather unselfconscious about expressing an interest in ecclesiastical matters, as we see in a letter he wrote to Bailey a few weeks after leaving the university. "So you have got a Curacy! good. . . . When do you preach your first sermon tell me—for I shall propose to the two Rs [John Reynolds and James Rice] to hear it so dont look into any of the old corner oaken pews for fear of being put out by us. . . . When you are settled I will come and take a peep at your Church" (I, 171ff.). Generally, Bailey impressed upon Keats that religion was a very serious matter and should never be treated with contempt or ridicule. Before the poet left for home, Bailey made him pledge that he would refrain from the kind of mockery that Hunt and his friends engaged in. "He promised me, & I believe he kept his promise, that he would never scoff at religion. And when he returned to London,—it was remarked to me afterwards by one of his

---

[10] See his reference to the singing of "the Chauntry boy," *Letters*, I, 152.

most intimate friends,—there was a decided change in his manner regarding religion."[11]

One indication of Keats's new attitude of respect for traditional religion may be found in Book IV of *Endymion*, which was written after the visit to Oxford. The introductory invocation to the presiding Muse of England includes a brief sketch of the history of poetry, which begins with a respectful reference to the Bible: "There came an eastern voice of solemn mood" (IV, 10). The line originally read "a hebrew voice" (*Letters*, I, 172). That Keats would give the Hebrew scriptures equal mention with Greek and Latin literature is surprising enough, but considering that Moses, David, and the Old Testament in general were often the subject of ridicule by Voltaire, most of the English Deists, and others among the enlightened, the reference is even more noteworthy. We have seen Hazlitt remarking on the refusal of "skeptics and philosophical unbelievers" to recognize the literary merits of the Bible (see p. 82f.), and Keats himself resisting Haydon's recommendation that he read the Scriptures. Bailey seems to have succeeded where Haydon failed. Keats was not only reading the Bible while at Oxford; under Bailey's direction he was even paying some attention to hermeneutic considerations, such as the problems involved in translation and the various levels, literal and figurative, on which a passage might be understood (*Letters*, I, 157).

Bailey made another contribution to Keats's religious development, less specific but perhaps more significant in the long run than any I have mentioned. He apparently succeeded in persuading Keats that poetry was not necessarily the greatest, most important thing in the world. This was quite an accomplishment, considering Keats's earlier attitude. Henry Stephens, the poet's roommate while he was studying at Guy's Hospital, recalled: "Poetry was to his mind the zenith of all his Aspirations—The only thing worthy the attention of superior minds—So he thought—all other pur-

[11] *KC*, II, 292f.

suits were mean & tame . . . The greatest men in the world were the Poets, and to rank among them was the chief object of his ambition."[12] The poetry of 1816 and early 1817 reveals a similar disposition. But by January, 1818, his views had changed considerably. He wrote to his brothers: "In a note to Haydon about a week ago . . . I said if there were three things superior in the modern world, they were 'the Excursion,' 'Haydon's pictures' & 'Hazlitts depth of Taste' So I do believe—Not thus speaking with any poor vanity that works of genius were the first things in this world. No! for that sort of probity and disinterestedness which such men as Bailey possess, does hold & grasp the tip top of any spiritual honours, that can be paid to anything in this world" (I, 204f.).

The phrase "in this world" is significant, I think. Spiritual honors were to be paid elsewhere too; Bailey had heightened Keats's awareness of this obligation. Religion was the center of Bailey's life. All that he was, all that he did, was related to it in some way (including even his amorous involvements: Keats described him wooing a young lady "with the Bible and Jeremy Taylor under his arm" [Letters, II, 67]). His "probity and disinterestedness" and the other qualities of his impressive character could not be seen in isolation from his commitment to Christianity. This fact challenged Keats. Perhaps the spiritual side of man's nature was not adequately nourished by "works of genius." Perhaps some system of religious faith was desirable, more coherent and more emotionally satisfying than the rather nebulous theism to which he had been subscribing. The full urgency of this question would not come home to Keats until the spring of 1818, when the circumstances of his life forced him to confront it directly. Through the winter of 1817–1818 he would continue to cultivate an intellectual detachment in the matter of religion, at times even slipping back into the kind of mockery that Bailey had urged him to

12 *Ibid.*, p. 208.

forego. But Keats had been disturbed by Bailey: he had been permanently dislodged from many of his comfortable, "enlightened" prejudices against orthodoxy. He would continue to be challenged by Bailey's character and by his arguments until the moment came when the noble stature of his clerical friend was suddenly and drastically diminished in his eyes.

Keats's letters to Bailey in the months following his visit to Oxford reveal the extent to which the poet had adopted the theology student's way of looking at things. I called attention earlier to the October 28 letter in which he expresses an interest in Bailey's curacy and a desire to be present at his first sermon. The letter of November 3 is also concerned with things ecclesiastical. It opens with a rather surprising diatribe against a member of the Anglican hierarchy—surprising because Keats professes to be shocked and dismayed at discovering that a bishop could be capable of oppression and impertinence. As a friend of Leigh Hunt and a regular reader of the *Examiner*, he should have been beyond being astonished at improper behavior on the part of Churchmen. The tone of shocked indignation, then, may best be explained as an example of Keats's tendency to enter into the feelings of his correspondent when writing a letter. He is probably expressing what he assumes Bailey must be feeling:

Before I received your Letter I had heard of your disappointment—an unlook'd for piece of villainy. I am glad to hear there was an hindrance to your speaking your Mind to the Bishop: for all may go straight yet—as to being ordained—but the disgust consequent cannot pass away in a hurry—it must be shocking to find in a sacred Profession such barefaced oppression and impertinence —The Stations and Grandeurs of the World have taken it into their heads that they cannot commit themselves towards and inferior in rank—but is not the impertinence from one above to one below more wretchedly mean than from the low to the high? There is something so nauseous in self-willed yawning impudence in the shape of conscience—it sinks the Bishop of Lincoln into a smashed frog putrifying: that a rebel against common decency should escape the Pillory! That a mitre should cover a Man guilty of the most coxcombical, tyranical and indolent impertinence! (I, 178.)

None of Keats's biographers has touched on the exact nature of Bailey's difficulties with the Bishop of Lincoln. But Keats's phrase "impudence in the shape of conscience" suggests one possible explanation—an explanation that casts some credit on the bishop.

I conjecture that Bailey, having been offered a curacy in the diocese of Lincoln,[13] applied to the local bishop, George Pretyman Tomline, for ordination to the deaconate. This was normal procedure at a time when, aside from the universities, there were no formal seminaries or houses of study for candidates for the ministry. The aspirant would see to his own education in theology—which is what Bailey was doing at Oxford—and then present himself to be examined by his future ordinary. In this period, the examination was usually a rather perfunctory affair, the really essential qualification being the possession of title to a benefice—the promise of an ecclesiastical position within the diocese. Having been promised a curacy that had recently fallen vacant, Bailey may have assumed that the examination would be a mere matter of form, and that there would be nothing to prevent his taking orders immediately. If this was his assumption, he did not know his bishop very well.

[13] Hyder Rollins (*Letters*, I, 171n.) seems to identify this curacy with the one Bailey eventually held at Carlisle. But Bailey was not given the latter position until July, 1818 (*KC*, I, 20), long after the trouble with the Bishop of Lincoln. If the curacy referred to by Keats was in Carlisle, it is doubtful that he would have offered so readily to attend Bailey's sermon, and bring Rice and Reynolds with him. It is much more likely that the curacy was in the diocese of Lincoln, which at this time extended south almost to Oxford.

George Tomline, Bishop of Lincoln, had been raised to the episcopacy through political influence, but once having assumed office he seems to have taken his duties very seriously. He took a particular interest in the training of the clergy, having been dismayed by "the great deficiency with respect to professional knowledge which he discovered in candidates for Holy Orders,"[14] and he drastically raised the standards in his own see. Only with reluctance would he admit to orders a man who had not taken a degree at one of the universities. He set up a two-day series of examinations for ordinands that, by the standards of the time, was unusually comprehensive and demanding, and that was pointed to as a model by those interested in Church reform.[15] So warm was his zeal for raising the educational requirements for ordination that he became involved in a celebrated dispute on the subject with a brother bishop, Henry Bathurst of Norwich, whom he criticized for his "facility in granting orders."[16]

It may have been the absence of this facility in Tomline that led to Bailey's disappointment. This would explain Keats's reference to "impudence in the shape of conscience," and his hope that "all may go straight yet—as to being ordained." Whether the Bishop thought Bailey insufficiently prepared, or, what is more likely, insisted that he take his degree before ordination, Bailey was prevented from receiving orders in time to accept the curacy he had been offered. In an historical perspective, Tomline's attitude is praiseworthy. But, like most reformers, he caused a good deal of inconvenience in individual cases, and his manner of refusing Bailey appears to have been unnecessarily brusque and highhanded.

At any rate, the event made Keats surprisingly angry. He

[14] *Elements of Christian Theology*, 16th edition (London: Cadell, 1826), I, vii.
[15] See the *Christian Remembrancer*, 3 (1821), 51.
[16] F. Thistlethwayte, *Memoirs and Correspondence of Dr. Henry Bathurst, Lord Bishop of Norwich* (London: Bentley, 1853), pp. 248-53.

wanted revenge—a concrete, down-to-earth, immediately satisfying revenge like the pillory. "O for a recourse somewhat human independant of the great Consolations of Religion and undepraved Sensations. of the Beautiful. the poetical in all things—O for a Remedy against such wrongs within the pale of the World! Should not those things be pure enjoyment should they stand the chance of being contaminated by being called in as antagonists to Bishops? Would not earthly things do?" (I, 179.) This passage has not received very much attention from the Keats critics, yet I think it is an important one. Keats is saying: In our earthly misfortunes, there are certain non-earthly recourses or consolations available to us. He distinguishes two types of consolation: one is derived from "religion" and the other from "undepraved sensations of the beautiful, the poetical in all things." While it may not be immediately apparent, it seems to me that Keats is actually speaking of two types of religious consolation here, one of them arising from Bailey's beliefs and the other appropriate to his own.

What Keats meant, or at least what Bailey would have understood, by "the great consolation of religion" may be determined from a passage in an essay the latter wrote at about this time. "There is ever a source of religious consolation in all our sorrows and misfortunes. Life we should never consider or value but as the infancy of an eternal existence. The chastisement, therefore, which we adjudge requisite for that early stage of this existence, in order to the perfection of its more mature stage, is by a parallel way of reasoning necessary in this life to our purification for the next. Thus temporary sorrow is converted into lasting joy— fading calamity into unfading bliss."[17] This thought—that our earthly sufferings prepare us for eternity in the way that the chastisement of a child prepares him for adulthood —will form the basis of Keats's conception of the earth as a vale of soul-making.

From Bailey's type of spiritual consolation, dependent

[17] *Discourse*, pp. 35f.

upon an orthodox faith in the afterlife, Keats distinguishes his own, dependent upon "undepraved sensations of the beautiful, the poetical in all things." It may seem farfetched to read religious significance into these words, but some background information and an analysis of the phrases may make the connection more apparent. At about the time Keats visited Oxford, Bailey was working on a short ethical treatise called "An Essay on the Moral Principle."[18] Basically, the essay is an attempt to explain the nature of conscience—the moral law within. The issues raised and the terminology employed in the course of the argument indicate that Bailey derived many of his ideas from the writings of that group of eighteenth-century ethical philosophers known as the "moral sense school." It appears that Bailey was reading the moral sense philosophers while Keats was at Oxford, and that he discussed their theories with his friend. The effect of these discussions will be seen most clearly in Keats's November 22 letter to Bailey, to be considered later, but an investigation of some of the terminology of the moral sense school also casts light on the letter now under discussion.

Francis Hutcheson (1694–1746), who produced the most impressive and systematic analysis of the moral sense, saw this instinctive sense of good and evil as analogous to man's sense of beauty. He calls our ability to perceive regularity, order, and harmony in the universe an "internal sense," distinct from the five external senses generally acknowledged. The perceptions of this internal sense of beauty he therefore calls "sensations."[19] Our sensations of the beauty of the world, he says, lead us to acknowledge the existence of a

---

[18] In May, 1818, Bailey wrote to John Taylor, telling him of the essay and hinting that it might be worth publishing along with some other essays he was planning to complete (*KC*, I, 26f.). Taylor apparently resisted the offer, and the work was never printed; it now exists in manuscript at Harvard University.

[19] *An Inquiry into the Original of our Ideas of Beauty and Virtue* (1725), in *Collected Works of Francis Hutcheson* (Hildesheim, Germany: Georg Olms, 1971), I, vi, 32.

benevolent deity, and this knowledge of God's benevolent design is a source of comfort and consolation in our earthly troubles and misfortunes:

> Under this Head of our Internal Sense, we must observe one natural Effect of it, that it leads us into *Apprehensions of a* DEITY. Grandeur, Beauty, Order, Harmony, wherever they occur, raise an Opinion of a MIND, of *Design*, and *Wisdom*. Every thing great, regular, or proportioned, excites *Veneration*, either toward itself, if we imagine it animated, if not animated, toward some apprehended Cause. . . . We cannot open our Eyes, without discerning *Grandeur* and *Beauty* everywhere. Whoever receives these Ideas, feels an inward *Veneration* arise. . . . Custom, Prejudice of Sense or Education, may confirm some foolish Opinion about the *Nature* or *Cause* of these Appearances: But wherever a superior MIND, a governing INTENTION or DESIGN is imagined, there *Religion* begins in its most simple Form, and an inward *Devotion* arises.[20]

> The *Beauty* apparent to us in *Nature* will not of it self prove *Wisdom* in the *Cause*, unless this *Cause*, or AUTHOR of *Nature* be suppos'd BENEVOLENT; and then indeed the Happiness of Mankind is desirable or *Good* to the SUPREME CAUSE; and that Form which pleases us, is an Argument of his *Wisdom*. And the Strength of this Argument is increased always in proportion to the Degree of *Beauty* produced in *Nature*, and expos'd to the View of any *rational Agent*; since upon supposition of a *Benevolent* DEITY, all the apparent *Beauty* produc'd is an Evidence of the Execution of a *Benevolent Design*, to give him the Pleasures of *Beauty*. . . . This is certain, "That we have some of the most delightful Instances of *Universal Causes* in the *Works* of *Nature*, and that the most studious men in these Subjects

[20] *An Essay on the Nature and Conduct of the Passions and Affections*, in *Collected Works*, II, 175f.

are so delighted with the Observation of them, that they always look upon them as Evidences of Wisdom in the Administration of *Nature*, from a SENSE OF BEAUTY."[21] Imagining the divine MIND as *cruel, wrathful, or capricious*, must be a perpetual Source of Dread and Horror; and will be apt to raise a *Resemblance* of Temper in the Worshipper, with its attendant *Misery*. A contrary Idea of the DIVINITY, as good, and kind, delighting in universal Happiness, and ordering all Events of the Universe to this End, as it is the most delightful Contemplation, so it fills the good Mind with a constant *Security* and *Hope*, amidst either public Disorders, or private Calamities.[22]

I think these passages from Hutcheson serve to show that the phrases of Keats I have been discussing had connotations for him and for Bailey that they do not have for us. By his reference to the "great consolation" to be derived from "undepraved sensations of the beautiful, the poetical in all things," Keats seems to mean that a clear perception of the beauty to be found everywhere in the universe—a beauty that is regular and orderly and therefore the work of a creator (a Divine Poet, he suggests)—is enough to convince anyone whose sensations are not depraved (perverted by miseducation or prejudice) that a benevolent Deity presides over our destiny, a loving God who, in the words of Leigh Hunt's hymn,

> we know, from things that bless,
> Must delight in loveliness;
> And who, therefore, we believe,
> Means us well in things that grieve.

The confidence that our earthly misfortunes are part of a divine plan that has our happiness as its ultimate goal is certainly a religious consolation in the usual sense of that word. But it seems that Keats preferred to confine his use

---

[21] *Collected Works*, I, 60, 62.
[22] *Collected Works*, II, 176f.

of the term "religion" to the sort of organized, systematic, theological faith practiced by Bailey. "You know my ideas about religion," he wrote to his friend four months later, and went on to make clear that while he respected Bailey's right to subscribe to such a faith, he himself could not do so. Similarly, he admits here that "religion" may provide great consolation for those who can accept it but points out that his own beliefs provide their own kind of comfort. As in the May 11 letter to Haydon,[23] he is insisting quietly but firmly on the sufficiency of natural religion as a faith to live by.

There are a few more things in the November 3 letter that deserve comment. Still venting his spleen against the Bishop of Lincoln, Keats says: "When we look at the Heavens we cannot be proud—but shall stocks and stones be impertinent and say it does not become us to kick them?" One cannot be sure that Keats was consciously alluding to Milton's sonnet on the Piedmont Massacre, with its reference to the pagan English worshipping "stocks and stones." But there does seem to be a suggestion that the veneration of bishops is not far removed, in Keats's view, from primitive superstition. In another remark he is less subtle: "At this Moment I take your hand let us walk up yon Mountain of common sense . . . now look beneath at that parcel of knaves and fools. Many a Mitre is moving among them." Attempting to calm himself a few lines later, he says: "I will speak of something else or my Spleen will get higher and higher—and I am not a bearer of the two egded Sword." This appears to be an allusion to Psalm 149, which contains the following lines:

Let the saints be joyful in glory: let them sing aloud
    upon their beds.
Let the high praises of God be in their mouth, and a
    two-edged sword in their hand;

[23] See pp. 107f.

To execute vengeance upon the heathen, and punishment
   upon the people;
To bind their kings with chains, and their nobles with
   fetters of iron.

Keats seems to be admitting wryly that, although he has
been threatening vengeance upon a particular "noble," his
credentials as one of the saints may be somewhat questionable.

Keats's next letter to Bailey, dated November 22, 1817,
has received about as much close attention from critics as
any of his poems. The letter is looked upon as a key docu-
ment in Romantic aesthetic theory, expressing Keats's views
on the nature of the poetic imagination and providing other
interesting insights into his understanding of the creative
process. Nevertheless, I believe that to read the letter primarily as a treatise in aesthetics or literary theory is to miss
the central point. I think Keats is addressing himself mainly
to a theological question, and when the letter is examined
in this light it reveals much about Keats's religious views at
the end of 1817. I will quote the well known passage and
then explain the grounds for my assertion:

I wish I was as certain of the end of all your troubles as
that of your momentary start about the authenticity of
the Imagination. I am certain of nothing but of the holiness of the Heart's affections and the truth of Imagination—What the Imagination seizes as Beauty must be
truth—whether it existed before or not—for I have the
same Idea of all our Passions as of Love they are all in
their sublime, creative of essential Beauty. . . . The Imagination may be compared to Adam's dream—he awoke
and found it truth. I am the more zealous in this affair,
because I have never yet been able to perceive how any
thing can be known for truth by consequitive reasoning—
and yet it must be—Can it be that even the greatest Philosopher ever arrived at his goal without putting aside

numerous objections—However it may be, O for a Life of Sensations rather than of Thoughts! It is "a Vision in the form of Youth" a Shadow of reality to come—and this consideration has further convinced me for it has come as auxiliary to another favorite Speculation of mine, that we shall enjoy ourselves here after by having what we called happiness on Earth repeated in a finer tone and so repeated—And yet such a fate can only befall those who delight in sensation rather than hunger as you do after Truth—Adam's dream will do here and seems to be a conviction that Imagination and its empyreal reflection is the same as human Life and its spiritual repetition. But as I was saying—the simple imaginative Mind may have its rewards in the repetition of its own silent Working coming continually on the spirit with a fine suddenness— to compare great things with small—have you never by being surprised with an old Melody—in a delicious place —by a delicious voice, felt over again your very specula- tions and surmises at the time it first operated on your soul—do you not remember forming to yourself the sing- er's face more beautiful than it was possible and yet with the elevation of the Moment you did not think so—even then you were mounted on the Wings of Imagination so high—that the Prototype must be here after—that deli- cious face you will see—What a time! I am continually running away from the subject—sure this cannot be exactly the case with a complex Mind—one that is imag- inative and at the same time careful of its fruits—who would exist partly on sensation partly on thought—to whom it is necessary that years should bring the philo- sophic Mind—such an one I consider your's and there- fore it is necessary to your eternal Happiness that you not only drink this old Wine of Heaven which I shall call the redigestion of our most ethereal Musings on Earth; but also increase in knowledge and know all things. (1, 184ff.)

The main subject of this discussion, the subject Keats is "continually running away from," is the reliability of the imagination as a means of getting at truth—an even greater reliability, he says, than that which is attributed to reason. What provoked the discussion, apparently, was an expression by Bailey of some doubt concerning the "authenticity of the Imagination." Those who assume that Keats's topic here is the poetic imagination have supposed that Bailey's "momentary start" must have involved some questioning of the "truth" of poetry. Yet there is really very little evidence to support such a supposition. Why should Bailey suddenly have suffered an attack of doubt concerning the authenticity of the poetic imagination? He wrote poetry himself and, what is more, he filled his religious writings with quotations from Milton, Wordsworth, and other English and classical poets, using them as he used passages of scripture to illustrate and reinforce his theological and moral arguments.

But the human imagination may function in ways that have no direct connection with the writing of poetry. As a student of theology Bailey was aware that the faculty played a part in speculation on religious matters. And there is evidence that he did not entirely trust its reliability in this area. In this very month of November, 1817, Bailey was engaged in writing a lengthy essay entitled *A Discourse Inscribed to the Memory of the Princess Charlotte Augusta*,[24] in which we find these words: "The extinguishment of the taper of old age we all expect, but that the shadows of death should put out the torch of youth, is abhorrent to the imagination. But our reason is constantly enforcing, and in a manner re-echoing her admonitions against our sophistications and self-deceit."[25] I think this passage indicates that Bailey's doubts about the imagination involved a subject far removed from the problem of poetic truth.

The reliability of reason and the deceptiveness of the imagination when dealing with death and its mysteries was a lesson Bailey may have learned from Bishop Joseph But-

[24] Princess Charlotte died on November 6. Since the *Discourse* was published before the end of the year, Bailey must have worked on it in November.
[25] *Discourse*, p. 27.

ler, the most eminent Anglican theologian of the eighteenth century. Butler was one of Bailey's favorite divines, and his greatest work, *The Analogy of Religion* (1736), was used as a standard text by theology students well into the nineteenth century. It is not unlikely that, when preparing his remarks on the Princess Charlotte's demise, Bailey consulted the chapter, "Of a Future Life," where Butler spurns the aid of imagination in formulating conceptions of the afterlife: "One cannot but be greatly sensible, how difficult it is to silence imagination enough to make the voice of reason even distinctly heard in this case; . . . we are accustomed, from our youth up, to indulge that forward, delusive faculty; ever obtruding beyond its sphere; of some assistance indeed to apprehension, but the author of all error."[26] The fact that Keats devotes so much attention to the nature of the afterlife in the November 22 letter reinforces my conviction that Bailey's doubt about the imagination concerned its reliability in speculation about death and the life that follows death.

Keats begins his argument with a rather sweeping assertion: "I am certain of nothing but of the holiness of the Heart's affections and the truth of Imagination." Probably because in his development of the statement he seems more interested in the second item—the truth of imagination— most commentators have all but ignored the first. They have generally equated the "Heart's affections" rather loosely with "love" and accepted "holiness" as just another example of Keats's fondness for religious vocabulary. But there is evidence that the phrase had a rich significance for Keats and Bailey, and that, in this context, it carries a great deal of theological meaning. I made reference earlier to "An Essay on the Moral Principle," on which Bailey was working at about the time Keats visited Oxford. There are certain statements in that essay that shed considerable light on the phrase of Keats now under examination.

[26] *The Works of Bishop Butler*, ed. J. H. Bernard (London: Macmillan, 1900), II, 17.

There are general affections and feelings over which the will (with which will I would identify moral principle) has a natural and proper control. That portion of knowledge, which is not suffered to be developed by our imperfect understandings, is mysteriously transferred to the feelings & affections of our hearts. The heart is first operated upon by the grace of God; and this is succeeded by an illumination of the understanding. The heart is the source & centre of devotion. From the heart emanate all christian graces.[27]

Some explanation of Bailey's (and Keats's) vocabulary may be in order. Once again we are dealing with the terminology of the "moral sense school" of ethics. The moral sense, man's ability to know good from evil, virtue from vice, is based on certain mental dispositions called affections and passions. These are feelings of pleasure or pain that result from reflection on our sensations. We develop affections toward those things which give us pleasant sensations, and revulsions from things that cause unpleasant sensations. Basically, then, an affection is a mental tendency toward or away from anything. The word may be applied to such widely varied impulses as compassion, parental love, patriotism, desire for wealth, and devotion to the arts. Generally, the moral sense philosophers seem to use "affection" and "passion" interchangeably; when a distinction is made, a passion is a stronger type of affection, one not entirely under the control of reason. Negative emotions like fear and envy are usually called passions.

Bishop Butler, one of the chief spokesmen of the moral sense school, was particularly interested in the religious ramifications of these theories. For him, the affections play a very important role in religion and morality. They are as essential as reason itself in forming a virtuous man. "Reason alone, whatever any one may wish, is not in reality a suffi-

[27] "An Essay on the Moral Principle," Bailey Scrapbook, Keats Collection, Harvard University, p. 7.

cient motive of virtue in such a creature as man; but this reason joined with those affections which God has impressed upon his heart: and when these are allowed scope to express themselves, but under strict government and direction of reason; then it is we act suitably to our nature, and to the circumstances God has placed us in."[28] The affections have an even higher purpose than to serve as guides to virtuous conduct: properly directed, they lead inevitably to the worship of God. "He hath given us certain affections of mind, which correspond to wisdom, power, goodness; i.e. which are raised upon view of these qualities. If then he be really wise, powerful, good; he is the natural object of those affections, which he hath endued us with, and which correspond to those attributes. . . . A Being who hath these attributes, must necessarily be the object of these affections: there is as real a correspondence between them, as between the lowest appetite of sense and its object."[29]

In the passage quoted earlier from Bailey's "Essay," one can see that Keats's friend also placed heavy emphasis on the part the heart's affections play in a man's religious life. They are indispensable aids to the mind in its attempt to comprehend that which lies beyond sense experience. When our imperfect understanding fails us, as sometimes it must, the heart's affections come into play, providing new insights into transcendent reality and giving the understanding new data with which to work. It is important to note that there is a "portion of knowledge" in the religious sphere that is denied to the understanding and that can be attained only by the heart. This "heart knowledge" would seem to be more practical than theoretical, related more to piety than to theology. Such "christian graces" as faith, hope, and charity, Bailey says, emanate from the heart alone. "In a more perfect state we may arrive at these through the understanding; but this is not the process upon Earth. Here we must surrender the mind into the keeping of the heart. Hence in scripture the Deity speaks to men in the language of the passions and affections: 'For no one hath seen God at any time.' That is, no one but God hath read, or can read the Eternal mind. It is presumptuous in such a creature as man to aspire to those dangerous heights 'where angels fear to tread.' "[30]

The point of Keats's juxtaposition of "the holiness of the Heart's affections" with "the truth of Imagination" is explained to some extent in the statements that follow in the letter. "What the imagination seizes as Beauty must be truth —whether it existed before or not—for I have the same Idea of all our Passions as of Love they are all in their sublime, creative of essential Beauty" (one should remember that for Bailey, as for the moral sense philosophers, "passion" and "affection" are usually synonymous). These lines, which have challenged scholars from the beginning and provoked many ingenious theories concerning Keats's concept of the poetic imagination, become somewhat less puzzling when one understands that Bailey's doubt about the imagination had to do with its ability to conceive the nature of post-mortal existence.

Traditional religion has always taught that those who go to heaven after death are made perfectly, totally happy. The nature of this beatitude is usually seen as involving the satisfaction of our noblest earthly desires and aspirations. This is necessary, since, if the happiness of heaven bears no relation to our earthly yearnings after happiness, we would be incapable of desiring it and would have no motivation to discipline and direct ourselves toward attaining it. If the happiness of heaven has nothing to do with earthly happiness, then our noblest human aspirations and desires are destined to be thwarted and frustrated. This cannot happen, of course, since these desires, these "affections," are put in our hearts by God himself.

So, what makes us happy here will, *mutatis mutandis*, make us happy hereafter, though probably according to a more refined standard of happiness. Likewise, what seems beautiful to us here will seem beautiful hereafter, perhaps according to a higher, more satisfying aesthetic. Furthermore, since our human imagination is creative, we can conceive of beauty that does not actually exist now, and that beauty will have to exist for us hereafter—since our happiness in heaven must be perfect and total, and the absence of any imaginable beauty would diminish our happiness. Our situation, Keats suggests, would resemble that of Adam, who, after seeing Eve in a dream-vision,

> wak'd
> To find her, or forever to deplore
> Her loss, and other pleasures all abjure.[31]

Perhaps the connection between the heart's affections and the imagination is now clearer. It was generally accepted by the moral sense philosophers that the mind could develop an affection for an imaginary good. As Shaftesbury put it: "Our passions and affections are known to us. They are certain, whatever the objects may be on which they are employed. Nor is it of any concern to our argument how those exterior objects stand: whether they are realities or mere illusions; whether we wake or dream."[32] It was also accepted, by Bishop Butler at least, that all our affections are destined to be satisfied in the hereafter. Keats draws the necessary conclusion: whatever the heart develops an affection for—even if it is a non-existent beauty conceived by the imagination—must be present in the afterlife, if mind and heart are to be totally at rest. "What the imagination seizes as Beauty must be truth—whether it existed before or not."

Keats goes on to say that he is particularly interested in

[31] *Paradise Lost*, VIII, 478-80. Bruce E. Miller (*N&Q*, 209 [1964], 423) argues that "Adam's dream" refers to his earlier vision of the garden (VIII, 309-11). But Keats's remarks further on in the letter about the singer's face ("that delicious face you will see") make it seem more likely that he was thinking of Adam's vision of Eve.

[32] Anthony, Earl of Shaftesbury, *Characteristics of Men, Manners, Opinions, Times*, ed. John M. Robertson (New York: Bobbs-Merrill, 1964), I, 336f.

proving the reliability of the affections and the imagination "because I have never yet been able to perceive how any thing can be known for truth by consequitive reasoning." Apparently Bailey had expressed to Keats an attitude similar to the one that appears in the *Discourse Inscribed to the Memory of the Princess Charlotte Augusta*—a preference for reason over imagination as a guide when contemplating the mysteries of death. In deference to the philosophical Bailey, Keats concedes that deductive reasoning must produce some truth, but he makes clear that this is not *his* way. "However it may be, O for a Life of Sensations rather than of Thoughts!"

Some critics have been mildly scandalized by the apparent irresponsibility of these words and have attempted to explain them away. They have assumed that Keats is choosing the pleasures of the senses over the life of the mind. But, as I pointed out earlier, Keats seems to use the word "sensation" in a special way, similar to the way it was used in the preceding century by the moral sense philosophers. Indeed, whether or not they were aware of it, Keats and Bailey were rearguing an old question that had been publicly debated by Francis Hutcheson and one of his rationalist critics in 1725. In his *Inquiry into the Original of Our Ideas of Beauty and Virtue*, Hutcheson suggested that a man's sense of good and evil was closely related to his aesthetic sense: it involved an immediate perception of the beauty of virtue that did not depend upon any process of rational deduction. This theory was challenged in the *London Journal* by Gilbert Burnet, because it seemed to place reason in an inferior or secondary position to a sense of beauty: "Things do not seem to us to be true or right because they are beautiful or please us, but seem beautiful or please us because they seem to us to be true or right. And always, in our apprehensions of things . . . the reason of the thing or the sense of its being true or right is antecedent to our sense of beauty in it or of the pleasure it affords us. . . . Beauty in the nature of things follows or depends upon our previous apprehension of truth or of right."[33] When Keats wrote, one year later, "I never can feel certain of any truth but from a clear perception of its Beauty" (II, 19), he was espousing the side of the argument that Hutcheson defended: the beauty of truth is recognized by man before the truth of beauty. Likewise, when he says here "O for a Life of Sensations rather than of Thoughts," he is choosing a mode of approaching truth that depends upon immediate perceptions of internal senses such as the aesthetic rather than upon the deductions of reason. If he is being irresponsible in this preference, he is in the company of some of the most eminent moral philosophers of the eighteenth century.[34]

Continuing his discussion of the hereafter, Keats suggests that a life of sensations is necessary not only for earthly happiness but also for one's eternal well-being. He offers another of his favorite speculations, "that we shall enjoy ourselves here after by having what we call happiness on earth repeated in a finer tone and so repeated." This is another aspect of a basic idea running through the letter—during our terrestrial life we lay the groundwork, create the pattern, for our celestial existence. Just as the affections

[33] "To Britannicus," London Journal, April 10, 1725; reprinted in Illustrations on the Moral Sense, by Francis Hutcheson, ed. Bernard Peach (Cambridge, Mass.: Belknap Press of Harvard Univ. Press, 1971).

[34] He may also be in the company of William Wordsworth, who was

> well pleased to recognise
> In nature and the language of the sense
> The anchor of my purest thoughts, the nurse,
> The guide, the guardian of my heart, and soul
> Of all my moral being.
> ("Tintern Abbey," ll. 107-11)

Wordsworth also describes how "the affections gently lead us on" to a kind of religious insight. It is possible, as Jack Stillinger suggests (The Hoodwinking of Madeline and Other Essays on Keats's Poems [Urbana, Ill., Univ. of Illinois Press, 1971], p. 152f.), that Keats's phrasing in this letter to Bailey owes something to "Tintern Abbey," a poem the two friends seem to have read carefully together at Oxford (KC, II, 275).

we develop on earth determine the kind of beatitude we experience in heaven, so the nature of our earthly joys will affect the nature of our eternal joy. He speaks particularly of the pleasures of sensation, which he says we will enjoy again in the afterlife, refined and intensified because free from physical limitations, and heightened by the creative expectations of the imagination. The thought here seems related to an idea of Bishop Butler (which Bailey may have discussed with Keats) that, although death puts an end to our powers of sensation, it does not affect our ability to reflect on sensation. "For, though, from our present constitution and condition of being, our external organs of sense are necessary for conveying in ideas to our reflecting powers . . . yet when these ideas are brought in, we are capable of reflecting in the most intense degree, and of enjoying the greatest pleasure, and feeling the greatest pain, by means of that reflection, without any assistance from our senses."[35] Using Butler's terms, one might paraphrase Keats's speculation in this way: our enjoyment hereafter will be based to a large extent on reflection. But the mind can reflect only on what sensation has fed into it. So, while we are alive and our power of sensation is active, we should use it to its fullest capacity, amassing as large a store of sense memories as possible.

Keats cautions Bailey that the happiness of which he is speaking "can only befall those who delight in sensation rather than hunger as you do after Truth." It was said of Bailey by one who knew him at this time that his keen search after truth tended to lead him into the "abstract and metaphysical."[36] But if the happiness of heaven involves repetition of the pleasures of sensation, one should not waste one's time on earth pursuing abstractions. One should rather lay up as large a treasure of sensations as possible. Driving home his point, Keats links together two curious metaphors: the juice of the grapes we gather on earth will

[35] *Works*, II, 24.   [36] *KC*, I, 20n.

ferment and grow richer in eternity; rather like ruminant animals, we will redigest in heaven what we have "mused on" in this world. "Therefore it is necessary to your eternal Happiness that you . . . drink this old Wine of Heaven which I shall call the redigestion of our most ethereal Musings on Earth."

The letters of November, 1817, show Keats in a rather confident state of mind regarding religion. His cool advice to a clerical friend that he learn to look upon his bishop from the lofty perspective of the "mountain of common sense," his readiness to instruct a theology student on what was necessary to his eternal happiness, seem to indicate a considerable degree of confidence in the merits of his own views. This new assertiveness may have derived in part from his discovery at Oxford that he could hold his own in discussion with Bailey. But I think it also has to do with his having defined more precisely for himself the nature of his own religious views. When Keats claimed to be certain of "the holiness of the heart's affections," he was identifying himself with a rich complex of beliefs and attitudes associated with a mode of religious thinking, developed in the eighteenth century, which found in the human heart—in man's instincts and emotions—the foundation of religion, the source of theology, piety, and morality. The basic premise of this faith, as phrased by Leigh Hunt, was that "God has written his religion on the heart, for growing wisdom to read perfectly, and time to make triumphant."[37] For a natural religionist like Hunt, these "heart-scriptures" provided a sufficient rule of life. For someone like Bailey, of course, they were only a foundation for a richer faith deriving from Biblical revelation. Yet, as we have seen, even Bailey was ready to agree that the heart was a quite reliable guide in religious matters, and "the source & centre of

[37] *The Religion of the Heart* (London: John Chapman, 1853), p. 1.

devotion." Bishop Butler's definition of "devotion" clarifies Bailey's meaning.

> The nature of it consists in the actual exercise of those affections towards God, which are supposed habitual in good men. He is always equally present with us: but we are so much taken up with sensible things, that *Lo, he goeth by us, and we see him not*. . . . Devotion is retirement from the world he has made to him alone: it is to withdraw from the avocations of sense, to employ our attention wholly upon him as upon an object actually present, to yield ourselves up to the influence of the divine presence, and to give full scope to the affections of gratitude, love, reverence, trust, and dependence; of which infinite power is the natural and only adequate object.[38]

So for natural religionist and Christian alike, the affections of the heart were indeed holy, providing foundation and motivation for a life of faith and piety. It is not clear whether his first catechist in this matter was the orthodox Bailey or the heterodox Hunt; he seems to have learned from both. From whatever sources it came, Keats adopted the teaching as the basis for his own personal form of religion. From this point on, the heart will figure prominently in his speculations, until, in that final formulation of his religious system—the "vale of soul-making" letter—he will designate it as one of the three grand materials from which God forms a mature human soul, and describe it as "the Mind's Bible."

Although Keats seems very confident in his November 22 theologizing, one should remember that he calls his ideas "speculations" and that in another place he tells Bailey "I have not one Idea of the truth of any of my speculations" (I, 243). Keats's normal tendency was to be extremely diffident in advancing his religious views. He generally culti-

[38] *Works*, I, 182.

vated a kind of intellectual humility that prevented him from claiming certainty in areas where no certainty was really possible. That tendency toward religious reticence may have been submerged to some extent during the period of his personal contact with Bailey, but it made itself evident again shortly after the November 22 letter was written.

On the day after Christmas, 1817, Keats went to see a pantomime at Drury Lane with two friends, Charles Brown and Charles Wentworth Dilke. Afterward, walking back to Hampstead, the three fell into a discussion, as a result of which a famous literary theory was formulated. As Keats recounted the event to his brothers,

> I had not a dispute but a disquisition with Dilke, on various subjects; several things dovetailed in my mind, & at once it struck me, what quality went to form a Man of achievement especially in Literature & which Shakespeare possessed so enormously—I mean *Negative Capability*, that is when man is capable of being in uncertainties, Mysteries, doubts, without any irritable reaching after fact & reason—Coleridge, for instance, would let go by a fine isolated verisimilitude caught from the Penetralium of mystery, from being incapable of remaining content with half knowledge. This pursued through Volumes would perhaps take us no further than this, that with a great poet the sense of Beauty overcomes every other consideration, or rather obliterates all consideration. (1, 193f.)

Although this passage and the ideas it contains have been the subject of much critical commentary, they demand further attention here. A man's ability and willingness to remain "in uncertainties, Mysteries, doubts" will necessarily have an influence on the quality of his religious faith. And it is my opinion that the connection between Keats's religious attitudes and "Negative Capability" is closer than has been generally noticed. I believe religious considerations were prominent among those things which "dovetailed" in his mind to precipitate the theory.

I do not suggest that the "disquisition with Dilke" was an argument on religion, although this is by no means unlikely ("disquisition" is a word that at this time was frequently applied to metaphysical or theological treatises). Dilke was a radical republican and a very free thinker in religious matters. Keats described him as a "Godwin-methodist" (*Letters*, II, 213), and the meaning of that phrase is probably explained in this characterization of Dilke by Bailey: "He is at best a Sceptic in his principles, & it rather arises from too much passion, & too little knowledge, than any cause which can assume the shape of natural conviction."[39] But I am interested in a more remote set of circumstances that, I think, worked to influence Keats toward his theory. One could, of course, begin at the beginning of his life. As J. R. Caldwell observed, "Negative Capability . . . although perversely called a philosophy and discovered to have a 'source,' was surely a native virtue of his mind."[40] In my first chapter I suggested that this natural tendency was reinforced by certain intellectual attitudes prevalent in the London medical schools. Still, granting the importance of native propensity and education, the fact is that Keats says his insight came to him at a particular moment, at a certain point in his life. It will be instructive, therefore, to examine some of the circumstances that may have contributed to his thought.

Keats names Shakespeare as the poet who possessed Negative Capability to a preeminent degree, and we must look first to that poet to understand the inspiration for Keats's theory. In 1817 Shakespeare was for Keats, in the words of John Middleton Murry, "the living centre of his thought and feeling, into which his deepest speculations on

[39] *KC*, I, 20.
[40] *John Keats' Fancy: The Effect on Keats of the Psychology of His Day* (1945; rpr. New York: Octagon Books, 1965), p. 7.

the nature of poetry and his most intimate sensations were inseparably merged."[41] But Keats first caught his enthusiasm for Shakespeare from the members of the Hunt circle—particularly Haydon. If there was one thing about the Bard that especially interested these men in 1817, it was the nature of his religious beliefs. I have made reference to the argument carried on by Shelley, Haydon, Severn and others about whether or not Shakespeare was a Christian. The debate seems to have lasted for months after the initial confrontations in January. On April 15, Haydon made an excited entry in his diary, citing what he felt was a conclusive argument for his side.[42] On May 10, Keats wrote to Hunt quoting two passages from Shakespeare, one supporting each side of the question (I, 138). It must have occurred to him, at this point if not before, that the most interesting aspect of the argument was that neither side was able to prove its case conclusively. One simply could not demonstrate from his writings where Shakespeare's religious sympathies lay.

Keats used Coleridge as an example of a man who lacked Negative Capability, who could not be comfortable in uncertainties, mysteries, and doubts, or remain content with half knowledge. George Watson, in his 1956 edition of *Biographia Literaria*, suggests that it may have been that work which inspired Keats's remark.[43] But Watson admits that there is no evidence that Keats ever read the *Biographia*, and, that being so, I would like to suggest another possibility. In a letter to Bailey two months earlier, Keats referred to the fact that his friend was reading, or was about to read, Coleridge's first "Lay Sermon," *The Statesman's Manual*, which had been published the preceding year (I, 175). We cannot be sure that Keats read the

[41] *Keats and Shakespeare* (1925; rpr. London: Oxford Univ. Press, 1949), p. 38.
[42] *The Diary of Benjamin Robert Haydon*, ed. Willard B. Pope (Cambridge, Mass.: Harvard Univ. Press, 1960), II, 108.
[43] S. T. Coleridge, *Biographia Literaria*, ed. George Watson (New York: Dutton, 1956; rpr., 1962), p. 256n.

work himself, but he might well have heard it discussed in the Hunt circle or read reviews such as Hazlitt's (see p. 99). There are certain passages in the "Sermon" that could have provoked his critique in the "Negative Capability" letter.

Toward the end of *The Statesman's Manual*, Coleridge takes issue with those who would evade the doctrinal implications of the Scriptures by claiming that one should not attempt to penetrate what is necessarily mysterious. He points out that "St. Paul repeatedly presses on his Hearers that thoughtful perusal of the Sacred Writings, and those habits of earnest though humble enquiry which if the heart only have been previously regenerated would lead them 'to a full *assurance* of Understanding.' . . (*to an entire assent of the mind; to a spiritual intuition, or positive inward knowledge by experience*) of the Mystery of God, *and* of the Father, and of Christ, in which . . . are hid all the treasures of wisdom and knowledge." (The italics are Coleridge's.) He goes on to say that "all effective Faith presupposes Knowledge and individual Conviction," and that "mere acquiescence in Truth, uncomprehended and unfathomed" is not sufficient for man. Not only does Scripture extol knowledge as "the Crown and Honor of a Man, but to seek after it is again and again commanded us as one of our most sacred Duties."[44] These are the words of a man who considers it intellectually irresponsible to remain satisfied with mystery, and who will not be content with half knowledge if he thinks he can get more. One indication that Keats's criticism of Coleridge has to do with religion is his use of the phrase, "Penetralium of Mystery." He appears to have picked up the Latin word (incorrectly) from Bailey: note its use—and the connection with religious mystery—in the following passage from a letter Bailey wrote in 1818: "Plato had 'the vision and the faculty divine.' He looked into

---

[44] *The Collected Works of Samuel Taylor Coleridge* (Princeton: Princeton Univ. Press, 1971-); vol. 6: *Lay Sermons*, ed. R. J. White, pp. 45-48.

'adyta,' the 'penetralia,' the inmost recesses of Truth; and wanted but the eye of Revelation to see *clearly* into the mysteries of Christianity, which he saw shadowed in the twilight."[45] Coleridge was not the only contemporary writer who helped Keats to clarify his ideas on negative capability. I think he also had Wordsworth very much in mind. While Keats was at Oxford, Bailey continually called his attention to a side of Wordsworth that he had apparently not noticed before. At first, Bailey recalled, Keats seemed "to value this great Poet rather in particular passages than in the full length portrait, as it were, of the great imaginative & philosophic Christian Poet, which he really is, & which Keats obviously, not long afterwards, felt him to be."[46] To have been made conscious of Wordsworth's identity as a "Christian Poet" at the very time he had been noticing Shakespeare's curious detachment from Christianity must have provided Keats with food for thought. Even more thought-provoking was an incident that took place a couple of weeks previous to the writing of the "Negative Capability" letter.[47] At what was probably their first meeting, Keats recited the "Hymn to Pan" for Wordsworth, only to hear the older man dismiss the poem as "a very pretty piece of Paganism." Recounting the event years later, Haydon explained that "Wordsworth's puling Christian feelings were annoyed."[48] It is interesting that Haydon went on to remark, "The Poet ought to have been a Pagan for the time"—ought, as one might paraphrase it, to have shown some Negative Capability. The painter recalled that Keats felt the affront deeply. Perhaps it occurred to him then that there was some great flaw in Wordsworth's poetic character, if he could let a personal religious bias so overcome his sense of beauty.

Shortly after this event, on December 22, Wordsworth sat

[45] *KC*, I, 9.   [46] *Ibid.*, II, 274.
[47] T. O. Mabbot (*Notes and Queries*, May 10, 1941, pp. 328f.) argues convincingly that the incident took place around December 15.
[48] *KC*, II, 144.

for Haydon at his studio. We do not know whether they discussed the "piece of Paganism" incident, but, after the poet left, Haydon wrote down some very interesting remarks in his diary. The passage is long but pertinent to this discussion.

December 22. Wordsworth sat to me today & I began to put his head into my Picture. He read all the book of "Despondence Corrected" in his Excursion in the finest manner.

Wordsworth's great power is an intense perception of human feelings regarding the mystery of things by analyzing his own, Shakespeare's an intense power of laying open the heart & mind of man by analyzing the feelings of others acting on themselves. The moral in Shakespeare is inferred from the consequences of conduct, that of Wordsworth is enforced by a previous devellopement of Duty. Shakespeare is the organ of Nature; Wordsworth of Piety, Religion, & Virtue. Wordsworth lays down the duty of man, from which to swerve is to do wrong. Shakespeare has no moral code, and only leaves it at the option of all how to act by shewing the consequences of such & such conduct in acting. Wordsworth tries to render agreable all that hitherto has alarmed the World, by shewing that Death, the Grave, futurity are the penalties only to go to a happier existence. Shakespeare seems reckless of any principles of guidance. He takes futurity, Death, & the Grave as materials to act on his different characters, and tho' one may be horrified one moment in reading what Claudio says of Death, we may be reconciled the next by attending to what the Duke has said of Life, and be uncertain which to believe, and leave off in intense and painful distraction.

In grief & the troubles of life Shakespeare solaces by our finding similar feelings displayed by others in similar situations; that is sympathy. In Grief & in misery the comfort & consolation Wordsworth affords is by consolidating the hopes & glimmerings man has from a higher power into a clear & perceptible reality. What we hope he assures us of. What we fear he exhibits without apprehension; of what we have a horror he reconciles us to, by setting it before us with other associations. Wordsworth is the Apostolic Poet of Piety & Pure thoughts, and Shakespeare, dear Shakespeare, the organ of nature herself, with all her follies & captivations & beauties & vices. Wordsworth's feelings are exclusive, because his intensity of purpose is so strong. His object is to reform the World, by pointing out to it how it *ought to be*; Shakespeare to delight it, by shewing Nature herself how she is. It would be the height of absurdity to say that the Power of dear Shakespeare, in its infinite variety, does not entitle him to the highest place over all Poets, but in moral scope & height of purpose, Milton & Wordsworth have greater intention & nobler views than Shakespeare has shewn; take any one power separately and compare it with theirs. They have *but one*, but that one is the highest on Earth; it is to guide Man to deserving, endless happiness in futurity.[49]

This is an acute analysis of the difference in character between the two poets, and it would have been unlike Haydon to keep such good thoughts to himself and not share them with the man with whom he enjoyed reading Shakespeare more "than with any other Human creature."[50] He must have seen or written to Keats shortly before December 28, to invite him to the "immortal dinner" that took place on that evening. These ideas on Wordsworth and Shakespeare may well have been among the things which dovetailed in Keats's mind to produce the theory of negative capability, that quality "Shakespeare posessed so enormously" and Wordsworth did not.

It seems to have taken a while for these thoughts to develop into an actual distaste for Wordsworth's poetry. On January 10, 1818, Keats wrote to Haydon: "I am convinced

[49] *Diary*, II, 171f.
[50] *Ibid.*, p. 318. Alternatively, a conversation with Keats may actually have been the source of the ideas.

that there are three things to rejoice at in this Age—The Excursion Your Pictures, and Hazlitt's depth of Taste" (I, 203). He may not at this moment have been aware that one could not have an unqualified admiration for both *The Excursion* and Hazlitt's taste, since the critic had damned the poem when it appeared in 1814 and was getting ready to damn it again (at least in part) in his Lectures on the English Poets. In the lecture delivered on January 27, Hazlitt contrasted Shakespeare and Milton with contemporary poets, attacking the "devouring egotism" of the moderns and making clear that he had Wordsworth very much in mind. Hazlitt's criticism appears to have helped crystallize Keats's feelings against the older poet. A week later he wrote to John Reynolds:

> It may be said that we ought to read our Contemporaries. that Wordsworth &c should have their due from us. but for the sake of a few fine imaginative or domestic passages, are we to be bullied into a certain Philosophy engendered in the whims of an Egotist—Every man has his speculations, but every man does not brood and peacock over them till he makes a false coinage and deceives himself—Many a man can travel to the very bourne of Heaven, and yet want confidence to put down his halfseeing. Sancho will invent a Journey heavenward as well as any body. We hate poetry that has a palpable design upon us —and if we do not agree, seems to put its hand in its breeches pocket. (I, 223f.)

This passage can be understood as a sweeping indictment of a whole approach to poetry; certainly a multitude of Wordsworthian sins are covered in the charge of egotism. But there are indications that Keats had in mind a particular fault: Wordsworth's tendency to assume the role of religious teacher. His mention of "the very bourne of heaven" might provide a hint that he was thinking of the "Hymn to Pan" and of the older poet's reaction to it. The statement, "Sancho will invent a Journey heavenward as well as any body," is significant in connection with Haydon's assertion that Wordsworth's poetic purpose was "to guide Man to deserving, endless happiness in futurity." When Keats remarks that "every man has his speculations," one recalls that he himself had views, expressed in the November 22 letter to Bailey, on what was necessary for eternal happiness. His reference to Wordsworth's "Philosophy" can also be interpreted as an allusion to his religious beliefs. The word was frequently used at this time to signify what is commonly called "natural theology"—an area of investigation dealing with those truths about God and human destiny which may be discovered by reason or instinct without recourse to revelation. Keats's correspondent would have understood the word used in this sense: Reynolds once wrote of Wordsworth, "He breathes the same air of philosophy that Milton and Jeremy Taylor breathed before him."[51]

The sort of "Philosophy" into which Keats felt Wordsworth was trying to bully his readers may be illustrated by the following passage from Book IV of *The Excursion*—a book Keats seems to have read with particular attention:

> The Wanderer said:—One adequate support
> For the calamities of mortal life
> Exists—one only; an assured belief
> That the procession of our fate, howe'er
> Sad or disturbed, is ordered by a Being
> Of infinite benevolence and power;
> Whose everlasting purposes embrace
> All accidents, converting them to good.
> The darts of anguish *fix* not where the seat
> Of suffering hath been thoroughly fortified
> By acquiescence in the Will supreme
> For time and for eternity; by faith,
> Faith absolute in God, including hope,
> And the defence that lies in boundless love
> Of his perfections.[52]

[51] "Mr. Wordsworth's Poetry," *The Champion* (December 9, 1815), p. 398. Quoted by Willard B. Pope, "Studies on the Keats Circle" (unpublished dissertation: Harvard University, 1932), p. 628.

[52] IV, 10-24. *The Poetical Works of Wordsworth*, ed. Thomas Hutchinson, rev. Ernest de Selincourt (London: Oxford Univ. Press, 1961), pp. 625f.

If Wordsworth had been content to leave his sermonizing unspecific and "non-sectarian," Keats might not have objected so strongly. But in other passages he makes clear his allegiance to one particular religious system.

> Hail to the State of England! And conjoin
> With this a salutation as devout,
> Made to the spiritual fabric of her Church;
> Founded in truth; by blood of Martyrdom
> Cemented; by the hands of Wisdom reared
> In beauty of holiness, with ordered pomp,
> Decent and unreproved.[53]

Doctrinal considerations may not have irritated Keats so much as the tone of certainty, of smug self-assurance, that pervades much of the poem. As Keats understood him now, Wordsworth was not content to remain in doubt and uncertainty. In his eagerness to solve the mysteries of human existence, he had seized upon a single, half-seeing faith and was willing to rest content with it, abandoning any further search for truth.

Keats's sudden revulsion against the poetry of Wordsworth seems to have coincided with a rebirth of his critical attitude toward "vulgar superstition." He appears to have forgotten, at least temporarily, his promise to Bailey that he would not engage in mockery of religion. In a letter to his brother on February 14, he copied out some lengthy extracts from a poem by Horace Smith, called "Nehemiah Muggs—An Exposure of the Methodists." The general character of the poem is conveyed by the following lines:

> Behold them in the Holy place
> With others all agog for Grace
> Where a perspiring preacher vexes
> Sundry old women of both sexes. (I, 229)

Smith's doggerel may have been responsible for stirring up the old fires of religious controversy among Keats's friends

[53] VI, 6-12. *Poetical Works*, pp. 653f.

in London. It seems that there was a fierce argument about the Methodists, involving at least Haydon and Keats, and this grew into a more general dispute. Things must have become fairly heated: a month after leaving London Keats was still disturbed by the memory. On April 8, he wrote to Haydon from Teignmouth: "I shall be in town in about a fortnight and then we will have a day or so now and then before I set out on my northern expedition—we will have no more abominable Rows—for they leave one in a fearful silence having settled the Methodists let us be rational—not upon compulsion—no if it will out let it" (I, 266).

The Methodists were not the only occasion for argument during this winter. The spirit of Voltaire returned to provoke more discord between Haydon and his friends. Keats had begun reading him again (I, 237), possibly inspired by Hazlitt's championing of him, in his February 17 lecture, against Wordsworth's attack in *The Excursion*. It was very likely at about this time that the following event occurred. As Haydon recalled it, "Never shall I forget Keats once rising from his chair and approaching my last picture ('Entry into Jerusalem'), he went before the portrait of Voltaire, placed his hand on his heart and bowing low . . . 'That's the being to whom I bend,' said he, alluding to the bending of the other figures in the picture, and contrasting Voltaire with our Saviour, and his own adoration to that of the crowd."[54]

Keats's readiness to trifle with Haydon's religious feelings is surprising when one recalls the respect and deference with which he treated Bailey's beliefs. It may simply be that he was less awed by Haydon than he was by Bailey. But I think one can discern a definite change of attitude in Keats between November, 1817, when he spoke of the "great Consolation of Religion," and February, 1818, when he attacked

[54] *The Life, Letters and Table Talk of Benjamin Robert Haydon*, ed. Richard Henry Stoddard (New York: Scribner, 1876), p. 208. W. J. Bate assigns an earlier date to this event (*John Keats*, p. 112), but Haydon did not "paint in" the head of Christ until February 1818 (*Diary*, II, 188f.).

Wordsworth and provoked Haydon. The change involves much more than a movement from reverence to irreverence or a return of anti-Christian prejudice. It seems to be a general abandonment of the concern with religious questions that he had developed in association with Bailey. Having decided that the proper intellectual attitude of a "man of achievement" was tolerance of doubt and mystery, he became more critical of those who were unable or unwilling to remain in this sort of uncertainty and who aspired or pretended to knowledge of things that, he felt, were essentially unknowable.

Keats's mood at this time can be seen in a letter he wrote to Reynolds on February 19, which is devoted entirely to the praise of "delicious diligent Indolence" (1, 231ff.). He counsels his friend: "Let us not therefore go hurrying about and collecting honey-bee like, buzzing here and there impatiently from a knowledge of what is to be arrived at: but let us open our leaves like a flower and be passive and receptive." He goes on to repeat what he imagined a thrush said to him:

> O fret not after knowledge—I have none
> And yet my song comes native with the warmth
> O fret not after knowledge—I have none
> And yet the Evening listens.

I think that this relaxed, indolent, and rather self-satisfied frame of mind has much to do with his personal circumstances at the time. He had completed *Endymion*, that enormously ambitious "trial of invention." It was not as good as it might have been, but it was done—he had written a long poem and demonstrated the seriousness of his commitment to his art. Having succeeded in climbing that mountain, the world of poetry was all before him, where to choose. At twenty-two years of age, he was at the peak of his physical powers. "He was in perfect health," recalls a witness who saw him at this time, "and life offering all things that were precious to him."[55] Never again would Keats be quite.so happy as he was in February, 1818.

When one is young and in good health, when one's prospects for a happy, successful life seem fair, the kind of questions that are usually associated with religion may easily be set aside. The nature of God and of man's relationship with him, the immortality of the soul, the problem of evil— such matters tend to intrude much more upon a man's consciousness in times of suffering and unhappiness. For Keats such a time was not far off. When it came, it would bring a revival of his interest in religious questions.

On March 4, 1818, Keats left London for Teignmouth in Devonshire, to be with his ailing brother, Tom. Apparently, neither he nor his other brother, George, had yet come to consider Tom's illness very serious, and the carefree mood that we observed in Keats during February continues to appear in the first letters written at Teignmouth. The concomitant distaste for things religious seems to have perdured also, as can be seen in a letter he wrote to Bailey on March 13. Two months earlier he had written, with reference to Bailey's *Discourse Inscribed to the Memory of the Princess Charlotte Augusta*, "I have not had your Sermon returned—I long to make it the subject of a Letter to you" (I, 212). Now in March, he has finally read the "Sermon," but his eagerness to talk about it has faded. "I have never had your Sermon from Wordsworth but Mrs Dilke lent it me—You know my ideas about Religion—I do not think myself more in the right than other people and that nothing in this world is proveable. I wish I could enter into all your feelings on the subject for one short 10 minutes and give you a Page or two to your liking" (I, 242). Note that in order to write something pleasing to his friend he would have to "enter into" Bailey's own feelings on the subject, to abandon his own identity—in short, to exercise

[55] *KC*, II, 158.

some degree of Negative Capability. This he seems unable or unwilling to do, but since Bailey is expecting some reaction to the *Discourse* he offers a few general remarks on the kind of intellectual activity involved in mental endeavors such as theology:

> I am sometimes so very sceptical as to think Poetry itself a mere Jack a lanthern to amuse whoever may chance to be struck with its brilliance—As Tradesmen say every thing is worth what it will fetch, so probably every mental pursuit takes its reality and worth from the ardour of the pursuer—being in itself a nothing—Ethereal things may at least be thus real, divided under three heads— Things real—things semireal—and no things—Things real—such as existences of Sun Moon & Stars and passages of Shakspeare—Things semireal such as Love, the Clouds &c which require a greeting of the Spirit to make them wholly exist—and Nothings which are made Great and dignified by an ardent pursuit—Which by the by stamps the burgundy mark on the bottles of our Minds, insomuch as they are able to *"consecrate whate'er they look upon."* (1, 242f.)

It should be emphasized that Keats in this passage is not questioning the value or validity of belief in God, but only of "religion"—by which he seems to mean theology or an organized, systematic approach to religious truth. A few weeks later he will write to Reynolds, "I have not the slightest feel of humility towards the Public—or to any thing in existence,—but the eternal Being, the Principle of Beauty,—and the Memory of great Men" (1, 266). So it is not the fact of God's existence nor the obligation of men to venerate Him that Keats is questioning, but rather the value of a systematic pursuit of knowledge about God.

The *Discourse* is devoted in large part to a defense of Christianity as the one true religion. Bailey appears totally convinced of the cogency of his arguments; he seems quite satisfied that his assertions are irrefutable. In the face of such conviction, Keats resists being drawn into the kind of dispute that would involve haggling over particular points of doctrine. His approach is much more radical, calling into question the absolute value of the entire "mental pursuit" in which Bailey is engaged. He does not attack formal religion as trivial, or pointless, or foolish. He simply points out that it has value and meaning only for those who can subscribe to it. His argument is almost tautological: those who are interested in religion find religion interesting: those who are not, do not. His characterization of it as a "nothing" is not at all an expression of contempt. In Book IV of *Endymion*, the hero describes his dream-goddess as a "nothing" (ll. 636ff.), and then begins praying to her. A "nothing," apparently, is a thing that does not have immediate, palpable, physical reality.

Keats admits that what is, absolutely speaking, a "nothing" can be "made Great and dignified by an ardent pursuit." But implicit in the admission is a suggestion that this greatness and dignity may be apparent only to the ardent pursuer. From the inside, religion may seem to be a coherent and satisfying system of truth. From the outside, its viability and plausibility may not be quite so obvious. "It is an old maxim of mine and of course must be well known that every point of thought is the centre of an intellectual world—the two uppermost thoughts in a Man's mind are the two poles of his World he revolves on them and every thing is southward or northward to him through their means—We take but three steps from feathers to iron" (I, 243). This is a rather astute analysis of the professional religious mind—or any mind that is committed to a particular ideology or thought-system. Rigid mental paradigms are set up according to which all knowledge and experience must be organized. Truth and falsehood, worth and worthlessness, are determined by reference to fixed categories. Within such a tightly organized thought-structure, relationship between ideas can be discovered more quickly (or, perhaps, assumed more facilely) than would be the case outside the structure. When Keats says, "We take but three steps from feathers to iron," he may be thinking of the facility with which Bailey, in the *Discourse*, moves from rather flimsy premises to hard dogmatic conclusions.

Conscious that Bailey may find this analysis of his mind offensive, Keats backs off in a characteristic fashion. "Now my dear fellow I must once for all tell you I have not one idea of truth of any of my speculations—I shall never be a Reasoner because I care not to be in the right, when retired from bickering and in a proper philosophical temper." Except when he is involved in argument (one thinks of the "abominable rows" with Haydon), he is not concerned with being in the right on religious matters. His attitude toward religious discussion has changed markedly since the previous November, when he eagerly shared "favorite speculations" with Bailey and lectured the theology student on what was necessary to his eternal happiness. Now, it seems, he is more interested in cultivating the capability "of being in uncertainties, Mysteries, doubts, without any irritable reaching after fact & reason," and in trying to remain content with half knowledge.

This is a difficult intellectual stance to maintain even in the best of circumstances. To an active, seeking mind, the existence of mysteries poses a challenge. When those mysteries begin to touch a man directly, when they become, as Keats would call them, a "burden," the mind grows increasingly less capable of ignoring them. Such a situation was about to arise in Keats's life. He would be forced by circumstances to come to grips with certain basic religious questions. In his search for answers he would do something that all of Bailey's arguments had not persuaded him to do— engage in a serious reexamination of the worth of Christianity as a faith to live by. His investigation would lead him to reject that faith again, clearly and definitively, but the rejection would come only after he had developed for himself a satisfactory alternative.

CHAPTER FOUR

The Burden of the Mystery

A T the end of the March 13 letter to Bailey, Keats wrote:
"My Brother Tom desires to be remember'd to you—he
has just this moment had a spitting of blood poor fellow"
(I, 244). Shortly afterward, Tom had a much more serious
hemorrhage, which apparently brought home to Keats for
the first time the possibility that his brother would not re-
cover from his illness. This realization shattered the mood
of carefree complacency he had been enjoying for several
months. Away from the distractions of London society, confined within doors by an almost continuous cold rain, and
confronted constantly by the spectacle of his brother's losing
fight for life, Keats's view of reality darkened perceptibly.
There is a distinct change in the tone of his letters: he can
still joke and write doggerel verses, but the cheerfulness
and optimism of the past are gone. In April, he wrote to
John Taylor: "Young Men for some time have an idea that
such a thing as happiness is to be had and therefore are extremely impatient under any unpleasant restraining—in
time however, of such stuff is the world about them, they
know better and instead of striving from Uneasiness greet
it as an habitual sensation, a pannier which is to weight
upon them through life" (I, 270).

Keats's new awareness of the "stuff" of the world about
him, and the uneasiness that followed from it, seems to have
had as one of its effects the undermining of his attempt to remain content with metaphysical uncertainty.
On March 24, he wrote to his friend, James Rice: "What a
happy thing it would be if we could settle our thoughts,
make up our minds on any matter in five Minutes and remain content—that is to build a sort of mental Cottage of

feelings quiet and pleasant—to have a sort of Philosophical
Back Garden, and a cheerful holiday-keeping front one—
but Alas! this can never be: for as the material Cottager
knows there are such places as France and Italy and the
Andes and the Burning Mountains—so the spiritual Cottager has knowledge of the terra semi incognita of things
unearthly; and cannot for his Life, keep in the check rein"
(1, 254f.). A similar thought appears in a verse epistle he
sent to John Reynolds on the following day.

> O that our dreamings all of sleep or wake
> Would all their colours from the sunset take:
> From something of material sublime,
> Rather than shadow our own Soul's daytime
> In the dark void of Night. (1, 261)

An interesting gloss for these lines may be provided from
Bailey's *Discourse*, which Keats had recently been reading.
Mourning the dead Princess Charlotte, Bailey found some
consolation in the fact that her death forced many Englishmen to consider more seriously the questions of mortality
and eternity. "When the sun sets, the moon and stars are
like serene thoughts: they stand as it were alone and visible
to all eyes and their own consciousness, in the same space
where they were but an hour before lost in the light of day.
A lesson is here taught us by the face of heaven. What is
apparently true, or fetched by the imagination out of the
material is but a shadow of the truth which exists in the
moral world."[1] What the eye can perceive in daylight reveals little of the enormous, complicated universe around
us; in the same way, what the imagination is able to construct out of material realities does not begin to suggest the
vast realm of non-material or spiritual truth. Consciously
or not, Keats seems to be borrowing Bailey's ideas and
images when he wishes that our human dreams ("of sleep

[1] *A Discourse Inscribed to the Memory of the Princess Charlotte
Augusta* (London: Taylor and Hessey, 1817), pp. 25f.

or wake") could be made up entirely of comfortable, material, "daytime" realities, and not be shadowed by darker mysteries.

More light is shed on the meaning of Keats's lines, and on the nature of his intellectual difficulties at this time, by a statement of another of his friends, William Hazlitt. Although the following words were written a year later, in 1819, they touch on and develop a theme that had long been a subject of discussion in Keats's circle of friends—the relative merits of Christianity and classical paganism as systems of belief. Hazlitt's description of Christianity in this passage might apply equally well to any modern faith in an invisible, transcendent Deity.

> The religion or mythology of the Greeks was nearly allied to their poetry: it was material and definite. The Pagan system reduced the Gods to the human form, and elevated the powers of inanimate nature to the same standard. . . . All was subjected to the senses. The Christian religion, on the contrary, is essentially spiritual and abstracted; it is "the evidence of things unseen." In the Heathen mythology, form is every where predominant; in the Christian, we find only unlimited, undefined power. The imagination alone "broods over the immense abyss, and makes it pregnant." There is, in the habitual belief of an universal, invisible principle of all things, a vastness and obscurity which confounds our perceptions, while it exalts our piety. A mysterious awe surrounds the doctrines of the Christian faith: the infinite is everywhere before us, whether we turn to reflect on what is revealed to us of the divine nature or our own.[2]

Perhaps one of the things Keats found attractive in Greek religion was this "material" quality that Hazlitt singles out. In modern religion, whether Christian or "natural," the

[2] *Complete Works of William Hazlitt*, ed. P. P. Howe (London: Dent, 1930-1934), VI, 353.

imagination is challenged but is given almost nothing to work with. Keats touches on this problem in the verse letter to Reynolds.

> Things cannot to the will
> Be settled, but they tease us out of thought.
> Or is it that Imagination brought
> Beyond its proper bound, yet still confined,—
> Lost in a sort of Purgatory blind,
> Cannot refer to any standard law
> Of either earth or heaven? It is a flaw
> In happiness to see beyond our bourne—
> It forces us in Summer skies to mourn:
> It spoils the singing of the Nightingale. (1, 262)

But, although he recognizes that seeing beyond our bourne brings frustration and discontent, he seems unable now to discipline his imagination. As he remarked to Rice, once we have knowledge of the "terra semi incognita of things unearthly," our minds cannot be reined in, cannot remain content with half knowledge.

The verse epistle of March 25 goes on to reveal a particular problem that was challenging and troubling Keats. It seems that, perhaps for the first time, he was confronting intellectually the questions raised by the existence of evil in the world.

> Dear Reynolds. I have a mysterious tale
> And cannot speak it. The first page I read
> Upon a Lampit Rock of green sea weed
> Among the breakers—'Twas a quiet Eve;
> The rocks were silent—the wide sea did weave
> An untumultuous fringe of silver foam
> Along the flat brown sand. I was at home,
> And should have been most happy—but I saw
> Too far into the sea; where every maw
> The greater on the less feeds evermore:—

But I saw too distinct into the core
Of an eternal fierce destruction,
And so from Happiness I far was gone.
Still I am sick of it: and though to day
I've gathered young spring-leaves, and flowers gay
Of Periwinkle and wild strawberry,
Still do I that most fierce destruction see,
The shark at savage prey—the hawk at pounce,
The gentle Robin, like a pard or ounce,
Ravening a worm. (I, 262)

This awful vision of what another poet would call "Nature red in tooth and claw with ravine" seems to have struck Keats suddenly, unexpectedly, and almost with the force of a revelation. Nothing like it appears before in his writings. In the earlier poetry, the natural world is all peace and harmony and "places of nestling green for Poets made." Nature, for the younger Keats, was a "fair paradise" where

the hurrying freshnesses aye preach
A natural sermon o'er their pebbly beds.[3]

The fish who inhabited these freshnesses were little silvery minnows, pretty and undistressing. A rather different kind of natural sermon, it now appears, is preached by a dark sea (and a suddenly darkened world) filled with insatiable and pitiless predators.

The proponents of natural religion had always had difficulty explaining the existence of natural evil. Moral evil—what man has made of man—was easily enough understood as the consequence of human perversity (though that perversity itself was not easy to account for when one denied Original Sin). But evils that seemed a necessary part of life, that were woven into the fabric of earthly existence, posed a serious theological problem. If the order of the universe proclaims a great Original, what is proclaimed by disorder? If God is revealed in his creation, what lessons are we to

[3] "I Stood Tip-toe," ll. 126, 70f.

learn about him from earthquakes and tidal waves, and from the suffering and death that are inseparable from our terrestrial existence? Those natural religionists who adverted to the problem at all either characterized it as an impenetrable mystery, as did Leigh Hunt, or tried to see it, rather illogically, as in some way man's fault. Rousseau took the latter position:

> Our cares, our sorrows, our sufferings are of our own making. Moral ills are undoubtedly the work of man, and physical ills would be nothing but for our vices which have made us liable to them. . . . O Man! seek no further for the author of evil; thou art he. There is no evil but the evil you do or the evil you suffer, and both come from yourself. Evil in general can only spring from disorder, and in the order of the world I find a never-failing system. Evil in particular cases exists only in the mind of those who experience it; and this feeling is not the gift of nature, but the work of man himself. Pain has little power over those who, having thought little, look neither before nor after. Take away our fatal progress, take away our faults and our vices, take away man's handiwork and all is well.[4]

But all is not well, and Keats knew it. Tom's hemorrhaging did not exist only in his mind. Keats points to one flaw in the arguments of men like Rousseau: the "eternal fierce destruction" that goes on within the brute creation is not in any way man's handiwork or the result of man's vices. It is part of the natural order of things, a natural order created by a supposedly benevolent Deity. And Keats seems to have seen an awful parallel between the suffering of animals and that of human beings. One year later, he would achieve an attitude of acceptance regarding human misery only after learning to accept the necessity of suffering in the animal world (II, 79). He came to see the condition of animals as

[4] *Emile, or Education*, trans. Barbara Foxley (London: Dent, 1911), pp. 244f.

symbolic of man's state: "Man is originally 'a poor forked creature' subject to the same mischances as the beasts of the forest" (II, 101). Even now, in March, 1818, he acknowledges that his meditation on "eternal fierce destruction" was provoked by the sufferings of those he held dear. He says to Reynolds,

> Do you get health—and Tom the same—I'll dance,
> And from detested moods in new Romance
> Take refuge. (I, 263)

Keats was well aware that orthodox religion offered what was at least a coherent explanation of the distressed condition of the world and the human race. Two months earlier, in January, he had written to Bailey: "One saying of your's I shall never forget—you may not recollect it . . . you were at the moment estranged from speculation and I think you have arguments ready for the Man who would utter it to you . . . merely you said: '*Why should Woman suffer?*' Aye. Why should she?" (I, 209.)

Bailey's "arguments" would probably have been to the effect that evil came into the world as a result of the sin of Satan and of the first human beings, and that all of us, women and men, are still suffering the consequences of those first cataclysmic offenses.[5] Recently, "feasting upon Milton," Keats had observed a great poet's attempt to justify the ways of God to men by recalling man's responsibility for bringing misery upon himself and his world, and God's generosity in offering man, despite his offense, a second chance, an opportunity for redemption. Keats could not accept the Christian analysis of man's situation, but he had to acknowledge that it did offer a systematic explanation of the state of the world, exculpating the Deity, and, more important, offering some consolation and hope to men. There was com-

[5] "The principle of evil which runs through the physical and moral world is so mighty a mystery, that . . . without revelation, it were impossible to obtain any clue by which it could be in the most minute point unravelled." *Discourse*, pp. 14f.

fort in the simple faith of most Christians which the natural religion of the enlightened did not offer, and Keats seems to long for that sort of comfort as he attempts to banish his fears.

> Away ye horrid moods,
> Moods of one's mind! You know I hate them well,
> You know I'd sooner be a clapping bell
> To some Kamchatkan missionary church,
> Than with these horrid moods be left in lurch.

One recalls the association Keats once made between churchbells and "vulgar superstition," and his hope that church religion would soon die "like an outburnt lamp." Now he seems to be suggesting that even a superstitious faith like that preached by the Christian missionaries in Kamchatka would be better than the uncharted speculations that have made him so unhappy.

I do not mean to assert that Keats was, at this time, seriously considering embracing Christianity as a faith to live by. But I think he was coming to realize the value of having some systematic view of the nature of things, some framework according to which he could organize his insights and experiences. "I have been hovering between an exquisite sense of the luxurious and a love for Philosophy," he wrote on April 24. "Were I calculated for the former I should be glad—but as I am not I shall turn all my soul to the latter" (I, 271). I pointed out earlier that, in Keats's time, "philosophy" often meant, or at least included, "natural theology"—the attempt to understand man's nature and destiny without reference to Biblical revelation. That Keats had this sort of philosophy in mind is hinted at in a letter to Reynolds written three days later, in which he announces his intention of preparing himself "to ask Hazlitt in about a years time the best metaphysical road I can take—For although I take poetry Chief, there is something else wanting to one who passes his life among Books and thoughts on Books" (I, 274). "Metaphysical" is a word of broad signification, but if Keats was using it as Hazlitt did he was looking for a thought-system that might provide an alternative to revealed religion. Hazlitt once remarked on "how impossible it is to reconcile the faith delivered to the saints with the subtleties and intricacies of metaphysics."[6] He saw metaphysics as an exercise of the reason, religion as a concern of the heart. Each strives to comprehend super-sensible reality, but their modes of investigation are totally different.

The conflicting claims of heart and head in "philosophical" speculation were a matter of interest to Keats as well. He hoped that the brain or the understanding would be able to provide him with answers to life's riddles, and bring the kind of mental serenity that religious faith brought to others. On May 3, he wrote to Reynolds: "An extensive knowledge is needful to thinking people—it takes away the heat and fever; and helps, by widening speculation, to ease the Burden of the Mystery. . . . The difference of high Sensations with and without knowledge appears to me this—in the latter case we are falling continually ten thousand fathoms deep and being blown up again without wings and with all the horror of a bare shoulderd Creature—in the former case, our shoulders are fledged, and we go through the same air and space without fear" (1, 277). But he is not quite certain that the kind of knowledge associated with the understanding or the reason is sufficient in all human situations: "When we come to human Life and the affections it is impossible how a parallel of breast and head can be drawn . . . it is impossible to know how far knowledge will console us for the death of a friend and the ill 'that flesh is heir to.'" In time of distress, it is man's heart that needs to be consoled; intellectual knowledge is cold comfort. So if

6 *Complete Works*, xx, 117f. Speaking of "that personification and abstraction of cross purposes—a Scotch metaphysical divine," Hazlitt said: "We do not approve of this method of carving out excuses or defences of doctrinal points from the dry parchment of the understanding or the cobwebs of the brain. Whatever sets or leaves the dogmas of religion at variance with the dictates of the heart, hardens the last, and lends no advantage to the first."

there is to be found any consolation for the sufferings of man to replace the "great consolation of religion," it will be found by investigating the nature and the needs of the human heart.

These thoughts lead Keats into a lengthy discussion of the relative merits of Milton and Wordsworth that ends, not surprisingly, in a comparison of the two as religious thinkers. His remarks on Wordsworth reveal that a considerable change has taken place in his attitude toward that poet. Three months earlier, in a more carefree mood, he had resented being "bullied into a certain Philosophy engendered in the whims of an Egotist" (1, 223). Now he begins to see some worth in that philosophy:

> We find what he says true as far as we have experienced and we can judge no further but by larger experience— for axioms in philosophy are not axioms until they are proved upon our pulses. We read fine things but never feel them to the full until we have gone the same steps as the Author. . . . You are sensible no man can set down Venery as a bestial or joyless thing until he is sick of it and therefore all philosophizing on it would be mere wording. Until we are sick, we understand not;—in fine, as Byron says, "Knowledge is Sorrow"; and I go on to say that "Sorrow is Wisdom." (1, 279)

Much of the "philosophy" of *The Excursion* is an attempt to provide consolation for the sufferings of human life. Keats now realizes that only when a man has known suffering intimately and is in need of consolation will such a philosophy appeal to him. He does not say he agrees with Wordsworth's conclusions. What he has come to admire is the older poet's intensive search for conclusions. This becomes clearer in a later, more famous passage in the May 3 letter, in which Keats compares human life to a "Mansion of Many Apartments."

One of those apartments he calls "the Chamber of Maiden-Thought"; among the effects of being in that chamber is

sharpening one's vision into the heart and nature of Man
—of convincing ones nerves that the World is full of Misery and Heartbreak, Pain, Sickness and oppression—
whereby This Chamber of Maiden-Thought becomes
gradually darken'd and at the same time on all sides of
it many doors are set open—but all dark—all leading to
dark passages—We see not the ballance of good and evil.
We are in a Mist—*We* are now in that state—We feel the
"burden of the Mystery," To this point was Wordsworth
come, as far as I can conceive when he wrote "Tintern
Abbey" and it seems to me that his Genius is explorative
of those dark Passages. Now if we live, and go on thinking, we too shall explore them. (I, 281)

Wordsworth's phrase, "the burden of the mystery," appears
twice in this letter; it had evidently captured Keats's imagination. What precisely did he mean by it? He provides a
clue in the sentence, "We see not the ballance of good and
evil." The presence of evil in the world was called a "mystery" by many of Keats's contemporaries, including some
of his close friends. Bailey, for instance, with whom Keats
had had lengthy discussions about the lines from "Tintern
Abbey" that contain the phrase in question,[7] speaks of the
origin of evil in these terms: "It is a mystery, and it were
impious to pursue it further, especially to our unbelief. It
is enough if we can understand that it *is* a mystery, and perceive what remains to be supplied to us in a future and
more perfect state."[8] Leigh Hunt's *The Religion of the
Heart* advises that "the solution of the mystery called evil
had better be left in God's own hands, to be given in his
own good time."[9] Keats himself had introduced his vision
of "eternal fierce destruction" in nature with the words, "I
have a mysterious tale." In the immediate context of the
May 3 letter to Reynolds, feeling the "burden of the Mystery" appears to be a consequence of realizing "that the
World is full of Misery and Heartbreak, Pain, Sickness, and
oppression."

[7] KC, II, 275.   [8] *Discourse*, p. 51.   [9] P. 123.

"The ballance of good and evil" was a very important concept in natural religion (for those of its exponents who conceded the reality of evil at all). If most of what can be known about God is discerned from his works, those who want or need to believe in a benevolent Deity must demonstrate that creation contains more good than evil, and that the evil that does exist is directed in some way to producing ultimate good. So religious thinkers devoted much attention to weighing the sum of good in the world against the sum of evil, in order to show that there was a preponderance of the former. Leigh Hunt is typical in this regard: "Nature is justified (to speak humanly) in the ordinary state of the world, granting it is never to be made better, because the sum of good, upon the whole, is greater than that of evil."[10] "What evils there are, I find, for the most part, relieved with many consolations: some I find to be necessary to the requisite amount of good and every one of them I find to come to a termination."[11] One year earlier, Keats had believed that "every evil has its share of good" (I, 142); now, apparently, he could no longer see such a balance. During the past few months of his life, the scales had seemed to tip on the side of evil. He had seen a vision of the natural world full of savagery and strife; he had known, in his personal affairs, great misery and distress. In another month he would write to Bailey: "Now I am never alone without rejoicing that there is such a thing as death —without placing my ultimate in the glory of dying for a great human purpose Perhaps if my affairs were in a different state I should not have written the above—you shall judge—I have two Brothers one is driven by the 'burden of Society' to America the other, with an exquisite love of Life, is in a lingering state . . . I have a Sister too and may not follow them, either to America or to the Grave—Life must be undergone" (I, 293).

[10] "Guesses on Human Nature," *The Indicator*, September 13, 1820; in *The Indicator and the Companion* (London: Bentley, 1834), p. 84.
[11] *The Autobiography of Leigh Hunt*, ed. J. E. Morpurgo (London: Cresset Press, 1948), p. 451.

These circumstances provide the background for the change in his attitude toward Wordsworth. He now recognizes and appreciates the efforts of the older poet to understand the human condition and to find, if possible, some source of consolation.

Here I must think Wordsworth is deeper than Milton—though I think it has depended more upon the general and gregarious advance of intellect, than individual greatness of Mind—From the Paradise Lost and the other Works of Milton, I hope it is not too presuming, even between ourselves to say, his Philosophy, human and divine, may be tolerably understood by one not much advanced in years. In his time englishmen were just emancipated from a great superstition—and Men had got hold of certain points and resting places in reasoning which were too newly born to be doubted, and too much opposed by the Mass of Europe not to be thought etherial and authentically divine—who could gainsay his ideas on virtue, vice, and Chastity in Comus, just at the time of the dismissal of Cod-pieces and a hundred other disgraces? who would not rest satisfied with his hintings at good and evil in the Paradise Lost, when just free from the inquisition and burrning in Smithfield? The Reformation produced such immediate and great benefits, that Protestantism was considered under the immediate eye of heaven, and its own remaining Dogmas and superstitions, then, as it were, regenerated, constituted those resting places and seeming sure points of Reasoning—from that I have mentioned, Milton, whatever he may have thought in the sequel, appears to have been content with these by his writings—He did not think into the human heart, as Wordsworth has done—Yet Milton as a Philosopher, had sure as great powers as Wordsworth—What is then to be inferr'd? O many things—It proves there is really a grand march of intellect—, It proves that a mighty providence

subdues the mightiest Minds to the service of the time being, whether it be in human Knowledge or Religion.
(I, 281-82)

Without a knowledge of contemporary religious vocabulary, one might easily make the mistake of interpreting this
passage as an expression of a preference for a kind of secular humanism over religion. But Keats is actually comparing
two approaches to religion, one of which rests content with
"Dogmas and superstitions" while the other "thinks into the
human heart." In the context of what was said earlier concerning the "heart" as the subject of much contemporary
theological comment, "thinking into the human heart" can
and, perhaps, must be understood as signifying religious investigation. The following remarks of Leigh Hunt will serve
to clarify and buttress this assertion:

> Upon this innermost heart of man, God, the Great First
> Cause, in the mysterious graduality of his ways, im-
> printed those first sentiments of good and just, to grow
> with his growth in knowledge, and strengthen with his
> strength in wisdom, which, however imperfectly read by
> conscience for a time, were never wholly overlooked by
> it. . . . These then and these alone, are the scriptures of
> which it can be said, that "not one jot or one tittle can
> pass away": these, and these alone, the texts that require
> no explanation, and give rise to no wars and heresies, in
> whatever book we meet with them: and to know thus
> much, and abide manfully and devoutly by the knowl-
> edge, is the only religion which men can cease finally to
> dispute, because it is the only one that can secure brother-
> hood on earth, and that preaches hope, without excep-
> tion, for all who die.[12]

God has written his religion in the heart, for growing wisdom to read perfectly, and time to make triumphant. . . .

[12] *The Religion of the Heart*, p. 113.

(171)

Doctrines revolting to the heart are not made to endure, however mixed up they may be with lessons the most divine.[13]

God's true religion is written in the heart, and Wordsworth, thinking into the human heart, is helping to clarify that religion and to make it triumphant. Milton was not as "deep" as Wordsworth because he was content with the dogmas and superstitions of Protestantism. Yet in his defense it can be said that he acted and thought as he had to, given the times in which he lived. His task and that of his contemporaries was to help stamp out the greater superstitions of Catholicism—this was their unique contribution to the progress of human enlightenment; this was the special role they were assigned in God's plan. In Keats's view, the development of theology and the development of all human thought is presided over and directed by a "mighty providence" that raises up prophets and reformers in each age to lead mankind toward a purer, more refined religious consciousness.

Mankind still had far to go. Compared with *Paradise Lost, The Excursion* preached a relatively enlightened theology, but Wordsworth still held on to some of the "dogmas and superstitions" in which Milton believed. However, the grand march of intellect was moving forward. Keats had remarked to Reynolds that they too, like Wordsworth, were involved in exploring the dark passages in the Mansion of Life, and they too might expect to make discoveries. During the months to come, Keats would be involved in a quiet search for a religious system "which does not affront our reason and humanity" (II, 103)—which, in short, would serve as a substitute for and improvement on Christianity. The most important requirement for that system would be an ability to provide an explanation and a measure of comfort for the miseries and pain of earthly existence.

[13] *Ibid.,* pp. 1f.

In June, 1818, Tom's health having taken a slight turn for the better, Keats began a walking tour of northern England and Scotland with his friend Charles Brown. His purpose was to enlarge his experience of men and things and to stock his memory with a new store of images on which to draw for future poems. Perhaps he was also seeking distraction from the anxiety and sorrow that had been burdening him. But if he thought that he could avoid being teased into disturbing speculations or that his imagination could be nourished without being challenged and troubled, he was mistaken.

From the beginning he was conscious of the religious ramifications of what he saw. Describing Windermere, he wrote: "The two views we have had of it are of the most noble tenderness—they can never fade away—they make one forget the divisions of life; age, youth, poverty and riches; and refine one's sensual vision into a sort of north star which can never cease to be open lidded and stedfast over the wonders of the great Power" (I, 299). But the works of the great Power are not all tender or beautiful; later on in the tour Keats caught a glimpse of creation's darker side. I quote from Brown's account of their visit to Staffa:

> We went into the cave, nearly to the end, and I shall never forget the solemn impression it made on me;—the pillars on each side, the waves beneath, and the beautiful roof,—all surpassed the work of man,—it seemed like a Cathedral, built by the Almighty to raise the minds of his creatures to the purest and grandest devotion,—no one could have an evil thought in such a place, We returned to Oban by a different road, and I ought to tell you of the strange sight we had of a swarm of sea gulls attacking a shoal of herrings, with now and then a porpoise heaving about among them for a supper,—I assure you that as our boat passed the spot, the water was literally spangled

with herring scales, so great had been the destruction by these Gulls.[14]

Brown was able to juxtapose these two scenes without drawing any metaphysical moral from the contrast. Perhaps the thought did not strike him that the same God who created the natural cathedral of Staffa "to raise the minds of his creatures to the purest and the grandest devotion" was also responsible, ultimately, for the carnage wrought by the gulls. But Keats, who had once before been horrified by looking "too far into the sea," may have been more sensitive than his friend to the theological implications of the contrast between the scenes. Returning from the "Cathedral of the Sea" (his own phrase—I, 350) which had evoked such serenely pious sentiments, at least in Brown, he came face to face with another example of "eternal fierce destruction" in the animal world. Which of these natural phenomena provided the more reliable evidence as to the character of the Deity? Confronted by such conflicting evidence, could man's reason or man's heart arrive at any conclusion at all about the nature of God, or about anything having to do with God? The experience at Staffa may help to explain the tone of helpless bewilderment which characterizes the sonnet Keats wrote a few days later, after having climbed to the top of Ben Nevis.

> Read me a lesson, Muse, and speak it loud
>   Upon the top of Nevis, blind in mist!
> I look into the chasms, and a shroud
>   Vaporous doth hide them,—just so much I wist
> Mankind do know of hell; I look o'erhead,
>   And there is sullen mist,—even so much
> Mankind can tell of heaven; mist is spread
>   Before the earth, beneath me,—even such
> Even so vague is man's sight of himself!
>   Here are the craggy stones beneath my feet,—

[14] *The Letters of Charles Armitage Brown*, ed. Jack Stillinger (Cambridge, Mass.: Harvard Univ. Press, 1966), p. 40.

This much I know that, a poor witless elf,
I tread on them,—that all my eye doth meet
Is mist and crag, not only on this height,
But in the world of thought and mental might!

Mist seems to have been a favorite symbol for Keats when he was speaking of metaphysical difficulties. In 1815, he wrote to a schoolmate that he was in a "mazy Mist" with regard to certain theological questions. More recently he had remarked to Reynolds, "We are in a Mist. . . . We feel the 'burden of the Mystery'" (I, 281). Now he says that mankind is blinded by mist when it attempts to comprehend Heaven and Hell. The allusion to Hell deserves comment, especially since it is the second such reference Keats has made in the space of four months. On April 27, he had written to Reynolds: "The most unhappy hours in our lives are those in which we recollect times past to our own blushing—If we are immortal that must be the Hell—If I am to be immortal, I hope it will be after having taken a little of 'that watery labyrinth' in order to forget some of my schoolboy days & others since those" (I, 273). Keats had been "feasting upon" Milton in April, and one might therefore see the reference to Hell as literary rather than theological. The same might be said of the allusion in the "Ben Nevis" sonnet, since Keats had brought a copy of the *Divine Comedy* along on the tour. But perhaps it is too easy to dismiss these references as purely literary. Perhaps Keats was in fact giving serious consideration to the possibility that Hell was a reality.

Leigh Hunt's refusal to accept the doctrine of eternal punishment was based largely on his understanding of the benevolent nature of God. The "Great Beneficence" could not be so cruel as to subject his creatures to everlasting torture. But Keats was being forced by experience to question the absolute benevolence of a God who allowed innocent creatures to suffer. If the Deity willingly presided over "eternal fierce destruction" in this world, why not in the

next? Haydon's argument against Hunt was: "Why may
there not be punishment hereafter as well as punishment
here?" He observed further: "You may as well argue there
is no God because we see the innocent suffer, as that
Xtianity cannot be of Divine Origin because the guilty are
threatened with punishment hereafter."[15] If Keats had once,
with Hunt, looked upon the doctrine of Hell as a major
stumbling block to the acceptance of Christianity by reasonable men, and if he was now more willing to grant the
plausibility of that doctrine, the time was coming closer
when he would feel compelled to rethink his whole attitude
toward the religion of Christ.

Just before leaving Scotland, Keats went with Brown to
Beauley Abbey, where they came upon some old skulls, supposedly the remains of long dead monks. Playing at craniol-
ogy, they collaborated on some verses speculating on what
the owners of the skulls were like in life. Brown, fervently
anti-clerical, wrote derisively of the monks, snickering at
their hypocrisy and unmonastic proclivities. One stanza will
suggest his general tone:

> A Toper this! he plied his glass
> More strictly than he said the Mass,
> And lov'd to see a tempting Lass
>   Come to confession,
> Letting his absolution pass
> O'er first transgression.

Keats's lines (he wrote only 20 to Brown's 76)[16] are strik-
ingly different in mood; he tends to sympathize rather than
mock.

[15] *The Diary of Benjamin Robert Haydon*, ed. Willard B. Pope
(Cambridge, Mass.: Harvard Univ. Press, 1960), II, 58.
[16] Lines 7 to 12 (the first stanza quoted here) were apparently
written by Keats, although Garrod does not so identify them. See
Jack Stillinger, *The Texts of Keats's Poems* (Cambridge, Mass.:
Harvard Univ. Press, 1974), pp. 201f.

The mitred ones of Nice and Trent
Were not so tongue-tied,—no, they went
Hot to their Councils, scarce content
    With Orthodoxy;
But ye, poor tongueless things, were meant
    To speak by proxy.

Poor Skull, thy fingers set ablaze,
With silver Saint in golden rays,
The holy Missal; thou did'st craze
    'Mid bead and spangle,
While others pass'd their idle days
    In coil and wrangle.

This lily-colour'd skull, with all
The teeth complete, so white and small,
Belong'd to one whose early pall
    A lover shaded;
He died ere Superstition's gall
    His heart invaded.

An artist devoting himself to his illuminations while those
around him argued theology; a young lover who died before the burden of life made him vulnerable to the appeal
of Christianity;—such things were on Keats's mind as he
turned his eyes toward home.

CHAPTER FIVE

The Vale of Soul-Making

I N the autumn, winter, and spring of 1818–1819—that most
remarkable period in his growth as a poet—Keats turned
and confronted directly the religious questions that had
been troubling him, as though with a new determination to
resolve them once and for all. We find expressions of renewed interest in the origin and history of Christianity—
indications, apparently, of a new, serious investigation of
the merits of that faith. We watch the slow development of
a new attitude toward the presence of suffering in the
world. Finally, we see these two lines of investigation
merge, when Keats explicitly rejects the Christian system
of redemption in favor of his own newly formulated system
of "soul-making."

As one reads the letters of this period, it very quickly becomes apparent that religion was assuming a central place
in Keats's consciousness. What one notices first, perhaps, is
a reappearance of the kind of piety that characterized some
of his early verse. In October, for instance, he writes to his
brother and sister-in-law in America to prepare them for
Tom's death, which was now inevitable: "You must my dear
Brother and Sister take example frome me and bear up
against any Calamity for my sake as I do for your's. Our's
are ties which independent of their own Sentiment are sent
us by providence to prevent the deleterious effects of one
great, solitary grief. . . . thank heaven for what happiness
you have and after thinking a moment or two that you suffer in common with all Mankind hold it not a sin to regain
your cheerfulness" (1, 391f.). Six months later, such sentiments are still appearing. In March, he concludes a section
of another letter to George and his wife in this way: "I must
fancy you asleep—and please myself in the fancy of speaking a prayer and a blessing over you and your lives—God

bless you" (II, 74). Perhaps in the context of their common sorrow the expression of such sentiments is not remarkable. But the statements serve to remind us that throughout his life, in joy as well as in suffering, Keats never abandoned his faith in a benevolent Deity.

Tom's death naturally raised the question of immortality, and it drew from Keats one of his more confident assertions of belief in an afterlife. "I will not enter into any parsonic comments on death—yet the common observations of the commonest people on death are as true as their proverbs. I have scarce a doubt of immortality of some nature or other—neither had Tom" (II, 4). A few months later doubts would begin to creep in again, but now he is confident enough to indulge in some speculation on the nature of post-mortal existence. "There you are with Birkbeck—here I am with brown—sometimes I fancy an immense separation, and sometimes, as at present, a direct communication of spirit with you. That will be one of the grandeurs of immortality—there will be no space and consequently the only commerce between spirits will be by their intelligence of each other—when they will completely understand each other—while we in this world merely comprehend each other in different degrees—the higher the degree of good so higher is our Love and friendship" (II, 5).[1]

---

[1] This description of communication in the post-mortal state is quite similar to an idea contained in some verses by Katherine Philips (1631-1664) that Keats copied in 1817 while he was visiting Bailey at Oxford (*Letters*, I, 164).

> Our chang'd and mingled souls are grown
>   To such acquaintance now,
> That if each would resume her own
>   Alas! we know not how.
> We have each other so engrost
> That each is in the union lost
>
> And thus we can no absence know
>   Nor shall we be confin'd;
> Our active souls will daily go
>   To learn each others mind.
> Nay should we never meet to sense
> Our souls would hold intelligence.

Speaking of immortality in the first passage quoted above, Keats remarked: "The common observations of the commonest people on death are as true as their proverbs." Two weeks later he expressed a similar sentiment, following a remark that, whether or not he realized it, was a restatement of a traditional argument for the existence of an afterlife. "The more we know the more inadequacy we discover in the world to satisfy us—this is an old observation; but I have made up my Mind never to take any thing for granted —but even to examine the truth of the commonest proverbs" (ii, 18). This new appreciation of the wisdom of the "commonest people"—at least with regard to belief in immortality—may have been one of the factors inspiring Keats to look more closely and more respectfully at that system of faith he had once dismissed as a superstition of the vulgar.

A further indication that some change was taking place in Keats's religious disposition at this time may be seen in a remark he made in December concerning Leigh Hunt, who, he complained, "is certainly a pleasant fellow in the main when you are with him—but in reallity he is vain, egotistical and disgusting in matters of taste and in morals" (ii, 11). Commenting on these words, Amy Lowell wrote: "Since Hunt's morals were nothing short of impeccable, we can see that Haydon had been one of the many people whom Keats had been seeing, for Haydon applied the word 'morals' to religious opinions, a subject on which he and Hunt were forever at odds."[2] This is an interesting observation, but it needs some qualifying. For one thing, Leigh Hunt's morals were not considered "impeccable" by many who knew him.[3] And it may be misleading to suggest that

[2] *John Keats* (Boston: Houghton Mifflin, 1925), ii, 124.
[3] In a rather distasteful passage in his Diary (ii, 82f.), Haydon describes Hunt's conduct toward his sister-in-law as lecherous, and speaks of his "indecent improper jokes." John Reynolds too refers to Hunt's "indecent discoursings" (*KC*, i, 156). Hunt's biographer, Louis Landré, points out that Hunt had liberal ideas on sexual freedom and that the subject was one of his favorite topics of conversation—conversation that shocked many who heard it. *Leigh Hunt* (Paris: Société d'Édition "Les Belles Lettres," 1936), ii, 43.

Keats was criticizing Hunt's religious *opinions*. It is true that Haydon, like many of his contemporaries, seemed at times to use "religion" and "morals" interchangeably. He was a member of a Church that, in its desire to avoid doctrinal strife, tended to underplay theology and emphasize the moral aspects of religion. But although "morals" had become the central concern of most religious commentators, it was never equated with "religion"—a larger, more comprehensive term embracing doctrinal considerations as well as rules of conduct. Keats was not describing Hunt's *theology* as "disgusting" (an odd word to choose, if he were), but rather certain attitudes and habits which he found distasteful. Yet, one would be justified in interpreting his words as an indirect judgment on Hunt's creed. It was generally agreed that the soundness of a man's religious views was revealed in the effect they had on his character (Hunt's critique of Christianity rested heavily on this proposition). Criticism of a man's morals implied a criticism of his religious principles. There is further evidence that Hunt's religious beliefs were on Keats's mind at this time. A few days earlier he had written a parody of conversation in the Hunt circle, in which Hunt is made to say, "I am rather inclined to the liberal side of things—but I am reckoned lax in my christian principles" (II, 14).

Miss Lowell was probably correct in sensing Haydon's influence at work in this period. Keats saw much of his old friend during the winter of 1818–1819, especially in the month following Tom's death. In his attempts to console the poet for the loss of his brother, it would have been unlike Haydon not to talk about Christianity. He had long believed that one of the things that made his religion superior to other forms of faith was the comfort it offered in time of suffering. As he once wrote in his diary, "Christianity is a religion adapted to give relief to the wretched & hope to the good, and Christ having suffered is a bond of sympathy between man & his Saviour that nothing in any other religion before or after affords. Do we not feel for others in proportion as we have suffered ourselves? Is it not an intense gratification to fall before a being who having taken on a human form, been liable to human troubles, can sympathize with human weaknesses?"[4] Later on, Keats would explicitly reject the necessity of this sort of mediation between God and men, but that would come only after he had carefully studied the character of Christ for himself. It is quite possible that it was Haydon who urged him, or at least influenced him, to undertake this study.

There was another argument in Haydon's apologia for Christianity to which Keats would have been particularly vulnerable at this time.

> Evil is in the World; it cannot be rooted out. . . . Bones will be broken, pain will ensue, men will spend their property, poverty will come, passions will command reason, consequences & pangs of mind will follow. Christianity is the only religion which affords consolation for these. It teaches to bear those evils of an imperfect Nature, of a World which will not be altered in system to please us, but being as it is, Xtianity is sent to help us through it. Prevent poverty!—prevent illness, prevent old age or any weakness of the body; prevent vice or any of the aberrations of mind; prevent them you cannot, but alleviate them you may, and shew me before Xtianity such alleviation of misery as since its belief.[5]

Having discovered for himself that natural religion provided neither explanation nor consolation for the sufferings that are inseparable from the human condition, Keats was more susceptible to such reasoning than he had ever been before.[6]

---

[4] *Diary*, II, 67.   [5] *Ibid.*, pp. 68f.

[6] A possible counterweight to Haydon's influence during this period was that of Charles Brown, with whom Keats took up residence after Tom died. Brown was a Deist, extremely critical and often contemptuous of Christianity—as the stanzas he wrote on the skulls in Beauley Abbey will indicate. This attitude perdured throughout his life. Joanna Richardson records that as he lay dying in New Zealand in 1842, "some Baptist emigrant attempted to com-

The influence of Haydon, the increased disenchantment with Hunt, the need for assurance about immortality, and, perhaps, a larger need for some coherent system of faith—these factors provide, if not an explanation, at least a context for the brief revival of Keats's interest in Christianity. On March 3, or thereabout, he announced to his brother and sister-in-law that he was "not unwilling" to read Church history (II, 70).[7] And two weeks later, he revealed that he had been reading the New Testament:

> I have no doubt that thousands of people never heard of have had hearts completely disinterested: I can remember but two—Socrates and Jesus—their Histories evince it—What I heard a little time ago, Taylor observe with respect to Socrates, may be said of Jesus—That he was so great a man that though he transmitted no writing of his own to posterity, we have his Mind and his sayings and his greatness handed to us by others. It is to be lamented that the history of the latter was written and revised by Men interested in the pious frauds of Religion. Yet through all this I see his splendour. (II, 80)

When Benjamin Bailey became aware of this letter in 1848, it indicated to him that Keats's mind had been "gradu-

---

fort him with thoughts of the Saviour. 'For the love of God, sir,' answered Brown, 'speak to me no more about that *man.*'" Because of his beliefs, Brown was denied burial in consecrated ground. *The Everlasting Spell: A Study of Keats and His Friends* (London: Jonathan Cape, 1963), p. 109.

[7] He refers specifically to Joseph Milner's *The History of the Church of Christ* (5 vols., 1794-1809), which he says "is reckoned a very good one." It would be interesting to know who recommended Milner's work to him. The announced purpose of the author was to write a new kind of history, one that would not call attention to the past imperfections of the Church and thus give comfort to Deists and Sceptics and encourage "infidel malice." "The honour of Christianity will be supported; the value of its essential doctrines will be ascertained; and we shall have frequent occasion to state what the Gospel is and what it is not. Hence the triumphs of the Sceptic will appear to be unfounded in truth." From an American edition (Philadelphia: Hogan and Thompson, 1835), I, 4f.

ally working itself round to the more healthy tone of a Disciple of Christ."[8] But while Keats's words do reveal that he was outgrowing certain prejudices and broadening his religious perspective, Bailey should have realized that a mere acknowledgment of the "greatness" and "splendour" of the man Jesus is not sufficient grounds on which to assume a tendency toward Christianity. Leigh Hunt, whom Bailey saw as an anti-Christian influence on Keats, always spoke of Jesus in glowing terms. William Hazlitt, even more of a skeptic than Hunt, in 1819 expressed his admiration for the character of Christ in words that make Keats's comments seem reserved. "There is something in the character of Christ . . . (leaving religious faith quite out of the question) of more sweetness and majesty, and more likely to work a change in the mind of man, by the contemplation of its idea alone, than any to be found in history, whether actual or feigned. This character is that of a sublime humanity, such as was never seen on earth before, nor since."[9] What enabled these men to admire Christ while rejecting the Christian religion was the belief (to which Keats evidently subscribed) that the authors of the New Testament either misunderstood the teaching of Jesus or deliberately revised it to suit their own purposes. This notion was popular among eighteenth-century rationalists; it allowed them to develop a radical critique of Christianity without directly impugning the character of Christ. Voltaire, for example, liked to point out the problems involved in the growth of the New Testament canon, and thereby cast doubt on the overall reliability of the gospel accounts (Keats's praise, "pious frauds" appears frequently in Voltaire's writings on the subject).[10] The questionable veracity of the evangelists was a favorite notion of Leigh Hunt's, and Keats must often have

[8] *KC*, II, 294.

[9] *Complete Works of William Hazlitt*, ed. P. P. Howe (London: Dent, 1930-1934), VI, 183.

[10] Stuart Sperry, "Keats's Skepticism and Voltaire," *Keats-Shelley Journal*, 12 (1963), 86.

heard him expressing an opinion like the following, which appeared in the *Examiner* in August 1819:

> There is great reason to suspect that Christ (in whom we have the noblest part of belief, the belief in his benevolence), preached no dogmas at all;—but only kindness and justice. But be this as it may, the writers of his life, whom we suspect to have grievously misunderstood him (just as might have been expected in similar followers of Plato and Pythagoras), amply supplied the omission; and the consequence has been what we all know;—that Christian charity has been swallowed up in Faith itself, and in Apostolic ambition and fighting.[11]

But, although Keats's sentiments closely resemble those of men whose appreciation of Christ's "sublime humanity" never developed into a belief in his divinity, it is impossible to dismiss Bailey's pious hope as totally unrealistic. Keats had come a long way since the time when, one year earlier, he had shocked Haydon by bowing to a likeness of Voltaire in preference to one of Christ. His new realization of the greatness and splendor of Jesus was not a quickly passing thing; there is evidence that the impression endured at least throughout the year 1819.[12] One is struck by the similarity of Keats's general religious sentiments in that year to those of Coleridge when he was the same age. "My Heart forced me to admire the 'beauty of Holiness' in the Gospel, forced me to *love* the Jesus, whom my Reason (or perhaps my *rea-*

[11] *Examiner*, August 8, 1819, p. 497.

[12] In a section of *The Anatomy of Melancholy* that Robert Gittings and Aileen Ward agree Keats did not read until the autumn of 1819, Burton remarks that the practice of fasting is a commendable one, since it was advised "by such parties as Moses, Elias, Daniel, CHRIST, and as his apostles made use of it." Referring in a marginal note to Burton's reverent capitals, Keats wrote: "I would decapitate these large letters but really they being in such very bad company have *without sneer* a right to preeminence." *The Complete Works of John Keats*, ed. H. Buxton Forman (Glasgow: Gowers & Gray, 1901), III, 275. Forman's citation of Burton is incorrect: the passage quoted is from Part 3, Sec. 4, Mem. 1, *Subs.* 2, not Subs. 1.

sonings) would not permit me to *worship*—my Faith, therefore, was made up of the Evangelists and the Deistic Philosophy—a kind of *religious* Twilight."[13] Granting the difference in emotional and intellectual make-up between the two men, one must at least acknowledge the possibility that, if sickness and death had not intervened, Keats would have followed Coleridge out of the religious twilight and into some richer form of faith, closer to Christian orthodoxy.

The fact that his friend's admiration for Jesus did not lead him immediately to embrace Christianity Bailey attributes to "rather a want of knowledge than of faith."[14] But another letter that Keats wrote in March, 1819—and that Bailey never saw—seems to indicate that he possessed considerable knowledge of the basic elements of Christian doctrine. During that Lenten period, his sister Fanny was undergoing instruction preparatory to her Confirmation. At one point in her course of study she was apparently given a homework assignment by her instructor, a local clergyman, and having found the task difficult turned to her brother for help. She sent him a list of eleven questions and on March 31 he answered them in order. The following selections will suggest his general approach.

4 There are two Sacraments of our Church—Baptisim and the Lord's Supper. The Church of Rome has seven Sacraments. . . . The reason why we have but two Sacraments is—that it is proved from the Scriptures by the great protestant reformers—that only two are commanded by god—the rest adopted by the Church of Rome are human institutions.

6 Look in Isaia for "*A virgin shall conceive*" &c—Look in the Psalms for "*The Kings of the Earth set themselves and the Princes take counsel together*" and "*they parted*

---

[13] *Collected Letters of Samuel Taylor Coleridge.* ed. Earl Leslie Griggs (Oxford: Clarendon Press, 1956–1971), I, 78.
[14] *KC*, II, 294.

my Garments among them &" and "*My god, my god why has thou forsaken me* &c" In Jeremia "*Comfort ye, comfort ye* &" In Daniel The stone cut out of the mountain without hands that breaks the image in pieces is a type of the Kingdom of Christ—Look at the 2nd Chat. Isaiah— Chap 7-9—"*For unto us a Child is born*" II—Jeremiah Chap xxxi Micah Chap 5—Zechariah Chap 6 and Chap 13 *verse 6.* Those I have marked will be sufficient—You will remember their completion in the new testament—

7th The communion of saints is the fruition they enjoy in heaven among one another and in the Divinity of Christ—

11th The Prophecy to our first parents is this—Genesis 3 Chapter—Verse 15 "And I will put enmity between thee and the woman and between thy seed and her seed; *it shall bruize thy head* and thou shall bruize his heel— Christ the Son of David by dying on the Cross triumphed over death and the grave from which he saved mankind; and in that way did he 'bruize the Serpent's head' " —(II, 50-51)

The letter is valuable, not for what it tells us of Keats's own creed (it tells us almost nothing), but because it reminds us that his rejection of Christianity was based upon a sound understanding of what he was rejecting. It is possible, of course, that he did some brushing up before writing to Fanny, but the letter does not give that impression. He seems to speak with an easy competence, to be quite comfortable in his knowledge of the essential doctrines of the Anglican faith and of their background in scripture.[15]

---

[15] Keats's doctrine is erroneous in one particular, and it is an interesting error. He says that the sacrament of Baptism was instituted by John the Baptist. Orthodox theologians have always insisted (and this insistence has caused many doctrinal controversies) that Jesus himself instituted the sacrament. This is the teaching of the Thirty-nine Articles and the answer that was expected of Fanny Keats. But the Unitarians, among others, believed (and Voltaire calls attention to this fact in the *Dictionnaire Philosophique*) that the sacrament

Even more interesting than the letter's content is its tone. Apart from the smiling close ("Your affectionate Parson, John"), there is not a single indication that the writer had any personal difficulty with the doctrines of which he was speaking. There is no mockery, no qualification, no self-conscious embarrassment—no attempt at all to disassociate himself from the conceptions he was dealing with. Indeed, if this were the only example we possessed of Keats's writing on the subject of religion, we would have to assume that he was an unquestioning believer and a loyal son of the Church. Evidently he did not wish to burden the young girl with questions and doubts that he had not satisfactorily resolved for himself. Perhaps he would have agreed with Rousseau that "as long as there is any true faith left among men, we must not trouble quiet souls, nor scare the faith of the ignorant with problems they cannot solve, with difficulties which cause them uneasiness, but do not give them any guidance."[16]

At the very time when he was expounding Christian doctrine to his sister and expressing to his brother renewed interest in Jesus and the Church, Keats was gradually developing for himself a view of the world that would enable him decisively to reject the Christian faith and that would provide him, at least temporarily, with an alternative "system of salvation." One motive, it would appear, behind his investigation of Christianity at this time was the desire to measure its worth against certain new insights of his own. Ironically, it seems to have been that friend of Keats who was professionally committed to advancing the interests of Christianity who indirectly and unwittingly provided the stimulus for this new line of investigation.

was not introduced by Christ himself but by John. One wonders if Keats had allowed his pure Church doctrine to be muddied by heterodox reading or associations.

[16] *Emile, or Education*, trans. Barbara Foxley (London: Dent, 1911), p. 274.

"I have a long story to tell you about Bailey," wrote Keats to his brother on February 19. He went on to report that Bailey had jilted a sister of John Reynolds in order to marry the daughter of Bishop Gleig, Primus of the Church of Scotland. In recounting the events, Keats's tone is surprisingly controlled—almost dispassionate. Yet it must have come as a tremendous shock to discover that the friend whom he had called "one of the noblest men alive at the present day" and whom he had praised particularly for his "disinterestedness" was capable of acting in so ignoble a manner—to serve (as it must have seemed) his own advancement in the Church. "No doubt," said Keats, "his conduct has been verry bad. The great thing to be considered is—whether it is want of delicacy and principle or want of Knowledge and polite experience—And again weakness—yes that is it—and the want of a Wife—yes that is it . . . but his so quickly taking to Miss Gleig can have no excuse—except that of a Ploughman who wants a wife" (II, 66f.). The bitter disillusionment that shows itself in those last words was probably part of the inspiration for another passage from this letter, written a few days earlier.

I begin to hate Parsons. . . . A Parson is a Lamb in a drawing room and a lion in a Vestry—The notions of Society will not permit a Parson to give way to his temper in any shape—so he festers in himself—his features get a peculiar diabolical self sufficient iron stupid expression—He is continually acting—His mind is against every Man and every Mans mind is against him—He is an Hippocrite to the Believer and a Coward to the unbeliever—He must be either a Knave or an Ideot—And there is no man so much to be pitied as an ideot parson—The soldier who is cheated into an esprit du corps—by a red coat, a Band and Colours for the purpose of nothing—is not half so pitiable as the Parson who is led by the nose by the Bench of Bishops—and is smothered in absurdities—a poor necessary subaltern of the Church. (II, 63)

Knave or idiot: under which heading did Keats now classify the man whom he had once so deeply respected and to whom he had confided his secret dreams and fears? The harshness of this diatribe, so uncharacteristic of its author, must owe something to a sense of betrayal, of confidence misplaced and admiration misdirected.

Yet Keats seems to have profited from his disillusionment. He drew from Bailey's behavior a lesson concerning the nature of man—a lesson on which he would build a new philosophy of life.

He had compared Bailey's conduct to that of "a Ploughman who wants a wife." Two weeks later, he wrote: "Parsons will always keep up their Character, but as it is said there are some animals, the Ancients knew, which we do not; let us hope our posterity will miss the black badger with tri-cornered hat" (II, 70). Keats's comparison of the parson with an animal and his sense of the impulsiveness of his old friend's behavior seem to have been the origins of a further insight he expressed on March 19. "Very few men have ever arrived at a complete disinterestedness of Mind," he wrote (and one thinks again of the "disinterested" Bailey):

> The greater part of men make their way with the same instinctiveness, the same unwandering eye from their purposes, the same animal eagerness as the Hawk—The Hawk wants a Mate, so does the Man—look at them both they set about it and procure one in the same manner—they get their food in the same manner—The noble animal Man for his amusement smokes his pipe—The Hawk balances about the Clouds—that is the only differences of their leisures. This it is that makes the Amusement of Life—to a speculative Mind. I go among the Feilds and catch a glimpse of a stoat or a fieldmouse peeping out of the withered grass—the creature hath a purpose and its eyes are bright with it—I go amongst the buildings of a city and I see a Man hurrying along—to what? The Crea-

ture has a purpose and his eyes are bright with it.
(II, 79f.)[17]

Men and animals being so much alike, disinterestedness is
no more to be expected among human beings than among
lower forms of life. "For in wild nature the Hawk would
loose his Breakfast of Robins and the Robin his of Worms
The Lion must starve as well as the swallow."

That last remark shows that a considerable change has
taken place in Keats's attitude toward the suffering that one
sees in nature. What, one year earlier, had horrified him as
"eternal fierce destruction" ("the gentle Robin, like a pard
or ounce,/Ravening a worm") he now sees as a necessary
part of life in the world. Although the parallel with human
suffering would not be drawn fully until a month later, even
now he begins to see a resemblance between the situation
of animals and that of men:

> Even here though I myself am pursueing the same instinc-
> tive course as the veriest human animal you can think of
> —I am however young writing at random—straining at
> particles of light in the midst of a great darkness—with-
> out knowing the bearing of any one assertion of any one
> opinion. Yet may I not in this be free from sin? May there

[17] Is Keats, perhaps, recalling something he heard once from
Bailey? His words bear an interesting similarity to a passage in one
of Bishop Butler's sermons:

> Now as brutes have various instincts, by which they are carried
> on to the end the Author of their nature intended them for: is
> not man in the same condition; with this difference only, that to his
> instincts (i.e. appetites and passions) is added the principle of
> reflection or conscience? And as brutes act agreeably to their
> nature, in following that principle or particular instinct which for
> the present is strongest in them: does not man likewise act agree-
> ably to his nature, or obey the law of his creation, by following
> that principle, be it passion or conscience, which for the present
> happens to be strongest in him? Thus different men are by their
> particular natures hurried on to pursue honour, or riches, or
> pleasure."

"The Works of Bishop Butler, ed. J. H. Bernard (London: Macmillan, 1900), I, 42.

not be superior beings amused with any graceful, though instinctive attitude my mind may fall into, as I am entertained with the alertness of a Stoat or the anxiety of a Deer? . . . By a superior being our reasoning may take the same tone—though erroneous they may be fine. (II, 80)

Clarence Thorpe assumed that "superior being" meant Supreme Being,[18] but I think the assumption is incorrect. Keats seems to be referring to the old theory that, just as there are many levels of existence below man on the chain of being, there may be many more above him. The idea was used by Pope in his *Essay on Man*—and Keats may have had Pope's lines in mind:

> Superior beings, when of late they saw
> A mortal Man unfold all Nature's law,
> Admired such wisdom in an earthly shape,
> And shew'd a Newton as we shew an Ape.[19]

Note that the "reasoning" that Keats thinks may amuse a superior being is religious reasoning. The passage above follows directly upon the comments, quoted earlier, on the splendor of Jesus and the pious frauds of religion. Keats admits that his ideas may be erroneous, but he hopes that his honest searching after truth will be pleasing and not sinful in the sight of heaven.

But Keats is not a relativist in this matter of truth. Although he believes that even erroneous reasoning may appear "fine" to a superior being, he affirms the reality of absolute truth and the obligation of men to search for it. A

[18] *The Mind of John Keats* (1926; rpr. New York: Russell & Russell, 1964), p. 96.
[19] *The Poems of Alexander Pope*, ed. John Butt (New Haven: Yale Univ. Press, 1963), p. 517. Keats may have heard about "superior beings" from another source. Soame Jenyns (1704-1787) worked Pope's idea into an organized explanation for human suffering (*Free Enquiry into the Nature and Origin of Evil*, published in 1757). Haydon knew Jenyns's work (*Diary*, I, 439), and perhaps he talked about it with his friend.

mere interest in fineness "is the very thing in which consists poetry; and if so it is not so fine a thing as philosophy—For the same reason that an eagle is not so fine a thing as a truth" (II, 81). He had expressed a similar idea five months earlier: "What shocks the virtuous philosopher, delights the camelion Poet" (I, 387). Now, apparently, he has come to feel that a delight in "fineness" is not enough for a man. And what he had once cautioned Bailey against, he is now doing himself: he is hungering after truth.

> Give me this credit—Do you not think I strive—to know myself? Give me this credit—and you will not think that on my own account I repeat Milton's lines
>
>> "How charming is divine Philosophy
>> Not harsh and crabbed as dull fools suppose
>> But musical as is Apollo's lute"
>
> No—no for myself—feeling grateful as I do to have got into a state of mind to relish them properly—Nothing ever becomes real till it is experienced—Even a Proverb is no proverb to you till your Life has illustrated it.
> (II, 81)

Although he admits that he himself has no claim to the title of philosopher, he has come to realize the importance and even the beauty of "divine Philosophy." It is not quite clear in what sense Keats understood the epithet "divine," but one should remember that he divided Milton's philosophy into "human and divine" (I, 281) and that, in the context of *A Mask presented at Ludlow Castle*, the "Philosophy" referred to is, in large part, moral theology. Keats's comments on Milton's lines are similar to his remarks on discovering the validity of Wordsworth's religious philosophy (I, 279) and the truth of common "proverbs" about immortality (II, 4). It would seem that Keats has become more appreciative of the ability of religious philosophers to cast "particles of light in the midst of a great darkness."

That great metaphysical darkness shadows a sonnet that Keats wrote at this time and included in the American letter. The poem reveals clearly the desperate need for some kind of spiritual comfort and enlightenment that he was feeling. It betrays such agony of soul that he was reluctant to transcribe it, lest his relatives think he was contemplating suicide, and he felt it necessary to assure them that he was sane at the time he composed it (II, 81f.).

> Why did I laugh tonight? No voice will tell:
>   No God, no Deamon of severe response
> Deigns to reply from heaven or from Hell.—
>   Then to my human heart I turn at once—
> Heart! thou and I are sad and alone;
>   Say, wherefore did I laugh? O mortal pain!
> O Darkness! Darkness! ever must I moan
>   To question Heaven and Hell and Heart in vain!
> Why did I laugh? I know this being's lease
>   My fancy to its utmost blisses spreads:
> Yet could I on this very midnight cease
>   And the world's gaudy ensigns see in shreds.
> Verse, fame and Beauty are intense indeed
> But Death intenser—Deaths is life's high mead.
>
> (II, 81f.)

We do not know the particular circumstances that inspired the sonnet, but Martin Halpern is probably correct in his analysis of the general emotional situation: "In the octave, Keats is asking, in effect: how was it possible for me to be overcome tonight by a mood of sudden and apparently causeless joy, when all conditions—my loneliness, ignorance, personal grief . . . conspire to make anguish and despair seem the proper mood?"[20]

In his search for an answer, Keats considers two possible sources of revelation: the realm of the supernatural, and the human heart. One cannot help being reminded of the two

[20] "Keats and the 'Spirit that Laughest,'" *Keats-Shelley Journal*, 15 (1966), 78f.

types of theological consciousness he described in his 1818 letter comparing Milton and Wordsworth as religious thinkers. Milton was content with a theology of God and Demon, while Wordsworth, sent by a mighty Providence to teach a more enlightened age, sought to lighten the burden of the Mystery by "thinking into the human heart" (1, 281f.).[21] Keats had learned from men like Hunt and Bailey that, in the absence of supernatural revelation, man could derive comfort and illumination from his own heart, whereon God had imprinted a revelation of himself. But now, having questioned his heart as well as Heaven and Hell, Keats has received no response. Even if he had not used the word "darkness" to describe his state, one would be justified in identifying this experience with the "dark night of the soul" of traditional religious writing, in which God withdraws himself, leaving man alone in a condition of spiritual aridity.

In the remainder of the sonnet, the poet seems to resign himself to the fact that no answer will come, at least not on this side of the grave. As in the "Ode to a Nightingale," he finds comfort in the thought of easeful death that brings an end to all earthly suffering—and all questioning. Yet in this very willingness to accept death as the ultimate solution, one detects a sense of release, of newly achieved calm. Once a man has come to look upon the greatest evil in life as a kind of good, all other troubles can be seen in a new perspective. As John Middleton Murry commented, "To accept death is to accept life; it is to accept the whole of one's mortal destiny, to see it as necessary and inevitable and beautiful."[22]

[21] It should be noted that Shelley was a more direct inspirer of these lines than either Milton or Wordsworth. They contain obvious echoes of the "Hymn to Intellectual Beauty":

No voice from some sublimer world hath ever
To sage or poet these responses given—
Therefore the names of Demon, Ghost, and Heaven,
Remain the records of their vain endeavour. (ll. 25-28)

[22] *Keats and Shakespeare* (1925; rpr. London: Oxford Univ. Press, 1965), p. 126.

The sonnet—or the mental crisis that inspired it—appears to have marked a turning point in Keats's life. Soon after writing it, he took hold again and began a slow climb out of the state of bewilderment and despondency into which he had been plunged by the events of the preceding months. Two or three days later, a renewed self-confidence appears as he writes to his brother: "I did not intend to have sent you the . . . sonnet—but look over the two last pages and ask yourselves whether I have not that in me which will well bear the buffets of the world. It will be the best comment on my sonnet; it will show you that it was written with no Agony but that of ignorance; with no thirst of any thing but knowledge when pushed to the point" (ii, 81). The "two last pages" contain his thoughts on the instinctual behavior of most men and their lack of disinterestedness, on the inevitability of suffering in the animal world, on Jesus, on superior beings, and on the importance of "divine Philosophy." Keats evidently realized that among those ideas was the foundation for a new philosophy of life.

That philosophy, and the theology with which it is inextricably mingled, was given expression a month later, on April 21. Keats introduces the subject in this way:

I have been reading lately two very different books Robertson's America and Voltaire's Siecle de Louis xiv It is like walking arm and arm between Pizarro and the great-little Monarch. In How lementable a case do we see the great body of the people in both instances: in the first, where Men might seem to inherit quiet of Mind from unsophisticated senses; from uncontamination of civilisation; and especially from their being as it were estranged from the mutual helps of Society and its mutual injuries—and thereby more immediately under the Protection of Providence—even there they had mortal pains to bear as bad; or even worse than Baliffs, Debts and Poverties of civilised Life. (ii, 100f)

It was a favorite belief of natural religionists that "the state of Nature was the reign of God"[23]—that natural man, under the eye of his Creator, enjoyed almost total freedom from bodily and social ills. Rousseau wrote: "How few sufferings are felt by man living in a state of primitive simplicity. His life is almost entirely free from suffering and from passion."[24] Rousseau and those who thought like him believed that, although God intended all his human creatures to remain in this state of beatitude, man—European man, at any rate—perversely forsook his original simplicity and with it his original happiness. Keats, apparently for the first time, finds himself questioning this view of man's history. Since he is not able to accept the Christian doctrine of an historic fall in which the entire human race was involved, he is forced to formulate a radically different theory about man's original state: "The whole appears to resolve into this —that Man is originally 'a poor forked creature' subject to the same mischances as the beasts of the forest, destined to hardships and disquietude of some kind or other. If he improves by degrees his bodily accommodations and comforts —at each stage, at each accent there are waiting for him a fresh set of annoyances—he is mortal and there is still a heaven with its Stars above his head" (II, 101).

Keats has gone the final step in his acceptance of the fact of natural evil. Having conceded the necessity of destruction in the animal world, he is now acknowledging that man's situation is basically similar to that of animals. He is subject to the same mischances as the beasts of the forest, and he is so *originally*: that is, he suffers not as a result of any primeval fall or degeneration but because God intentionally created him subject to suffering. On that account, it is idle to hope that man will ever achieve complete happiness on earth. The dream of human perfectibility is always being undercut by the fact of death and by the knowledge that man's stature and power are of an essentially inferior

[23] *Essay on Man*, III, 148; *Poems of Alexander Pope*, p. 530.
[24] *Emile*, p. 244.

order.[25] Keats paints a fairly bleak picture of the human situation: man is created susceptible to suffering and placed in a world where suffering can be neither avoided nor eradicated. How can one subscribe to such a view and still believe in a Supreme Being who is essentially benevolent? Where in this dispensation is the balance of good and evil? These are the questions Keats sets out to answer.

Of course, such questions provide no difficulty for those who see the world as a place of exile, full of sin and corruption, from which a forgiving God has mercifully opened avenues of escape. Keats dismisses this attitude contemptuously: "The common cognomen of this world among the misguided and superstitious is 'a vale of tears' from which we are to be redeemed by a certain arbitrary interposition of God and taken to Heaven—What a little circumscribed straightened notion! Call the world if you Please 'The vale of Soul-making' Then you will find out the use of the world." It is fairly clear that by "the misguided and superstitious" Keats means most Christians.[26] The phrase "vale of tears" has a very long history in Christian writing, and "interposition" was a word frequently used by religious writers of the period to describe the redemptive mission of

[25] The meaning of "there is still a heaven with its Stars above his head" becomes clearer when it is compared with Keats's remark to Bailey: "When we look at the Heavens we cannot be proud" (i, 179), and Leigh Hunt's statement: "Religion is as natural to man as his sight of the stars, and his sense of a power greater than his own." *The Religion of the Heart* (London: Chapman, 1853), p. 76.

[26] Shelley's "Hymn to Intellectual Beauty" describes the world as "this dim vast vale of tears," and it is possible that Keats meant to include in his condemnation the Platonic view of the earth as a prison from which the human spirit longs to escape (this might explain his reference to the "misguided" as well as the superstitious). But despite its use in the "Hymn," the phrase does not seem to have been closely identified with Shelley. Earlier in 1819 Leigh Hunt, who was among Shelley's greatest admirers, spoke scornfully of "those who call, and make, this beautiful world a *vale of tears*" (*Examiner*, January 17, 1819, p. 34). H. W. White and Neville Rogers discuss the history of the phrase in "The Vale of Tears in Keats, Shelley and Others," *Keats-Shelley Memorial Bulletin*, 24 (1973), pp. 16-18.

Christ.[27] Keats had revealed his distaste for the doctrine of
the Atonement in 1817 (*Letters*, I, 137), and his recent reexamination of Christianity had apparently not changed his
opinion. He found that it is possible to admire the human
character of Jesus without subscribing to the belief that he
was the Son of God, sent to redeem by his death a fallen
humanity and reopen to them the gates of heaven. Note that
what Keats is rejecting is, apparently, a Calvinist understanding of the Redemption (perhaps derived from the
Thirty-nine Articles), emphasizing man's powerlessness to
cooperate in his own redemption. He does not seem to be
aware that there are other authentic theological traditions
—the Catholic and the Arminian Protestant, for example—
that place a higher value on personal spiritual development
and that, on that account, are closer to his own system.[28]

That system is based on some interesting theological
premises.

I say "*Soul making*" Soul as distinguished from an Intelligence—There may be intelligences or sparks of the divinity in millions—but they are not Souls till they acquire
identities, till each one is personally itself. Intelligences
are atoms of perception—they know and they see and
they are pure, in short they are God—how then are Souls
to be made? How then are these sparks which are God
to have identity given them—so as ever to possess a bliss
peculiar to each ones individual existence? How, but by
the medium of a world like this? (II, 102)

Keats's concern with the question of "identity" can be better understood in the context of a dispute that occupied
religious thinkers during the eighteenth century. The question had been raised: what is it that constitutes a man's

[27] See, for instance, Butler, *Works*, II, 181, 273.
[28] D. G. James, in *Scepticism and Poetry* (1937; rpr. New York:
Barnes & Noble, 1960, p. 202), calls Keats's system "virtually a
statement of the true Christian view." This seems to me an over-
statement. A system that so totally disregards the importance of
Jesus Christ can hardly be called Christian in any meaningful sense.

continuing identity; what is there about him that allows us to say he is the same person now that he was twenty years ago? It is not the body, since (it was thought) the flesh is completely replaced every seven years. It is not, as some suggested, self-consciousness, since an infant or a man asleep is not conscious and yet has an identity. The discussion was not purely academic: it was intimately involved with the question of immortality. If a man could not be sure he would possess the same identity after death, he would have little motivation to discipline himself in this life to gain a reward in the next. Bishop Butler refers to this problem in his essay on "Personal Identity": "Whether we are to live in a future state, as it is the most important question which can possibly be asked, so it is the most intelligible one which can be expressed in language. Yet strange perplexities have been raised about the meaning of that identity or sameness of person, which is implied in the notion of our living now and hereafter, or in any two successive moments."[29]

If individual identity is to survive the death of the body, the principle of identity must be located in the soul. This is where Butler placed it, and Benjamin Bailey shared his view. "Man was formed out of the earth and he returns to it; and his bones are reconverted into that soil which sustains his progeny. His 'spirit returns unto God who gave it.' Thus our very bodies are by a wonderful dispensation made a part of our sustenance through continual change;— and we have not at this moment one particle of the same matter we had at our first formation. Our only identity, therefore, is our soul; our only existence, our moral being."[30] From this thoroughly orthodox association of identity with the soul, Keats draws a rather unorthodox conclusion: that the soul does not come into being when the body

[29] *Works*, II, 279.

[30] *A Discourse Inscribed to the Memory of the Princess Charlotte Augusta*, p. 44. Bailey's idea that man's "bones are reconverted into that soil which sustains his progeny" may have inspired Keats's reference, in the "Ode to a Nightingale," to hungry generations treading down the sod that once was the poet's body.

does, but only when the human being achieves his unique personal identity. It is doubtful that Bailey could have agreed with Keats in this opinion, but Leigh Hunt did. Three months later (July, 1819), in a letter of condolence to Shelley on the death of his son, Hunt wrote: "I do not know that a soul is born with us; but we seem, to me to *attain* to a soul, some later, some earlier; and when we have got that, there is a look in our eye, a sympathy in our cheerfulness, and a yearning and grave beauty in our thoughtfulness that seems to say, 'Our mortal dress may fall off when it will; our trunk and our leaves may go; we have shot up our blossom into an immortal air.' "[31]

The conception of God on which Keats bases his new system is rather surprising. In the past, in the few instances when he spoke in any direct way of the nature of God, his Divinity has sounded rather like the Great Artificer of natural religion, the "mighty providence" who cares for but remains essentially aloof from his creatures. Now we find him describing the Deity and his relationship with humanity in rather different terms—terms apparently derived from the Platonic tradition in theology. It may be that he is simply writing down for the first time opinions that he had entertained over a long period. There is evidence that these ideas were commonplaces within his circle of friends.[32] But one cannot rule out the possibility that they resulted from a recent, specific intellectual influence.

[31] *The Correspondence of Leigh Hunt*, ed. Thornton Hunt (London: Smith, Elder & Co., 1862), I, 130.

[32] Bailey described God as "pure Mind" in *Discourse*, p. 48. Hunt, too, characterized the Deity as "a Divine Mind governing the universe" (*Religion of the Heart*, p. 99), and suggested that each man contains a "divine particle" (p. 82). Haydon likewise believed that geniuses possess a "spark" of the Divinity (*Diary*, II, 92). There is another passage in *The Religion of the Heart* which bears strong similarity to Keats's thought: "For though the mind of man is so constituted, that it cannot, without violence, but think its powers derived from a greater mind . . . yet our intellect is so poor a thing compared with our hearts, that it becomes ashamed of being appealed to in this excessive and final manner, as though it were the greatest and most heavenly faculty which God has given us" (p. 213f.).

Ten days earlier, while on an Easter Sunday walk, Keats met Samuel Taylor Coleridge for the first and last time. Among topics on which Coleridge discoursed during a long, slow perambulation were, as Keats listed them, "Metaphysics . . . First and second consciousness . . . so many metaphysicians from a want of smoking the second consciousness" (II, 88f.). It is probable that what Keats calls "first and second consciousness" was Coleridge's important distinction between reason and understanding (he blamed the proliferation of erroneous theologies and philosophies in his time on undiscriminating use of the understanding).[33] I think it possible that some of Coleridge's "metaphysical" remarks concerning reason ("first consciousness") left a lasting impression on his young companion. The relationship that Keats posits between human intelligences and the Divine Intelligence is not unlike the relationship the older man understood to exist between the individual human reason and Divine Reason: the first was seen as a mental analogue or counterpart of the second.[34] Moreover, Coleridge was willing to speculate that human creatures might enjoy some type of existence in God before their earthly conception, but insisted that these preexistent entities could not be considered fully human since they would lack the kind of individual identity that comes only during life on earth.[35]

Whenever or wherever he found them, Keats was interested in these doctrines primarily because they provided a foundation and gave a kind of theological legitimacy to the system that he was offering as an alternative to Christianity.

I think it a grander system of salvation than the chrystain religion—or rather it is a system of Spirit-creation—This is effected by three grand materials acting the one upon

[33] James D. Boulger, *Coleridge as Religious Thinker* (New Haven: Yale Univ. Press, 1961), pp. 8f.

[34] Walter Jackson Bate, *Coleridge* (New York: Macmillan, 1968), pp. 185f.

[35] Boulger, p. 230. See also *Collected Letters of S. T. Coleridge*, IV, 545.

THE VALE OF SOUL-MAKING

the other for a series of years—These three Materials are
the *Intelligence*—the *human heart* (as distinguished from
intelligence or Mind) and the *World* or *Elemental space*
suited for the proper action of *Mind and Heart* on each
other for the purpose of forming the *Soul* or *Intelligence
destined to possess the sense of Identity.* I can scarcely
express what I but dimly perceive—and yet I think I perceive it—that you may judge the more clearly I will put
it in the most homely form possible—I will call the *world*
a School instituted for the purpose of teaching little children to read—I will call the *human heart* the *horn Book*
used in that School—and I will call the *Child able to read,
the Soul* made from that *school* and its *hornbook.* Do you
not see how necessary a World of Pains and troubles is
to school an Intelligence and make it a soul? A Place
where the heart must feel and suffer in a thousand diverse ways! Not merely is the Heart a Hornbook, It is the
Minds Bible, it is the Minds experience, it is the teat from
which the Mind or intelligence sucks its identity—As
various as the Lives of Men are—so various become their
souls, and thus does God make individual beings, Souls,
Identical Souls of the sparks of his own essence. (II, 102f.)

The distinction between the heart and the mind as means
of discovering truth has been a constant element in Keats's
thought. In the letter to Bailey of November 22, 1817, he
grudgingly acknowledged that some truth might be discerned by reason but he made clear his own reliance on the
insights of the heart. Later on, with the "burden of the Mystery" beginning to weigh upon him, he came to see that extensive knowledge might be useful, but still doubted the
final worth and relevance of the discoveries of the intellect:
"When we come to human Life and the affections it is impossible how a parallel of breast and head can be drawn . . .
it is impossible to know how far knowlege will console us
for the death of a friend and the ill 'that flesh is heir to' "
(I, 277f.). Now, finally, he is able to draw the parallel. He

THE VALE OF SOUL-MAKING

still recognizes the heart's preeminence, but he understands that its relationship with the head is not a matter of conflict or rivalry. The intellect can and must increase in knowledge, but it acquires this knowledge only under the guidance and tutelage of the heart. This applies to all branches of knowledge, and certainly to religion. When Keats describes the heart as "the Minds Bible" he is succinctly reaffirming one of the central premises of his religious faith—that the heart is the best and most reliable source of revelation concerning God and his purposes. One thinks again here of Leigh Hunt and his preference of "Heart-Scripture" over the Bible of orthodoxy. Keats's debt to Hunt becomes even more apparent in the following passage from *The Religion of the Heart*: "The progress of the best and wisest in the love of God must be entirely that of children in the love of their mortal father; till having arrived at intellectual man's estate, and read thoroughly what has been written in their hearts, they learn to love him so well in what they know of his works, as to be prepared to know and to love him more and more, in new stages of existence."[36]

Ironically, it appears that Benjamin Bailey made another large contribution to the development of the system his friend adopted as a substitute for Christianity. When Keats likens the development of the soul to the education of a child, he seems to be building upon an idea Bailey used in his *Discourse Inscribed to the Memory of the Princess Charlotte Augusta*: "Life we should never consider or value but as the infancy of an eternal existence. The chastisement, therefore, which we adjudge requisite for that early stage of this existence, in order to the perfection of its more mature stage, is by a parallel way of reasoning necessary in this life to our purification for the next."[37] Bailey may have borrowed the idea from Butler's *Analogy of Religion*, where it appears as part of an attempt to explain "why we are placed in a state of so much affliction, hazard, and diffi-

[36] P. 58.   [37] P. 35.

culty."[38] In that attempt, Butler offered another possible explanation that also bears strong similarity to Keats's thought. One can only speculate on whether Bailey discussed the passage with his friend. "There is a third thing which may seem implied in the present world's being a state of probation; that it is a theatre of action for the manifestation of persons' characters with respect to a future one; not, to be sure, to an all-knowing Being, but to his creation or part of it . . . It is not impossible, that men's showing and making manifest what is in their heart, what their real character is, may have respect to a future life, in ways and manners which we are not acquainted with."[39] Even when direct lines of descent cannot be plotted, it is clear that Keats's system of soul-making developed out of a fairly old and well established theological tradition.

Having described his own alternative system in detail, Keats returns to his critique of Christianity.

This appears to me a faint sketch of a system of Salvation which does not affront our reason and humanity. . . . It is pretty generally suspected that the christian scheme has been coppied from the ancient persian and greek Philosophers. Why may they not have made this simple thing even more simple for common apprehension by introducing Mediators and Personages in the same manner as in the hethen mythology abstractions are personified—Seriously I think it probable that this System of Soul-making —may have been the Parent of all the more palpable and personal Schemes of Redemption, among the Zoroastrians the Christians and the Hindoos. For as one part of the human species must have their carved Jupiter; so another part must have the palpable and named Mediatior and saviour, their Christ their Oromanes and their Vishnu. (II, 103)

[38] *Works*, II, 77.   [39] *Ibid.*, p. 98.

In using comparative religion as the basis for an attack on Christianity, Keats is adopting an old strategy of eighteenth-century natural religionists. Voltaire, for example, delighted in pointing out that the really praiseworthy elements in Christianity were not devised by Christians at all, but were taken over from earlier traditions. Stuart Sperry has demonstrated convincingly that Voltaire is the likely source for much of Keats's knowledge of the subject—particularly Voltaire's *Essai sur les moeurs*, a copy of which was among Keats's books when he died. Sperry writes:

> What the earlier part of the *Essai* presents is, as much as anything, an elaborate study of the earliest religions which traces the growth and transmission of certain common practices and beliefs so as to suggest a pattern of evolutionary development culminating in Christianity. More specifically Keats would have found here general discussions of the religious beliefs of the ancient Persians and the Greek sects, as well as particular accounts of the Hindu Brahmans and the Zoroastrians, including references to Vishnu and something very close to "Oromanes." . . . In the *Essai* Voltaire pays lip-service to the truth of divine revelation, but the historical perspective through which he compares the development of earlier religions continually emphasizes the derivative nature of Christianity and diminishes its authority.[40]

Sperry believes that Keats's venture into comparative religion reveals his primary objection to Christianity. "He cannot embrace it because he sees it as derivative—partly from earlier religions and partly from the needs of its adherents—and therefore a half-truth."[41] Commenting on the same passage, Roger Lloyd drew somewhat different conclusions. "He would have no religion which in any way separated him from the rest of mankind, and he would have only the God who is worshipped by all religions alike. To

40 "Keats's Skepticism and Voltaire," pp. 87, 89.
41 *Ibid.*, p. 86.

find Him, the basic God, he must go deeper than any manifestation of Him which appeals to any exclusive religion, for such a religion, by its very partiality, can apprehend God only in part."[42] Both of these opinions have some validity. Keats certainly subscribed to the basic principle of natural religion that there was one authentic form of faith prescribed by the Creator for all men and that most traditional religious systems were either unnecessary complications or superstitious corruptions of that original simple faith. He, like many before him, found it hard to believe that the Supreme Being chose an obscure Semitic people to be the recipients of a special revelation and the purveyors of salvation to the world. But Keats had held views like these for a long time before April, 1819, and I doubt that they provided the particular impetus behind the creation of his new system. He saw the simplicity and universality of that system as added proofs of its validity, but they were not central in his mind.

If there was one particular aspect of Christianity that made Keats feel the need for an alternative, it was probably the one he refers to so impatiently at the very beginning— the Christian response to earthly suffering. This problem of suffering had been troubling Keats for more than a year. During that time he had been continually challenged by the claim of Christianity (advanced by both Bailey and Haydon) that it alone could provide a satisfactory explanation and a measure of consolation for the existence of evil in the world. Now at last he had come to understand that what Christianity offered was not a solution but an evasion of the problem. Unwilling to face the fact that God created man to suffer, Christians blamed the human condition on a human sin and then invented an arbitrary divine interposition to effect man's salvation. Having irreparably fouled his own nest, man's only hope is that he will be taken one day to a better world. It is this desire to flee from the reality of the

[42] "Keats and the Limitations of Pantheism," *Quarterly Review*, 290 (1952), 258.

world rather than come to grips with it that Keats saw as little, circumscribed, and an affront to our humanity.

His own system, involving salvation through adversity rather than from it, is based on a more flattering view of human potential. Man is not the victim of his own stupidity nor a supine petitioner for release from its consequences. He works out his own salvation by coming to terms with his natural condition. The system also implies a new outlook on the nature of the world. Accepting the fact that "the World is full of Misery and Heartbreak, Pain, Sickness and oppression" (I, 281), Keats insists that God intended it to be so. Therefore, even though suffering is woven into the very fabric of creation, that creation must be seen as essentially good—and essentially beautiful. Perhaps this insight contributed to the philosophy that is concentrated in the words of the Grecian Urn: "Beauty is truth, truth beauty—that is all/Ye know on earth, and all ye need to know."

Keats was proud of his new system—proud enough to claim "seriously" that he had discovered the foundation upon which the great world religions were constructed. But he does not seem to have quite realized that what he had discovered was only a foundation and not actually a religion in itself. It could not, for instance, seriously be considered a substitute for Christianity. It offered nothing to match the scriptures, the liturgy, the doctrinal system, the hagiology, the history and traditions of the Christian faith. Religion is rather more than a "system of salvation": it is a way of life, offering encouragement to the spirit and nourishment to the imagination. If Keats desired only some type of justification for earthly suffering, his system provided it. Beyond this, the theory of "soul-making" did little to make his own brand of natural religion a more satisfying faith to live by.

Even as an approach to the problem of suffering, the system had a serious flaw. It rested upon a premise that was not a matter of absolute certainty for Keats. At the very start of his discussion, he qualifies all that is to come after by saying, "I am speaking now in the highest terms for human nature admitting it to be immortal which I will here take for granted." Without a belief in immortality "soul-making" is pointless: it is only from the perspective of eternity that the sufferings of an earthly existence can be judged as finally purposeful or beneficial. Keats seems fairly confident about immortality at this time, but doubts had troubled him before and they would become even stronger as his life drew to a close.

But a man of twenty-three who is not face to face with death can afford to leave the question of immortality open; one does not have to settle all metaphysical problems at once. The insights contained in the "Soul-making" discourse enabled Keats to resolve what had been his most serious religious dilemma—the problem of suffering—and with that resolution he seems to have regained a measure of spiritual serenity. The quality of that new inner peace, which apparently endured for several months, comes across most clearly in the letters Keats wrote in the fall of 1819. That is the season, of course, that inspired the ode "To Autumn," and the poem itself, with its quiet acceptance of change and death as inseparable from earthly life, is a reflection of his mood. The letters show us a man in love with the world, filled with a renewed delight in men and things. "I never liked stubble fields so much . . . O how I admire the middle siz'd Devonshire girls of about 15 . . . How glorious the Blacksmith's shops look now!" (II, 167ff.) He has found a new contentment within himself: "It strikes me tonight that I have led a very odd sort of life for the two or three last years—Here & there—No anchor—I am glad of it . . . I have lately shirk'd some friends of ours, and I advise you to do the same, I mean the blue devils—I am never at home to them"; "I am as far from being unhappy as possible" (II, 167f., 181).

He is nearly as far from being unhappy as he was in the

winter of 1817–1818, that carefree time when he felt "capable of being in uncertainties, Mysteries, doubts, without any irritable reaching after fact & reason." I do not think it entirely coincidental that now the Negative Capability mood returns. Once again, Charles Wentworth Dilke is the subject of his remarks. Dilke is a man, Keats says, "who cannot feel he has a personal identity unless he has made up his Mind about every thing. The only means of strengthening one's intellect is to make up ones mind about nothing—to let the mind be a thoroughfare for all thoughts. Not a select party . . . Dilke will never come at a truth as long as he lives, because he is always trying at it" (II, 213). Keats has come a long way since that dark night in March when, in an agony of ignorance, he questioned Heaven and Hell and Heart in vain. But that experience and the circumstances that produced it have left their trace. For although his present mood resembles that of early 1818 in many ways, one element has changed—his attitude toward orthodox religion.

On September 18, Keats decided to transcribe and send to America part of the journal letter he had written to Tom from Scotland during the summer of 1818. As he was copying a description of the island of Iona, he made at one point an interesting change in the text. The original 1818 letter read: "The Beginning of these things was in the sixth Century under the superstition of a would-be Bishop-saint" (I, 347). Now he wrote simply "under the Chaperonage of a Bishop-saint" (II, 197). The petty prejudice is gone. This does not mean that Keats was any more willing to accept the validity of the Christian faith than he was a year earlier. But perhaps he was more willing to understand and appreciate the honest efforts of religious men to lighten the burden of the Mystery, having felt that burden at its heaviest, and having discovered that answers and solutions are painfully hard to find. It seems that now he has given up the struggle and retired from the arena of religious speculation, making another try at remaining content with limited knowledge. Knowledge was not, after all, necessary for faith, and Keats's belief in God seems, if anything, more steady now than it ever was before. In a mood of autumnal serenity, he could look toward an uncertain future and say, "The whole is with Providence" (II, 211).

The serenity did not last: mortal illness and an obsessive passion combined to destroy his equanimity and unbalance his mind. We know almost nothing of Keats's thoughts on religion during the period of decline leading to his death. For a variety of reasons, he stopped writing the kind of long, thoughtful letter on which this study has depended for most of its evidence. Only at the very end of his life is it possible again to get anything like a clear idea of his religious dispositions, and their character, like their context, is so special that they must be treated separately.

The Last Days

"MISERABLE wretch I am—this last cheap comfort—
which every rogue and fool have—is deny'd me in
my last moments—why is this—O! I have serv'd every one
with my utmost good—yet why is this—I cannot understand this." That anguished cry, we are told, broke from the
lips of John Keats one month before his death on February 23, 1821; it was the cry of a man in spiritual despair.
The religious equilibrium that he had achieved with such
effort in 1819 had apparently broken down completely
under the onslaught of disease. As his companion Joseph
Severn described his state, "This noble fellow lying on the
bed—is dying in horror—no kind hope smoothing down his
suffering—no philosophy—no religion to support him—yet
with all the most knawing desire for it—yet without the
possibility of receiving it" (*Letters*, II, 368). Severn's impression is confirmed in the more dispassionate account of
Dr. James Clark, Keats's physician in Rome: "He has no religion—he has been robbed of that—& philosophy I fear is
seldom sufficient to produce tranquillity of mind under
such sad circumstances as he is placed—his certainly is not
sufficient."[1]

To say that Keats was without religion does not mean
that he no longer believed in a Supreme Being: it seems
that he held on to that faith until the very end. What Severn
and Clark appear to have meant by "religion" was a confident belief in an afterlife—a "kind hope" that would enable him to see his sufferings in an eternal perspective.
Leigh Hunt, who had cared for Keats during his last
months in England, sensed that this was the source of his
friend's mental anguish. He wrote to Severn: "Tell him . . .

[1] *KC*, I, 194.

that, Christian or Infidel, the most sceptical of us has faith
enough in the high things that nature puts into our heads
to think all who are of one accord in mind or heart are jour-
neying to one and the same place, and shall unite some-
where or other again, face to face, mutually conscious, mutually delighted. Tell him he is only before us on the road,
as he was in everything else."[2] In December 1818, Keats had
seemed fairly certain about immortality "of some nature or
other," but, only five months later, among the otherwise
confident assertions concerning "soul-making," doubts were
already creeping in. By 1820 his belief had diminished into
a desire for belief, inspired primarily by his love for Fanny
Brawne. He wrote to her: "I long to believe in immortality.
I shall never be able to bid you an entire farewell. If I am
destined to be happy with you here—how short is the long-
est Life—I wish to believe in immortality—I wish to live
with you forever" (II, 293). Later that year, he expressed
similar sentiments to Charles Brown: "The thought of leaving Miss Brawne is beyond every thing horrible—the sense
of darkness coming over me—I eternally see her figure
eternally vanishing. Some of the phrases she was in the
habit of using during my last nursing at Wentworth Place
ring in my ears—Is there another Life? Shall I awake and
find all this a dream? There must be we cannot be created
for this sort of suffering" (II, 345f.).

The remark, "We cannot be created for this sort of suffering," shows that the problem of evil was still on Keats's
mind. If God has allowed such suffering to exist, he once
believed, it must exist for some good purpose that will become clear in the hereafter. As long as he could hold on to
the belief that a benevolent Deity controlled our destiny,
he could remain confident that, despite present appear-
ances, all would be well in the end. But while he lay dying
in Rome a thought came to undermine even that last, essential hope. Perhaps our sufferings are not ordained by God

[2] Quoted by William Sharp, *The Life and Letters of Joseph Severn*
(New York: Scribner, 1892), p. 87.

(213)

for a good purpose; perhaps they have nothing to do with God at all. "I think a malignant being must have power over us—over whom the Almighty has little or no control."[3] Human suffering, then, is simply the product of gratuitous cruelty, having no meaning and bearing no fruit in eternity.

It was a horrible thought and, as Severn realized, the product of a morbid fancy. "The want of some kind faith to feed his voracious imagination leaves him to the wreck of ideas without purpose—imagination without philosophy."[4] Keats had long been afraid of "imagination brought beyond its proper bound"; he knew that his speculations needed an anchor of some sort, and he was aware that there was one available to him should he choose to grasp it. "You know Severn I cannot believe in your book—the Bible—but I feel the horrible want of some faith—some hope—something to rest on now—their must be such a book—and I know that is it—but I can't believe it—I am destined to every torment in this world—even to this little comfort on my death bed."[5] Severn was more than willing to share his own "kind faith" with Keats, but he was sensitive enough to realize that the matter had to be handled delicately. "I dont for a moment push my little but honest Religious faith upon poor Keats . . . I fall into his views sometimes to quiet him and tincture them with a somewhat of my own."[6] Actually it was less by word than by example—the quiet, diligent manner in which he performed his duties as nurse and companion—that Severn succeeded in impressing Keats with the quality of his faith. He recalled one incident in particular:

I had made him some coffee, and he threw it away. I then made some more, and he threw that away also. But when I cheerfully made it a third time, he was deeply affected, and confessed "that he had no agony but what he felt for me," and that he was sure my endurance of his "savageness" arose from my long prayers on his behalf and from

[3] KC, I, 181.   [4] Ibid.   [5] Ibid.   [6] Ibid.

my patient devotion to him. "Severn," he said to me one day, "I now understand how you can bear all this—'tis your Christian faith; and here am I, with desperation in death that would disgrace the commonest fellow! How I should like it if it were possible to get me some of Jeremy Taylor's works for you to read to me, and I should gain consolation, for I have always been a great admirer of this devout author."[7]

The reminiscences Severn wrote later in his life cannot be trusted completely, but Keats's desire to have Jeremy Taylor read to him is noted in contemporary letters as well. His choice of the seventeenth-century divine is not surprising. He was Bailey's favorite spiritual writer and was admired by Hunt and Hazlitt as well. Hazlitt may have put his finger on the nature of Taylor's appeal for Keats when he said: "His writings are more like fine poetry than any other prose whatever."[8] Fortunately Dr. Clark was able to procure a copy of Taylor's *Holy Living and Dying*, and during the last weeks Severn read from it to Keats every day. He believed that these readings worked a change in his dying friend; he thought he could see a new tranquillity coming over him. In later years, when he looked back upon these scenes, he liked to think that Keats finally accepted the Christian faith: "Thus he gained strength of mind from day to day just in proportion as his poor body grew weaker and weaker. At last I had the consolation of finding him calm, trusting, and more prepared for his end than I was. . . . In all he then uttered he breathed a simple Christian spirit; indeed I always think that he died a Christian, that 'Mercy' was trembling on his dying lips and that his tortured soul was received by those Blessed Hands which alone could welcome it."[9]

[7] Sharp, p. 85.
[8] *Complete Works of William Hazlitt*, ed. P. P. Howe (London: Dent, 1930-34), VI, 342.
[9] "The Vicissitudes of Keats's Fame," *Atlantic Monthly*, 11 (1863), 403.

These impressions, recorded in 1863, were colored, no doubt, by time and pious sentiment. Severn's letters from Rome in the winter if 1820–1821 give no clear indication that Keats ever became more disposed to accept Christianity. The poet had friends in England who would have rejoiced at such news,[10] and one suspects that if Severn could have provided it he would have done so. There is, however, some evidence that in the last weeks of his life Keats did come to accept his condition and his fate with greater serenity. Severn wrote to Charles Brown on February 8: "He is very calm. He is more and more reconciled to his horrible misfortunes."[11] Six days later the letter continued: "Little or no change has taken place since the commencement of this,—except this beautiful one, that his mind is growing to great quietness and peace. I find this change hath its rise from the encreasing weakness of his body; but it seems like a delightful sleep to me." It is possible that this new tranquillity had something to do with a change in religious disposition (Severn would have been reluctant to mention the matter to Brown, who was extremely critical of Christianity), but the contemporary evidence is lacking. H. N. Fairchild thought that "anything like a deathbed conversion" was "utterly foreign to Keats's nature."[12] In fact, so little is known about what Keats's nature had become in the last days of his life that one can not make any such statement with assurance. Apparently he died thanking God for his death,[13] but his innermost thoughts of and expectations

[10] Keats's publisher, James Augustus Hessey, was one of them. He wrote to Severn in Rome: "I have always, even when I have heard poor Keats utter the most extraordinary and revolting opinions, had hopes of him—I always trusted that he would think & feel differently, and I cannot but still encourage the hope that you may have witnessed the change in his Sentiments, and seen its happy effect on his feelings." *More Letters and Poems of the Keats Circle*, ed. H. E. Rollins (Cambridge, Mass.: Harvard Univ. Press, 1965), p. 117.

[11] *KC*, II, 91.

[12] *Religious Trends in English Poetry* (New York: Columbia University Press), vol. III (1949), p. 501.

[13] *KC*, II, 94.

of that God are as hidden from us as they probably were from Severn himself.

To the Church of England, which still recognized him as a member, such considerations were no longer a matter of concern; only the suicide and the excommunicate were excluded from her final blessing. Probably at Severn's request, the English chaplain at Rome, the Reverend Mr. Wolff, officiated at Keats's funeral service.[14] And so it was that the Church that had once welcomed him into the world now presided over his departure from it. Much of what was said at the service was not especially relevant to the life and accomplishments of John Keats, or concordant with the religious faith he had adopted for himself. But to those who were present, some of the words must have seemed poignantly appropriate: "Man that is born of a woman hath but a short time to live, and is full of misery. He cometh up, and is cut down, like a flower."

[14] *Ibid.,* I, 227.

Bibliography

Abernethy, John. *Physiological Lectures, Exhibiting a General View of Mr. Hunter's Physiology and of his Researches in Comparative Anatomy; Delivered before the Royal College of Surgeons in the Year 1817.* 2nd ed. London: Longmans, 1822.

Adami, Marie. *Fanny Keats.* London: Murray, 1937.

Altick, Richard. *The Cowden Clarkes.* London: Oxford University Press, 1948.

Bailey, Benjamin. *A Discourse Inscribed to the Memory of the Princess Charlotte Augusta,* by an Undergraduate of the University of Oxford. London: Taylor and Hessey, 1817.

——. "An Essay on the Moral Principle." Bailey Scrapbook, Keats Collection, Houghton Library, Harvard University.

Baker, Herschel. *William Hazlitt.* Cambridge, Mass.: Harvard University Press, 1962.

Balleine, George R. *Past Finding Out: The Tragic Story of Joanna Southcott and Her Successors.* London: S.P.C.K., 1956.

Barrell, Joseph. *Shelley and the Thought of His Time: A Study in the History of Ideas.* New Haven: Yale University Press, 1947.

Bate, Walter Jackson. *Coleridge.* New York: Macmillan, 1968.

——. *John Keats.* Cambridge, Mass.: Harvard University Press, 1963.

Boas, George. *French Philosophies of the Romantic Period.* New York: Russell & Russell, 1964.

The Book of Common Prayer and Administration of the Sacraments and other Rites and Ceremonies of the Church, according to the Use of the Church of En-

gland; together with the Psalter or Psalms of David, pointed as they are to be sung or said in Churches. Oxford: Clarendon Press, 1803.

Boulger, James D. *Coleridge as Religious Thinker.* New Haven: Yale University Press, 1961.

Briggs, Asa. *The Age of Improvement, 1783–1867.* 1959; rpt. New York: McKay, 1962.

Brilioth, Yngve. *The Anglican Revival.* London: Longmans, 1933.

Brown, C. K. Francis. *A History of the English Clergy, 1800–1900.* London: Faith Press, 1953.

Brown, Charles Armitage. *The Letters of Charles Armitage Brown,* ed. Jack Stillinger. Cambridge, Mass.: Harvard University Press, 1966.

Buck, Albert H. *The Dawn of Modern Medicine.* New Haven: Yale University Press, 1920.

Bullock, F. W. B. *A History of Training for the Ministry of the Church of England in England and Wales from 1800 to 1874.* St. Leonard's-on-Sea: Budd & Gillat, 1955.

Burnet, Gilbert. *History of His Own Time,* ed. Martin Joseph Routh. Oxford: Clarendon Press, 1833.

Butler, Joseph. *The Works of Bishop Butler,* ed. J. H. Bernard. 2 vols. London: Macmillan, 1900.

Byron, George Gordon, Lord. *The Works of Lord Byron, Letters and Journals,* ed. Rowland E. Prothero. London: Murray, 1898–1901; rpt. New York: Octagon Books, 1966.

Caldwell, James Ralston. *John Keats' Fancy: The Effect on Keats of the Psychology of His Day.* 1945; rpr. New York: Octagon Books, 1965.

Carpenter, S. C. *Church and People, 1789–1889.* London: S.P.C.K., 1933.

Clarke, Charles Cowden. *Recollections of Writers.* 1878; facs, rpr. Fontwell, Sussex; Centaur Press, 1969.

Clarke, Mary Cowden. *My Long Life.* New York: Dodd, Mead & Co., 1896.

BIBLIOGRAPHY

Coleridge, Samuel Taylor. *Biographia Literaria*, ed. George Watson. New York: Dutton, 1956; rpr. 1962.
——. *Collected Letters of Samuel Taylor Coleridge*, ed. Earl Leslie Griggs. 6 vols. Oxford: Clarendon Press, 1956–1971.
——. *The Collected Works of Samuel Taylor Coleridge*. Volume 6: *Lay Sermons*, ed. R. J. White. Princeton: Princeton University Press, 1972.
——. *The Poems of Samuel Taylor Coleridge*, ed. Ernest Hartley Coleridge. London: Oxford University Press, 1912; rpr. 1961.
Colvin, Sidney. *John Keats: His Life and Poetry, His Friends, Critics, and After-Fame*. London: Macmillan, 1920.
The Constitutions and Canons of the Church of England. Oxford: Clarendon Press, 1825.
Cooper, Bransby Blake. *The Life of Sir Astley Cooper, bart.* 2 vols. London: Parker, 1843.
Cox, J. Charles. *The Parish Registers of England*. London: Methuen, 1910.
Cragg, Gerald R. *The Church and the Age of Reason, 1648–1789*. Baltimore: Penguin Books, 1966.
Elliott-Binns, L. E. *The Evangelical Movement in the English Church*. London: Methuen, 1928.
——. *Religion in the Victorian Era*. London: Lutterworth Press, 1936.
Evert, Walter H. *Aesthetic and Myth in the Poetry of Keats*. Princeton: Princeton University Press, 1965.
The Examiner: A Weekly Paper on Politics, Literature, Music and the Fine Arts. London, 1808–1881.
Fairchild, Hoxie Neale. *Religious Trends in English Poetry*. Volume 3: *1780–1830, Romantic Faith*. New York: Columbia University Press, 1949; rpr, 1956.
Finney, Claude Lee. *The Evolution of Keats's Poetry*. 2 vols. Cambridge, Mass.: Harvard University Press, 1936.
Ford, Newell F. *The Prefigurative Imagination of John Keats*. 1951; rpr. Hamden, Conn.: Archon Books, 1966.

(221)

Froude, James Anthony. *Short Studies on Great Subjects.* Fourth Series. New York: Scribner, 1883.

Gaudin, Albert Charles. *The Educational Views of Charles Rollin.* New York: Columbia University Press, 1939.

Gittings, Robert. *John Keats.* London: Heinemann, 1968.

Gittings, Robert. *John Keats: The Living Year, 21 September 1818 to 21 September 1819.* London: Heinemann, 1954.

Grean, Stanley. *Shaftesbury's Philosophy of Religion and Ethics: A Study in Enthusiasm.* Athens, Ohio: Ohio University Press, 1967.

Halévy, Elie. *The Growth of Philosophic Radicalism,* trans. M. Morris. 1900; new ed., 1949; rpr. Boston: Beacon, 1955.

———. *A History of the English People in 1815,* trans. E. I. Watkin. 2nd rev. ed., New York: Smith, 1949.

Halpern, Martin. "Keats and the 'Spirit that Laughest.'" *Keats-Shelley Journal,* 15 (1966), 69-86.

Hampson, Norman. *A Cultural History of the Enlightenment.* New York: Pantheon Books, 1968.

Hans, Nicholas. *New Trends in Education in the Eighteenth Century.* London: Routledge & Kegan Paul, 1951.

Hanson, Lawrence. *The Life of S. T. Coleridge: The Early Years.* London: G. Allen, 1938.

Haydon, Benjamin Robert. *The Autobiography and Memoirs of Benjamin Robert Haydon,* ed. Tom Taylor. 2 vols. London: Davies, 1926.

———. *The Diary of Benjamin Robert Haydon,* ed. Willard B. Pope. 5 vols. Cambridge, Mass.: Harvard University Press, 1960-1963.

———. *The Life, Letters, and Table Talk of Benjamin Robert Haydon,* ed., Richard Henry Stoddard, New York: Scribner, 1876.

Haynes, Jean. "John Jennings: Keats's Grandfather," *Keats-Shelley Memorial Bulletin,* 13 (1962), 18-23.

Hazlitt, William. *Complete Works of William Hazlitt,* ed. P. P. Howe, 21 vols. London: Dent, 1930-1934.

BIBLIOGRAPHY

Hill, G. Birkbeck, ed. *Johnsonian Miscellanies*. 2 vols. Oxford: Clarendon Press, 1897.
Hinckley, Edward B. "On First Looking into Swedenborg's Philosophy." *Keats-Shelley Journal*, 9 (1960), 15-25.
Hodgson, Robert. *The Life of Bishop Porteus*. London: Cadell, 1823.
Horne, Thomas. *Deism Refuted, or Plain Reasons for Being a Christian*. London, 1819; rpr. Philadelphia: Littell & Henry, 1820.
Hunt, James Henry Leigh. *The Autobiography of Leigh Hunt*, ed. J. E. Morpurgo. London: Cresset Press, 1948.
———. *The Correspondence of Leigh Hunt*, ed. Thornton Hunt. 2 vols. London: Smith, Elder & Co., 1862.
———. *The Indicator and the Companion*. London: Bentley, 1834.
———. *The Poetical Works of Leigh Hunt*, ed. H. S. Milford. London: Oxford University Press, 1923.
———. *The Religion of the Heart*. London: Chapman, 1853.
Hutcheson, Francis. *Collected Works of Francis Hutcheson*. 7 vols. 1756; facs. rpr. Hildesheim, Germany: Georg Olms, 1971.
———. *Illustrations on the Moral Sense*, ed. Bernard Peach. Cambridge, Mass.: Belknap Press of Harvard University Press, 1971.
James, D. G. *The Romantic Comedy*. New York: Oxford University Press, 1948.
———. *Scepticism and Poetry: An Essay on the Poetic Imagination*. 1937; rpr. New York: Barnes & Noble, 1960.
Jarvis, William A. "A Cousin of John Keats." *Keats-Shelley Memorial Bulletin*, 14 (1963), 37-42.
Jeffrey, Lloyd N. "Keats and the Bible." *Keats-Shelley Journal*, 10 (1961), 59-70.
Jenyns, Soame. *The Works of Soame Jenyns*. 4 vols. 2nd ed. London: Cadell, 1793.
Kaufman, Paul. "The Leigh-Browne Collection at the Keats Museum." *The Library*, Fifth Series, 17 (1962), 246-50.

Keats, John. *The Complete Works of John Keats*, ed. H. B. Forman, 5 vols. Glasgow: Gowers and Gray, 1901.

——. *John Keats's Anatomical and Physiological Note Book*, ed. M. B. Forman. London: Oxford University Press, 1934.

——. *The Letters of John Keats*, ed. H. E. Rollins. 2 vols. Cambridge, Mass.: Harvard University Press, 1958.

——. *The Poetical Works of John Keats*, ed. H. W. Garrod. Oxford: Clarendon Press, 1958.

Lamb, Charles. *The Letters of Charles Lamb*, ed. Alfred Ainger. 2 vols. London: Macmillan, 1904.

Landré, Louis. *Leigh Hunt (1784–1859): Contribution à l'Histoire du Romantisme Anglais.* 2 vols. Paris: Société d'Édition "Les Belles Lettres, " 1935–1936.

Lawrence, William. *An Introduction to Comparative Anatomy and Physiology: Being the Two Introductory Lectures Delivered at the Royal College of Surgeons, on the 21st and 25th of March, 1816.* London: Callow, 1816.

——. *Lectures on Physiology, Zoology, and the Natural History of Man, Delivered at the Royal College of Surgeons.* London: Benbow, 1822.

Legg, J. Wickham. *English Church Life from the Restoration to the Tractarian Movement.* London: Longmans, 1914.

Lloyd, Roger. "Keats and the Limitations of Pantheism." *Quarterly Review*, 190 (1952), 252-61.

Lowell, Amy. *John Keats.* 2 vols. Boston: Houghton Mifflin, 1925.

Lucas, E. V. *The Life of Charles Lamb.* 2 vols. 5th ed., rev. London: Methuen, 1921.

Mabbott, T. O. "Haydon's Letter Arranging for Keats to Meet Wordsworth." *Notes & Queries*, 186 (1941), 328f.

Macilwain, George. *Memoirs of John Abernethy F.R.S., with a View of his Lectures, Writings, and Character.* New York: Harper, 1853.

Mathieson, William Law. *England in Transition, 1789–1832.* London: Longmans, 1920.

——. *English Church Reform, 1815–1840.* London: Longmans, 1923.

Miller, Bruce E. "Keats and 'Adam's Dream.'" *Notes & Queries,* 209 (1964), 423.

Milner, Joseph. *The History of the Church of Christ.* 5 vols. London, 1794–1809; rpr. Philadelphia: Hogan and Thomson, 1835.

Moore, Thomas. *The Letters of Thomas Moore,* ed. Wilfred S. Dowden. 2 vols. Oxford: Clarendon Press, 1964.

More, Hannah. *The Works of Hannah More.* 5 vols. London: Fisher, 1834–1835.

Mossner, Ernest Campbell. *Bishop Butler and the Age of Reason.* New York: Macmillan, 1936.

Murchie, Guy. *The Spirit of Place in Keats.* London: Newman Neame, 1955.

Murry, John Middleton. *Keats.* London: Cape, 1955.

——. *Keats and Shakespeare: A Study of Keats' Poetic Life from 1816 to 1820.* London: Oxford University Press, 1925; rpr. 1949.

Newman, John Henry. *Apologia Pro Vita Sua,* ed. Charles F. Harrold. New York: Longmans, 1947.

Ollard, S. L. "Confirmation in the Anglican Communion," *Confirmation or the Laying on of Hands.* London: S.P.C.K., 1926.

Overton, John Henry. *The English Church in the Nineteenth Century (1800–1833).* London: Longmans, 1894.

Pettet, E. C. *On the Poetry of Keats.* Cambridge: Cambridge University Press, 1957.

Pope, Alexander. *The Poems of Alexander Pope,* ed. John Butt. New Haven: Yale University Press, 1963.

Pope, Willard B. "Studies on the Keats Circle." Unpublished dissertation: Harvard University, 1932.

Priestley, Joseph. *A Catechism for Children and Young Persons.* 4th ed. London: J. Johnson, 1781.

Priestley, Joseph. *Miscellaneous Observations Relating to Education.* London: J. Johnson, 1788.

Quinlan, Maurice. *Victorian Prelude: A History of English Manners, 1700–1830.* 1941; rpr. Hamden, Conn.: Archon Books, 1965.

Rennell, Thomas. *Remarks on Skepticism, Especially as it is Connected with Organization and Life: Being an Answer to the Views of M. Bichat, Sir T. C. Morgan, and Mr. Lawrence, upon these Points.* London: Rivington, 1819.

——. Review of "Lawrence's Introductory Lectures." *British Critic*, 8 (July, 1817), 63ff.

Reynolds, John Hamilton. "On the Opening of the Ports of St. Paul's Cathedral." *New Monthly Magazine*, 79 (1847), 162ff.

——. *Selected Prose of John Hamilton Reynolds*, ed. Leonidas M. Jones. Cambridge, Mass.: Harvard University Press, 1966.

——. Review: "Warner's Church of England Theology, a Series of Ten Sermons." *London Magazine*, 4 (1821), 516ff.

Richardson, Joanna. *The Everlasting Spell: A Study of Keats and His Friends.* London: Cape, 1963.

——. "New Light on Mr. Abbey." *Keats-Shelley Memorial Bulletin*, 5 (1953), 26-31.

Robinson, W. *The History and Antiquities of Enfield.* 2 vols. London: Nichols, 1823.

Rollins, Hyder Edward, ed. *The Keats Circle: Letters and Papers, 1816–1878.* 2 vols. Cambridge, Mass.: Harvard University Press, 1965.

——. *More Letters and Poems of the Keats Circle.* Cambridge, Mass.: Harvard University Press, 1955.

Rosen, George. "The Philosophy of Ideology and the Emergence of Modern Medicine in France." *Bulletin of the History of Medicine*, 20 (1946), 329-39.

Rousseau, Jean Jacques. *Emile, or Education*, trans. Barbara Foxley. London: Dent, 1911.

Ryland, John Collet. *The Character of the Reverend James Hervey M.A.* London: Robarts, 1791.

———. *Contemplations on the Divinity of Christ.* 3 vols. Northampton: Dicey, 1782.

———. *A Key to the Greek New Testament.* London: Keith, 1777.

Schneider, Elizabeth. *The Aesthetics of William Hazlitt: A Study of the Philosophical Basis of His Criticism.* Philadelphia: University of Pennsylvania Press, 1933.

Severn, Joseph. "The Vicissitudes of Keats's Fame." *Atlantic Monthly*, 11 (1863), 401-7.

Shaftesbury, Anthony, Lord. *Characteristics of Men, Manners, Opinions, Times*, ed. John M. Robertson. New York: Bobbs-Merrill, 1964.

Sharp, William. *The Life and Letters of Joseph Severn.* New York: Scribner, 1892.

Shelley, Percy Bysshe. *The Complete Poetical Works of Percy Bysshe Shelley*, ed. Thomas Hutchinson. London: Oxford University Press, 1943; rpr. 1960.

Shryock, Richard Harrison. *The Development of Modern Medicine.* New York: Knopf, 1947.

Sperry, Stuart M. *Keats the Poet.* Princeton: Princeton University Press, 1973.

———. "Keats's Skepticism and Voltaire." *Keats-Shelley Journal*, 12 (1963), 75-93.

Stillinger, Jack. *The Hoodwinking of Madeline, And Other Essays on Keats's Poems.* Chicago: University of Illinois Press, 1971.

———. *The Texts of Keats's Poems.* Cambridge, Mass.: Harvard University Press, 1974.

Sykes, Norman. *Church and State in England in the XVIIIth Century.* Cambridge: Cambridge University Press, 1934.

BIBLIOGRAPHY

Taylor, Jane and Ann. *Original Poems for Infant Minds*, by Several Young Persons. Boston: House, 1808.

Thistlethwayte, F. *Memoirs and Correspondence of Dr. Henry Bathurst, Lord Bishop of Norwich*. London: Bentley, 1853.

Thorpe, Clarence DeWitt. *The Mind of John Keats*. 1926; rpr. New York: Russell & Russell, 1964.

Tomline, George Pretyman. *Elements of Christian Theology*. 2 vols. 16th ed. London: Cadell, 1826.

Underwood, A. C. *A History of the English Baptists*. London: Baptist Union Publ. Dept., 1947.

Vaux, James Edward. *Church Folklore: A Record of Some Post-Reformation Usages in the English Church, Now Mostly Obsolete*. London: Griffith, 1894.

Vidler, Alec. *The Church in an Age of Revolution: 1789 to the Present Day*. Baltimore: Penguin Books, 1962.

Voltaire, François Marie Arouet. *Philosophical Dictionary*, trans. Peter Gay. New York: Basic Books, 1962.

Ward, Aileen. *John Keats: The Making of a Poet*. New York: Viking Press, 1963.

——. "Keats and Burton: A Reappraisal." *Philological Quarterly*, 40 (1961), 535-52.

Wasserman, Earl R. *The Finer Tone: Keats' Major Poems*. Baltimore: Johns Hopkins University Press, 1953.

White, H. W. and Neville Rogers. "The Vale of Tears in Keats, Shelley and Others." *Keats-Shelley Memorial Bulletin*, 24 (1973), 16–18.

White, R. J. *Waterloo to Peterloo*. London: Heinemann, 1957.

Willey, Basil. *The Eighteenth Century Background: Studies on the Idea of Nature in the Thought of the Period*. 1940; rpr. Boston: Beacon Press, 1962.

——. *The Seventeenth Century Background: Studies in the Thought of the Age in Relation to Poetry and Religion*. New York: Columbia University Press, 1935; rpr. 1958.

BIBLIOGRAPHY

Wordsworth, William. *The Poetical Works of Wordsworth*, ed. Thomas Hutchinson, rev. Ernest de Selincourt. London: Oxford University Press, 1936; rpr. 1961.

———. *The Prose Works of William Wordsworth*, ed. W.J.B. Owen and Jane Worthington Smyser. 3 vols. Oxford: Clarendon Press, 1974.

Yost, George, Jr. "Keats's Early Religious Phraseology." *Studies in Philology*, 59 (1962), 579-91.

Index

INDEX

natural religion, 4, 17, 23–25,
48, 51–54, 69, 98–101, 107–108,
128, 140–41, 160, 162, 165, 169,
182, 197, 206–207, 209. *See
also* deism
Negative Capability, 6, 51, 83,
142–48, 153, 155, 157, 162, 210
Newman, John Henry, 49, 118
Newton, Isaac, 54, 87, 192

*Original Poems for Infant
Minds*, 32–33, 69n
original sin, 162, 164, 197, 207
Oxford Movement, 13, 28, 118

Paine, Thomas, 10, 21
Paley, William, 15
Petrarch, 87
Philips, Katherine, 179n
philosophy, 149–50, 165–67,
193, 212
piety, Keats's, 72, 99–101, 178–79
Plato, Platonism, 5, 145, 185,
198n, 201
Plutarch, 111
Pope, Alexander, 192, 197
Porteus, Bishop Beilby, 14, 15
Priestley, Joseph, 34, 35
Pythagoras, 185

Raphael, 88, 104
Rennell, Thomas, 58–59
Reynolds, John Hamilton, 18n,
83, 114–16, 118, 122n, 149–50,
153, 159, 161, 164–66, 168, 172,
175, 180n, 189
Rice, James, 118, 122n, 158, 161
Richardson, Joanna, 47, 182n
Robertson, William, 196
Rogers, Neville, 198n
Rollin, Charles, 35
Rousseau, Jean Jacques, 108, 163,
188, 197
Ryland, John Collet, 33–35, 37,
95n

Schneider, Elizabeth, 83
sensation, 124–27, 137–40
Severn, Joseph, 84–85, 93–94,
144, 212–17

Shaftesbury, Anthony, Earl of,
136
Shakespeare, William, 83, 87,
92–93, 104, 107, 109, 142–44,
146–48, 155
Sharp, William, 84
Shelley, Percy Bysshe, 25n, 85,
91–94, 96, 103, 144, 195n,
198n, 201
Sidney, Philip, 110–11
Smith, Horace, 92, 151
Socrates, 111, 183
Southcott, Joanna, 11, 98
Spenser, Edmund, 48, 70
Sperry, Stuart M., 49n, 206
Spurgin, John, 45, 53, 72
Stephens, Henry, 67–68, 119–20
Stillinger, Jack, 138n
supreme being, Keats's belief in,
5, 67, 69, 100–101, 103, 107–108,
127, 156, 174, 197–202, 207,
212–14, 217
Sykes, Norman, 13

Tasso, Torquato, 87
Taylor, Jeremy, 120, 150, 215
Taylor, John, 30, 158
Tennyson, Alfred, Lord, 56n,
162
Tertullian, 110–11
Thelwall, John, 63
Thorpe, Clarence DeWitt, 192
Tomline, George Pretyman,
121–23, 128–29
Turner, George, 98

unitarianism, 34, 71, 73, 110,
187n
universalism, 75

vale of soul-making, 112, 117–18,
124, 141, 198–201
Virgil, 87
Voltaire, François M. Arouet de,
49–51, 53, 54, 69, 73, 87, 98,
105, 119, 152, 184, 185, 187n,
196, 206

Wakefield, Gilbert, 36
Ward, Aileen, 47, 49n, 95, 185n

(234)

Library of Congress Cataloging in Publication Data

Ryan, Robert M   1941–
    Keats : the religious sense.

    Bibliography: p.
    Includes index.
    1. Keats, John, 1795–1821—Religion and ethics.
PR4838.R4R9   821'.7 [B]   76–3019
ISBN 0–691–06316–8